£10

THE ENGLISH FAIR

DAVID KERR CAMERON

SUTTON PUBLISHING

First published in 1998 by
Sutton Publishing Limited · Phoenix Mill
Thrupp · Stroud · Gloucestershire · GL5 2BU

British Library Cataloguing in Publication Data
A catalogue record for this book is available from the British Library.

ISBN 0-7509-1772-5

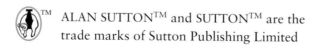
™ ALAN SUTTON™ and SUTTON™ are the
trade marks of Sutton Publishing Limited

Typeset in 10/14 pt Sabon.
Typesetting and origination by
Sutton Publishing Limited.
Printed in Great Britain by
Butler & Tanner, Frome, Somerset.

CONTENTS

ACKNOWLEDGEMENTS

This book owes an immeasurable debt to the staffs of county record offices, local history libraries, museums and galleries, the length and breadth of the land, who willingly and enthusiastically delved into their archives to uncover much of the information and many of the illustrations relating to the fairs once held in their respective regions. The author wishes to thank all those involved for their help and advice, so unstintingly given. In acknowledging the copyright of material he wishes particularly to thank Rosemary Gwynne-Jones for generously allowing inclusion of Allan Gwynne-Jones's vibrant painting 'Tottenham Fair' and the Sir Alfred Munnings Art Museum, Castle House, Dedham, Essex, for permitting the use of the artist's 'The Horse Fair, 1904'. For permission to quote from published work he would like also to thank the following: Longmans (Arthur Redford's *The Economic History of England, 1760–1860*); Heinemann (J.B. Priestley's *English Journey*); and Robert Hale (Sir William Addison's *Portrait of Epping Forest*). The illustrations are individually attributed. To the people and sources who located and loaned them to enhance this work the author expresses his deep gratitude, in particular to the National Fairground Archive and its assistant director, Dr Vanessa Toulmin.

LIST OF ILLUSTRATIONS

Page

A beacon in the dark. The vertiginous Big Wheel, towering high into the night sky, lured folk to the fair

CHAPTER ONE

HURDY-GURDIES
AND HOT PIES

They were colourful, vulgar and raucous and they were, at one time, almost the only entertainment of the *hoi polloi*. They are still plebeian, brash and raw with the passions of earthy enjoyment – occasions for the bizarre and outrageous. They exploded, the fairs of Old England, across the firmament of the year like star-bursts on bonfire-night, punctuating the rural calendar and changing destinies – beacons that marked the passing of the seasons and quietly regulated the country's economy. Kings were concerned about them and sometimes attended them. There was, after all, a touch of magic about the fair: one day here, next day there, spirited away in the night, its departure as secret as its arrival. It enhanced its mystery and excitement.

The fair was always transient; it blossomed briefly. The great sheep fairs when England's wealth was wool claimed the bleak tors of the downlands – and then were gone, leaving a hill that had been a heaving hive of activity, of men and livestock, once again silent, the loneliest place on earth. Even the most famous fair of them all, Stourbridge, obeyed the rule, claiming the Cambridgeshire stubble and fitting into the country calendar but fleetingly before autumn's ploughs again claimed the ground.

Now the fair has moved on from its early revels. Mostly those vivid and wonderful occasions that once choked the ridgeways and the green roads of England with droves of animals and itinerant traders, lost their purpose and all importance about the middle of last century, eclipsed by the coming of the railway, better roads and the desire of all to use them to widen the horizons of their world. Some would survive, nobly and against the odds, in something remotely like their original form: among them Barnet, Appleby – both of them horse fairs that have managed to retain a little of their sweaty vigour – and Priddy, that famous yearly sheep fair that defied the Black Death; some would unashamedly shrug off the past to transform themselves into the fair as we now know it, an occasion of high spirits and carnival gaiety; a few, worthy revivals, would strive to maintain their names and a piece of the proud past, the charade, alas, serving only to remind us of what once was rich in our heritage, their ancient ritual and period-costume earnestness a melancholy anachronism. Some, like Oxford's St Giles, would continue unchanged, their purpose, as it always was, the unfettered pursuit of pleasure. All of them, at some time, have attracted the poet, the artist, the novelist and even the composer, drawn by their riot of movement and shadows and perhaps even more by the spectacle of thronging humanity with its hair down. On them, as on the rest of us, the fair exerted its fascination; all have helped to record its often turbulent story.

It is a hurdy-gurdy history only partly revived by today's carnival on the Easter common, or on high days and holidays on the village moor, by the unbridled sound of the travelling funfair in full-throated cry. Before the imperious needs of motorised traffic mainly banished it to the outskirts of town – to waste land or some hedonistic farmer's field – the fair took over the town's market-place, coming to riotous life as dusk fell on a hard day's bargaining in goods and livestock. For the travelling fair, from its earliest time, clung tenaciously to the coat-tails of commerce and the country occasions that engendered it. But only when he had the notes from the sale of his beasts in his hand could a man give his mind to the fair's uninhibited jollity.

There have always been folk who 'followed the fair': traders in search of the incautious shilling, and with them the tumblers, clowns, jugglers, rhymesters and musicians – all who could command a moment's attention in its fevered atmosphere and attract the small change of the day (or night, when the heart had softened); they travelled on foot, or more thankfully on the back of some scrawny donkey. They took their acts round the countryside from one venue to the next, sleeping rough or in somebody's barn. It was the early 1800s before the old showmen really got their cavalcades on the move – a series of sideshows at first perhaps, and maybe a small menagerie – courtesy of Telford and Macadam. For the travelling fair, as we fondly remember it before its popularity withered and its ethos was changed by the lure of rival entertainments, had to wait for the construction of reasonable roads.

Time would extend the early attractions, with the rides, the terrifying big wheel, the cakewalk, the waltzer, the merry-go-round and, later than we usually suppose, the dodgems adding their magical fascination. The arrival of steam transcended all that had gone before and brought the travelling fair into its heyday from the mid-nineteenth century up to the Second World War. With the ability to generate electricity, the itinerant showmen could light up the night sky – and most of them did, festooning every bare surface of equipment with thousands of multi-coloured light bulbs. The big wheel towered, a blaze of light, a fiery beacon visible for miles around (as it was meant to be), while the merry-go-round made its madcap gallop under a rainbow of dazzling iridescence.

Perhaps it was the exuberance of the colours that drew the fair crowds as much as the thrill of the rides, the sideshows or the throbbing splendour of the giant traction engines. Their heady, oily smell and the hot hiss of steam assaulted the senses. Over the fair their tall smoke-stacks threw a haze of mystery in which the arc lights hung like distant galaxies. (The old showmen were fond of their engines; they christened them with dour and valiant names that would not have been out of place on the bows of a battleship, and advertised their imagined degree of superiority with titles that sometimes embraced royalty.) From the scenic rides shouts and shrieks rent the night, piercing above the brassy blare of the mechanical organ. The cries of the spielers and the hucksters rose ever and again, increasingly insistent. It was after dark that the old travelling fairs took on their strange magnetism: for one night reality was left behind.

The fair came to riotous life as dusk fell on a hard day's dealing

WIZARDS on the WALL

TOWER GARDENS,
— New Brighton —

YOU MUST SEE

Fearless Fred Farrow

and

Cyclone Billy Bellhouse

THE ENGLISH WIZARDS.

Riding and Stunting on High Power Motor Cycles on an Upright Wall.

A SUPER THRILL
THE AUSTRALIAN PURSUIT RACE.

Two Riders on the Wall at the same time Racing at Terrific Speeds.

CONTINUOUS DEMONSTRATIONS
(Including Sundays)

ADMISSION NOW REDUCED TO
ADULTS 6d. CHILDREN 3d.

Wallasey Printers Ltd., Belle Vue-road, Wallasey.

Billed to thrill. The wall-of-death riders, daring girls as well as men, defied gravity to shock and electrify fair-goers of the 1930s. One of the most spectacular of the fair's attractions, the wall of death, an import from America, made its first appearance at Southend's Kursaal in the late 1920s

They fly through the air . . . The chairoplanes, depicted here in a superb explosion of colour and light in painter Allan Gwynne-Jones's 'Tottenham Fair' shortly after the First World War, was among the first of the white-knuckle rides. It swung its riders in a twisting, giddy spin above the heads of the fair-goers. Tottenham Court and Tottenham Fields, long famous for their multitude of greens and inns, were once popular venues for Londoners' entertainment; the three-day fair in its eighteenth-century heyday was held in May – beside the Kings Head Tavern

Sphere of danger. A circular variant of the 'Wall', the Globe of Death was at Nottingham's 1929 Goose Fair. One of its dare-devil riders was 'Cyclone' Billy Bellhouse, whose show career ended in 1935 after an accident in the Globe

The old showmen who owned and managed the fairs orchestrated the escape of England's labouring and industrial classes, freeing them momentarily from the lathe and the loom, the gloomy and dangerous pit face, the squalor of the farmstead and the hammer music of the shipyard to enjoy a brief, garish interlude in their dull lives. They broke the calendar monotony of the workers' daily grind. Once, folk numbered the days to their arrival, whether for Newcastle's June Fair – sometimes piquantly called the Temperance Festival – on the town moor, an eight-day affair held beside the Great North Road, and one of the biggest fairs in the country on the country's largest fairground site (its last Saturday coinciding with the nearby Pitman's Derby), or for Oxford's St Giles, almost certainly the most cramped and congested. Steeped deep in our economic history the street fair may well be, and a potent reminder of how things were – like its moor equivalent, a boisterous fling that broke the drudgery of the downstairs maid, became a polite talking-point in genteel drawing-rooms and later a subject for scandalous gossip for days after the rides and gallopers had moved on – but today (unless you are a fond and nostalgic devotee) it can seem an indefensible nuisance, shutting public thoroughfares in the name of questionable revelry.

Londoners had their own fairs, fiestas where they came to breathe a kind of freedom, on Hampstead Heath and Blackheath Common – they ringed the capital round, from Greenwich to Pinner. In Epping Forest, the Cockney's paradise, a fair-like atmosphere continued almost all summer long, with weekends of cheerful fun and donkey rides, unprincipled drinking and moments of passion secretly unbridled in the undergrowth. South of the Thames, Mitcham's fair was held in August, giving itself unwarranted airs with the kind of civic opening that suggested a proud pedigree. The fair began – and still does – with the mayor giving his proclamation from some commanding platform or coign of vantage while brandishing aloft a 4½ ft long, gold-coloured symbolic key, known always as the charter key. It's the kind of raffish braggadocio that gives a fair a good name – and brings the crowds flocking expectantly.

As the between-the-wars pleasure-fair season swung into its stride the engines of rival showmen – those stately Burrells and formidable Fowlers, Avelings & Porters and purposeful Fodens – would race each other to the next

Luring lovelies. Diaphanous and decorative, the sinuously inviting dancing girls portrayed on the gigantic front of this early waltzer at a 1930s fair cast their spell on the punters, beckoning them on to the fair's newest ride of the time

The hiss of steam, the gleam of brass. The showmen's engines, festooned with multi-coloured lights, gave the old-time fair its after-dark magic – and powered it through a golden age

Galloper bird: the ostrich

big fair. Under their gilt-lettered canopies and barley-sugar pillars, their red-faced drivers in equally red neckerchiefs and well-greased waistcoats strove, sleeves rolled, to summon the last ounce of steam so that they could secure the best position for their rides. But wherever the fair pitched up it was the merry-go-round that took centre stage, constantly whirling, a romantic metaphor for life itself. Its invention was pioneered by a one-time mayor of King's Lynn, Frederick Savage, whose engineering genius revolutionised the fair and arguably kept it alive when it might have died. A smith and carpenter, Savage began by repairing fair machinery. But soon he was harnessing the steam of the new age to the rides and the roundabouts. His carousels had gallopers (wooden horses) three and occasionally four abreast. Sometimes he made them roosters which fair-goers could ride in tandem, or even flying pigs, all of them gaily painted. (At the start of the twentieth century, at Oxford's St Giles you could ride the pigs for an old-time penny.) Savage's home town became the hub – the very font – of fairground engineering and it is entirely fitting that its 800-year-old fair should now start Britain's travelling-fair season, on St Valentine's Day. What better day for stepping on to the merry-go-round, for succumbing to its dizzying excitement!

Savage also upped the thrills quotient with the switchback – or scenic ride – most famously with his gondolas replacing the gallopers on an undulating track and powered by steam from a central engine. The chairoplane, too, spun its exciting whirl, its chairs suspended on chains, hurtling the daring over the heads of the fair crowd; it was the first of the new white-knuckle machines to join older favourites like the helter-skelter and the highly vertiginous big wheel. Few were enticed who did not tremble.

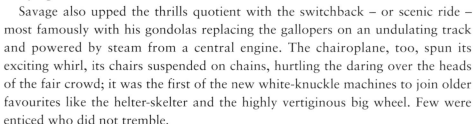

Yet hardly had the 1900s dawned than the cakewalk added to the fun of the fair: the ride encapsulated the name of a negro dance and incorporated several oscillating platforms that publicly challenged you to stay upright while making sure you had very little chance of doing so. Nottingham's Goose Fair, long a landmark in the fair year, saw its first cakewalk in 1909; the others cannot have been far behind. Punters seeking further excitement headed for the steam yachts, a descendant of the steam swing and still an old-penny ride as Britain headed for the endless and bloody attrition of the First World War. The dodgems came late on the scene into the disillusioned world that followed the war and have never lost their appeal. Generations of kindly aunts would uncomplainingly finance hair-raising rides in which they were hurtled from one jarring collision to the next.

There were other diversions, of course, ones that required no audience involvement or risk to decorum; that demanded only the price of one's ticket and an ability to gawp and wonder. The thrills came second-hand but put a catch in the breath, all the same, as the crowd watched the wall-of-death riders – daring men defying gravity on their motorbikes or in midget cars. To spice the appetite some of them used lions as sidecar passengers, a stunt likely to quicken the heartbeat on two counts. There was also the globe of death: an even more breathtaking spectacle in which men on much-modified Harleys rode furiously and at cross purposes inside a steel sphere. Understandably, it is said that they preferred to prepare their own machines.

Less dangerously, risking only outpourings of critical scorn, strolling players – in spirit the descendants of those early minstrels who had strummed through the Middle Ages from one great fair to the next – set up their boards alongside the

Showmen supreme. The 'duo' whose names combined to symbolise the ultimate in spectacle. Phineas Taylor Barnum (1810–1891) was the world's most famous showman; Bailey made his contribution

The shouts, the shrieks, the strident blare of the mechanical organ . . . Blazing light, and gilt-encrusted, the gallopers make their mapcap whirl as the traditional hub of the fair in a re-enactment at Great Dorset Steam Fair

Crowd scene, Hull Fair,
c. 1907. The teeming fair
could be frightening and
frequently volatile. The
fair's legendary characters
include Chicken Joe, whose
sideshow gave prizes of
fresh chickens and groceries
instead of the usual fair
baubles. In the early 1900s
the fair had as many as
seven bioscope shows

fair's usual distractions in a bid to introduce serious culture such as the can-can and even the striptease to occasions like the Stratford mops and those who would never have dared to darken a theatre door, exposing to the public gaze in the supposedly strict Thirties vaster areas of lusciously plump and suspendered thigh than most men then saw within the contract of marriage. If it all lacked a little of the panache of the Moulin Rouge, what matter: it gave many a farmboy the kind of education he would have had difficulty gaining elsewhere and no doubt created an addiction he may well have found it impossible to satisfy. With these variety shows, as with the more serious plays often staged at the fair, the actors would tickle the spectators' fancy with a front-of-house foretaste of the delights to come – inside the marquee, of course.

The barker's voice rode strident on the night air and in the clamour of it all bioscope shows stole the bystanders from puppet shows and performing dogs and monkeys, taking the movies into the travelling fairground some time before they settled in the high street cinema, the steam engine yet again providing the power, cleverly concealed – apart from its stack – in an elaborate frontage of quite superb kitsch. And when it all palled, there were the freaks who paraded themselves to the public stare and the embarrassed giggle: the five-legged ewe, the three-legged man, bearded ladies, twisted dwarfs, the tattooed lady, the world's ugliest woman, the eternally intriguing hermaphrodite. They vied with the Aunt Sally sideshows and the coconut shies, these tragic mutants, with lying machines that spoke your weight and with the venal lure of the penny arcade. Truly, the old showmen knew a thing or two about human nature and how to ensnare it.

They knew, too, that the fairground appealed to the competitive spirit, that it was a beckoning arena for the exhibitionist. Boxing and wrestling, those manly arts, drew the bold and the thoughtless into the ring in the hope of the ephemeral glory that could be theirs by besting the booth's champion, who travelled from fair to fair in the region fighting perhaps eight bouts a day, and sometimes twice that number, challenging all-comers. It was bruising, bare-knuckle stuff that spilt gore on the canvas and tingled the raw nerve of the crowd. Many were gulled and not a few were carried out again to a quiet place to recover their pride. The shooting galleries also exerted their pull on the exhibitionist – and as often led him into a distemper of disenchantment: were the barrels deliberately twisted, the foresights subtly tampered with, one wondered.

Bare-knuckle stuff spilt gore and tingled the raw nerve of the crowd

And there were the fortune-tellers, invariably in the plural, so that there was no problem if a prognosis proved unpalatable. One could always find a second opinion. Their tents held mystery and, if not, certainly a giggle. Silver crossed palms and the floodgates opened on the banalities of life and doubtless undid the unwary. Tall dark men, almost certainly, benefited unfairly and undeservedly from many a young woman's visit to the fortune-teller's tent.

Through the summer fair throng as they good-naturedly bumped and jostled, nibbling their jellied eels and whelks – the instant fair food of the 1920s, before the hotdog and hamburger assumed their fatty supremacy – the hawkers cried their wares, just as they had done through those ancient fairs by the river's edge or on the bleak hilltop. Their cheap goods might have a practical use, but most, in keeping with the spirit of the occasion, were tawdry and mainly for amusement: there were pedlars who pre-empted comedian Ken Dodd by half a century or more with his naughty tickling stick! They chatted and chaffed those fair-goers of yesteryear: mothers in their matronly cloches, young girls in their flowery frocks, men boatered and bowlered, wing-collared and perhaps expensively waistcoated. And that once-ubiquitous vest, removed to swing the mallet of the try-your-strength machine, could reveal with pride and without stigma braces of a prodigious breadth and quite awesome dependability. . . .

All that, though, was before our own candyfloss age, before the travelling fair became complex and computerised. The world was different then, the fairs in their heyday, gaudy and mainly good-humoured. Even then, however, they were but the flamboyant tail of a long tradition that dipped its roots in the pagan past and stretched dimly from the ancient mists. The purpose of the fair then was serious: it knitted the social and economic fabric of the nation.

CHAPTER TWO

TRADING ON THE TORS

The old fairs were in the gift of kings, who anciently owned the land. They swelled royal revenues. For the nobles and bishops and abbots of Old England they came with the territory or were granted after discreet lobbying at court; they were much coveted and zealously guarded. They were occasions when commodity met credit or coin – before that, they were venues of barter. They flourished by the river crossing, where the old ridge trails met or the green roads converged, their reputation a coincidence of history; or they took annual root on desolate stretches of moor. Conversely they may have helped to shape the countryside by threading its trackways towards the tentative centres of commerce. But wherever they convened their purpose was trade. They were most probably born as men ceased to be purely nomadic hunters and settled to an existence as primitive farmers. With fairs, man took his first serious step towards an economically integrated society.

There has been conjecture, not outlandish, that neolithic 'camps' of 4000 to 3000 BC on England's chalkland ridges were in fact 'fairgrounds' of a kind, great meeting points where the farmer-hunters might have traded pelts and primitive tools. Again, it is contended that these camps could have been the scene of religio-pagan festivals that honoured the ancient gods or heroes. It is impossible to say now, one way or the other. Almost certainly, though, tribal man from his early hillfort or tor – the setting for so many of the later sheep fairs – looked down on a countryside that would not have seemed so very different from our own, and with cows, sheep and pigs already domesticated it is entirely feasible that regular gatherings took place where a man could barter for the needs he could not fashion for himself. There was already in place some integrated system of agriculture – arable as well as pastoral, and with a field arrangement, according to experts, that evolved and changed with farming's needs. What is highly probable is that those early fairs coincided with the old festivals of the land: rites of fertility and the rituals of a pagan harvest.

The first meaningful farmers were the Celts, but it was not until the immediate pre-Christian era that the land began, finally and determinedly, to be put under the plough. The first skilful smiths and ironmasters, and the primary implement they fashioned, would radically change man's perception of himself. Thenceforward he would live by his sweat as much as by his courage. Meeting places would multiply as men gathered increasingly to trade not only foodstuffs but also the livestock they had reared in their stock-pens. The smiths came with the elemental ploughs they had made; stone-carvers brought the quern-stones

A minor affair. Lancashire's Cowhill Fair, from the eloquent brush of John Richardson (1782–1859) in 1835, when the event's best times were evidently behind it. The scene is one that poignantly conveys the decline of the rural fair, along with the then poverty of the English countryside

they had fashioned to grind the grain crops. Tribe traded with tribe, when there was peace between them; a tired pedlar on the old trackway might rest his pack and spread his wares in the sun – and find that he had established a settlement. Such was the teetering, eclectic advance of civilisation, the vagaries that created early society.

It was the itinerant traders' tramping feet that helped to trace out those early dusty paths along the country's ridgeways; it was probably they who first realised the benefit of gathering at recognised meeting points and at agreed times, rather than stomping, heavily burdened, from farmstead to farmstead, settlement to settlement. The locations of the ancient fairs strongly suggest this. The great gathering of St Giles Hill at Winchester, the old capital, was one of the earliest, meeting under the frown of its long barrow, a well-known landmark; Stourbridge, at Cambridge, equally historic, came to life beside the Icknield Way, the ancient route that ran from near Avebury in Wiltshire, along the downs of Berkshire and the Chiltern Hills, and crossing the Thames at Streatley, over the heights of East Anglia and down into Norfolk. Strete fair burgeoned by a busy ford of the River Test on the Roman road going through Salisbury and Winchester to the lead mines of Somerset. Shalford's ancient fair, near Guildford, grew also at a river crossing; Cornwall's Summercourt – at the centre of the county – sprang up where two major arteries crossed. Thus was the fair brought into being, given its status and a place in the year. Such gatherings at first were local, constrained by poor communications, the lack of a network of serviceable trails. The Romans would change all that as they sent their well-engineered and dismally unwavering roads like arrows across the land, linking one village with its neighbour and the one beyond that. And the Anglo-Saxons would not be idle: East Anglia's important fairs of later centuries, for instance, would be foreshadowed in such settlements as Bury St Edmunds, Beccles, Stowmarket, Ipswich, Hoxne, Sudbury and Haverhill. But they increased dramatically in number those early trading occasions after the Norman Conquest, spreading a significant and ever-widening network through the land. By the end of the 1200s Old England's markets and fairs would be well established against the background of a functioning agrarian countryside.

Meanwhile, town craftsmen – the protectionist guildmen – met regularly to sell their goods, so that slowly the twin foci of community commerce became the fair and the market cross, the latter symbolising the Church's role in encouraging honesty in the dealing that took place in its shadow. Many of these crosses remain, venerable monuments that still delight the eye, some of them so built as to give cover to the priest who collected the market dues – to enrich the Church's coffers. The cross would endure as the centre that nucleated the burgeoning town. The dominance of the great trading fairs, however, would continue only until the late Middle Ages, when the growth of towns began slowly to diminish their economic importance, though not their standing as the social landmarks of the year.

The provenance of the old fairs – mostly confirming occasions that were already a *fait accompli* – were the royal charters granted to lords of the manor, the prelates of the Church and the heads of other religious houses, almost all of whom exploited their franchises, with their imposition of tolls and taxes, to the full. Noblemen who had shown courage in the king's cause were often suitably rewarded in this way – with permission to stage a fair or market (not infrequently both) and a right also to hold an associated court of piepowder – from the quaintly distorted French *pied poudre*, describing the dusty feet of those early pioneers, the itinerant cheapjacks and chapmen who travelled their wares on the country's trackways. (In granting the charter for Southwark Fair to the 'Mayor and Commonality' of the City, Edward VI is helpfully compendious on the court's scope and rewards: i.e., that the 'Mayor, Commonality and Citizens' have 'all the liberties to such fairs pertaining; and that they may have and hold there at their said courts, during the said three days, from day to day, hour to hour, and from time to time, all occasions, plaints, and pleas of a Court of Piepowders, together with all summons, attachments, arrests, issues, fines, redemptions, and commodities and other rights whatsoever, to the same Court of Piepowders in any way pertaining, without any impediment, let or hindrance of us, our heirs or successors or other our officers and ministers soever.') At Weare in Somerset, in 1298, a fair on the Feast of the Assumption was granted to a certain John Adam 'in service with the king in Scotland', an example of the brave

Lords of the manor exploited their franchises with tolls and taxes

Dusty justice. In an upstairs room of Smithfield's Hand and Shears Inn, complainant and defendant argue their respective cases before Bartholomew Fair's piepowder court. A guilty verdict could mean being lodged in the pillory

warrior's reward. Watton-at-Stone had a yearly fair on the vigil, feast and morrow of the Nativity of the Virgin Mary, granted to Robert Aguillon, the local manor of Watton being held for the sending of just one foot soldier (complete with bow and arrows) to the army of the king in Wales for forty days. Kings so frequently acknowledged valour in this way that in Somerset alone, at the end of the Scottish campaign in 1304, no fewer than half a dozen new fairs were granted. Others followed in subsequent years. The 'greate faire' of Whitedown (or Whydown), a long-established Whitsun rendezvous for the West Country's fellmongers, was extended from two days to four for Stephen Preston, the lord of Cricket St Thomas's manor in 1467; Preston was the king's serjeant.

The piepowder court held the palm for justice with a duty to see 'fair play' (an expression of diminishing return still with us) and 'sort out' trading disputes and perhaps the rolling drunk and the pickpocket who came to find rich dippings amid the throng. The sharp-practice merchant faced trial by a jury of his fellow-traders; justice was summary, as it had to be before the whole cavalcade of trade moved on to the next country fair. The piepowder court had immediate jurisdiction over 'contracts, trespass, covenants, debts' and other matters pertinent to the fair. Penkridge's court, at the Michaelmas Fair of 1598, had power over waif and stray, felons' goods, toll, 'picage', stallage, and other matters belonging to the fair within the manor of Penkridge. Some of these courts would

Inn of court. The tailors' rendezvous and site of swift justice, the Hand and Shears Inn in Smithfield's Cloth Fair, once the venue for Bartholomew's piepowder court, is still a landmark link with the area's disreputable past

remain in the hands of the fair-owners until the late nineteenth century. Through its wicked worst, London's infamous Bartholomew Fair maintained its piepowder court to the last, while Hemel Hempstead's survived until 1898!

As lords of the manor, one noble family, a particular favourite with the king, might be granted several fairs. Abbeys and cathedrals could become the beneficiaries of charters given to assist their development in some way and hospitals, colleges and charities might likewise be endowed with manors – and their accompanying fairs – to fund their good works and profit from their tolls. Famous Stourbridge, for instance, was instituted in 1211 to fund a lepers' hospital. The Magdalen Fair, at Hedon, near Beverley, was granted by Henry II to the hospital of St Mary Magdalen and continued as one of the most popular North Country fairs into the nineteenth century. Bishops and abbots, and sometimes abbesses and priors, fared exceedingly well from charters to what in many cases would become the great fairs of Old England.

As lords of the manor – indeed, often of many manors – they acquired dominion over vast tracts of feudal England. Bath, the ancient city of the Romans, was once host to four fairs – one for the king, one for the bishop, one for the prior and the convent and one for the city-dwellers themselves, an amicable arrangement that could have been copied with advantage elsewhere in the cause of harmony. By 1156 Bishop Robert of Bath and Wells was being granted papal protection for his church, the Abbey of Saints Peter and Paul, along with the 'customs, markets, tolls and fairs on either feast of St Peter'. In 1178 Bishop Rainaud was enjoying the same privileges from a later Pope and for all we know earlier bishops may have enjoyed a similar dispensation. Royal sanction came a century later in 1284 from Edward I for a fair on the 'vigil, feast and morrow' of the saints (June 29) and the seven days following. A later bishop, Jocelin, is said to have 'procured' Cheddar's two fairs, originally on St George's and St Luke's Days, from Henry III; both would continue into the 1700s. The Bishops of Bath seem all to have shared the same high royal esteem for they also had the lordship over Axbridge's St Barnabas's Fair, a transfer apparently of a fair earlier given by the same monarch to William Longsword (given his name we can assume the service rendered). It would become a popular cattle and sheep occasion in Somerset's fair calendar. The Bishop of Salisbury was favoured by a two-day fair for the vigil and feast of the Assumption (14–15 August) in 1221 (in a charter to the city six years later its reign was stretched to ten days). By the high point of the 1500s we find the bishop owning three fairs: on the Tuesday after Epiphany; Lady Day; and Michaelmas, though some at least of the profits percolated to the city. The first two became important cloth fairs. The thirteenth century in fact was a frantic time for the granting of fairs. Lords of the manor clamoured to buy fair charters to profit from the tolls. The Crown was keen: if they generated tolls for the lord of the manor, they also brought much-needed revenue for the monarch.

The Cistercians were the country's great sheepmen, washing and grading their wool

Manors, contrary to our general perception, could be large or ridiculously small. Most indeed were quite modest, the exceptions usually being ecclesiastical spreads. The manorial structure, too, was an infinitely variable thing; the new monastic houses of the twelfth century might have many scattered parcels of land instead of the traditional demesnes, their ground seldom close to home. The manorial system was not tidy, but fragmented, and had a web of administration through several layers. The Bishop of Winchester's estates extended from Taunton in Somerset to Witney in Oxfordshire, Farnham in Surrey and Crawley in Sussex, Farnham being the largest; Canterbury Cathedral Priory's manors were located in Surrey, Kent, Buckinghamshire, Oxfordshire, Norfolk and Essex. In the north the great feudal landlords were the Bishop of Durham and the Earl of Northumberland. Late in the thirteenth century sheep grazed every available pasture, heath and down; in 1259 the Bishop of Winchester's flocks alone numbered 29,000. Abbeys such as Fountains and Bolton maintained enormous pastures. At the close of the century some 30,000 sacks of wool (each weighing 364 lb) were coming off the backs of the country's eight million sheep for export to the seemingly insatiable Italian and Flemish cloth-makers. This figure excludes the home market. Old England's economy then was mainly in the hands of the abbots and bishops, and particularly perhaps of the Cistercian abbeys who so actively promoted the wool trade. The Cistercians, with sixty-five compact granges, were the country's great sheepmen, washing and grading their wool (unlike the Benedictines) to tempt the market and push up prices.

Before it acquired fame with its goose fair, Tavistock had an earlier fair on the feast of St Rumon that boosted the funds of the local Benedictine abbey of St Mary and St Rumon. As well as the historic Tor Fair, the Abbot of Glastonbury, as lord of the manor, had a fair from 1332 at Wrington in the lee of the Mendips; held in early September at the feast of St Mary, it continued until at least 1729. In about 1280, the Abbess of Shaftesbury claimed the right of a fair at the wool town of Bradford on the vigil and feast of the Holy Trinity, which was still the town's fair into the 1800s. The abbess, about the same time, was also the patron of Cold Berwick's fair, held on St Leonard's Day (6 November).

Both lay and ecclesiastical lords would found fairs that would carry their name to future glory: Penkridge's 1316 charter to hold an eight-day horse fair in September was granted by Edward II to Hugo de Blount, who could hardly have foreseen its later fame; Horncastle's 'greatest horse fair in the world' on the August eve of St Lawrence, which would put kings and princelings and distinguished generals into the saddle, was first granted to the Bishop of Lincoln in 1229; its arch rival Howden, modestly claiming its September fair only to be the 'largest in England', had already been granted to the powerful Bishop of Durham in 1200; Brigg Fair began its long history and journey into English orchestral fame with a charter granted to Ernisius Neville in 1236; on the fringe of Lincolnshire's Folkingham, Stow Green fair would flourish down the years under Henry III's 1268 charter to the prior and convent of Sempringham at their manor of Stow for the vigil, feast and morrow of St John the Baptist. The men of the monasteries it seems also knew a thing or two about giving what today is called a sweetener: in recognition of a right to hold a market and fair at Abbot's Bromley, the Abbot of Burton, as lord of the manor, gifted two palfreys to the then youthful Henry until such times as he came of age.

Robert de Cadomo, son of the lord of Horsford, could hardly have envisaged the cattle fair fame of St Faith's when he founded the Benedictine priory at Horsham St Faith's dedicated to St Faith, the virgin, martyred in France in the third century. Returning through France from a pilgrimage to Rome, de Cadomo and his wife Sibilla were attacked by robbers and imprisoned. Only their belief and their prayers, they believed, enabled them to escape, and they vowed, after visiting the saint's shrine at Conches, to give their manors of Horsford and Horsham to build a monastery in the saint's honour. The priory installed just two monks from the saint's shrine at first but it expanded when de Cadomo's son John gifted it 60 acres of land. The famous fair took root in the reign of Henry I about 1100, honouring the saint's day and beginning a story that would link the far corners of Britain. Even by the reign of Edward I the priory was said to be holding a 'considerable fair' of several days' duration to which drovers 'out of Scotland' and from the north of England were bringing cattle. For the monks, however, it was primarily a sheep fair and it remained so until the droving breakthrough of the seventeenth century settled it into its role of giant cattle fair, described in 1679 as 'the greatest in these parts'. Nor could the Abbot of St Albans, in accepting King John's offer in 1199 of a market beside the church at Barnet, have dreamed that it too would grow to become a mecca on the Great North Road for the droving trade and later for horsey folk. Or that its cattle and horse fair, prospering long before it received a charter from Elizabeth I in 1588, would extend down to our own time.

Fairs did not always come singly, as once-a-year affairs. At times there was an embarrassing plurality. Four was remarkably common but Tamworth had five;

The Bishop of Lincoln's fair would put kings and princelings and generals into the saddle

Newcastle under Lyme had six a year 'for the sale of horses, cattle and woollen cloths'; Leek, in the same region, had seven 'chiefly for cattle and pedlars' goods' and neighbouring Longnor, like Berkshire's Newbury, claimed the right to stage eight. Northern Northallerton's, on the other hand, were too numerous to count – and came close at times to being continuous. The result of such frequency and proximity would have been dire but for the protectionist measure that avoided damaging competition between such occasions: no two fairs could be held within 6⅔ miles of each other – a curious stipulation based, as it turned out, on the not unreasonable premise that this was the distance a man might comfortably drove his beasts, sell them and walk home again for a late supper the same day. A political dimension, too, might come into play in the granting of a fair charter. Shrewd monarchs played Church against nobles; court favourite against unruly baron. Sometimes they pacified a troublesome situation; occasionally they must surely have inflamed it. But there was a need, still, for someone to keep an eye on any gathering of size and, in a time of burgeoning trade – when hard currency was often in short supply and long before the country had an adequate banking system – for the increasingly complex transactions of business to take place at an authorised assembly and, even more importantly, before witnesses.

Shrewd monarchs played off Church against nobles, court favourite against unruly baron

Henry III (1207–72) reigned for fifty-six years and granted fairs at an astonishing rate. In England and Wales in the span of a couple of centuries, the thirteenth to the fifteenth, nearly five thousand royal charters were given for fairs or markets, often granted simultaneously. Most existed primarily for the sale of livestock, mainly cattle. Horses and sheep, also important, would generate their own special fairs. Together they instituted a complex pattern of trading that would endure down the centuries. Down from the Michaelmas trysts in Scotland in time, slow-moving and bellowing on the hoof, would come herds of black stots (neutered bullocks) to the rich pastures of Norfolk to be fattened for the capital's market; sheep in surging, milling flocks would meet heavy purses at such memorable venues as Yarnborough Castle and Wilton and Priddy and Weyhill. And when the oxen finally quit the plough the horse fair would flourish as never before, heaping further fame on those venerated venues: Horncastle, Howden, Brigg, Penkridge, Yorkshire's Lee Gap, and Lincoln and Lavenham among others. Their names were a byword for incident and excitement – and also for sharp practice. Buying a horse could be a hazardous affair for there were wily old copers who had the knack of making even the most miserable nag, gone in the legs and broken in the wind, look like a champion – until the deal was done.

It is important here to make a distinction between fairs and markets, though once, in the Dark Ages, there had been little difference. Fairs were big, mainly once-a-year occasions of the old landscape; well publicised, they were part of the wider, national economy, seldom seriously concerned with the small beer of everyday needs; they were for trade in quantity whether it was wool, livestock or the victuals some bleak and isolated monastery would lay up for the winter; a select few were international in outlook, presaging the trade fairs of our own age; they needed space and drew their custom at times from even the far limits of Europe and beyond. The market was integral to town life, supplying its

Proclaiming the fair. This simple ceremony at the market cross opens Corbridge's fair as the horse-copers trot their animals into town. The painting, in oils, by Ralph Hedley (1848–1913), delightfully conveys the low-key start of the rural Northumberland fair in the shadow of the Hadrian's Wall

immediate needs; the fair was on the fringe, extraneous and extravagant, perhaps – reflecting that obscure link with the past – on the line of some old boundary where two or three shires met: Reach Fair, at the Fenland limit of Devil's Dyke, some seven miles from Cambridge, straddled an old border between kingdoms.

The town market would be largely immune from the forces that influenced the fair's story and it continues to prosper, long after the true fair has been eclipsed. One of the factors that forced the latter beyond the town's walls was the high stallage and toll charges imposed, and the reluctance of the craft guilds to tolerate 'foreigners' in a market-place they 'protected' for their own. The medieval fair would help to break that stultifying monopoly and give trading a fresh mobility. Essentially it was the greed of the guildmen that made the fair the main focus of international trade. The fair, too, would have a social dimension the weekly market could never aspire to. It was a tremendous happening. For days beforehand converging roads would be thronged by badly herded beasts, and lumbering, cumbersome carts drawn by horse and bullock. All this and packs of itinerant traders – pedlars and chapmen – the drunken fiddlers and others, purveyors of even more dissolute pleasures. Within the fair the beasts mulled, the throng milled; it was a living, undulating mass, an anthill of frenetic activity in which the merchandise would have delighted Aladdin. There were quacks with miraculous cures, potions and elixirs, gingerbread stalls with their figures of favourite saints

Pulling strings. The puppeteer comes to town. This study by the nineteenth-century painter J.T. Lucas typifies the precarious life of the itinerant entertainers who took their modest talents round the villages and old-time fairs – sometimes to delight and amuse only a small audience

and there were the booths, seething with a strange exotic excitement. It would have been a bad business to lose money at the fair and few of their owners did so, whatever the fate of the nomadic souls who made their pitch there.

The fair's role changed little from medieval times up to the seventeenth century. Arthur Redford in *The Economic History of England: 1760–1860* neatly capsules its place in the national economy: 'The marketing of manufactured goods in the home market was still very largely carried on at periodical fairs, such as those of Stourbridge, Winchester, Boston and Beverley. Travelling merchants, with their caravans of pack animals, were still the chief wholesale link between the fairs and the retail trade. The retail trade itself was for the most part carried on by pedlars or chapmen. This persistence of primitive trading conditions was due mainly to the tardy development of banking and transport.'

Many of the old fairs came late in the year, at the end of summer and in early autumn, their place in the country calendar dictated by the patterns of pre-mechanised agriculture. Most waited for the harvest, shorn then by sickle and scythe, to be gathered safely home and into the big barn. They came in particular around Michaelmas. That was the traditional time for the old countryside to take stock: when livestock sales flourished and the labourers shook the dust of one farm from their stout landsman's boots and hired their skills and countryman's wisdom to another. It was the time, too, when an old farmer would finally and reluctantly give up the acres that had been his care – that he had wooed more amorously than a wife – and sever for ever connection with the thing that had sustained him, rich or poor, through the days of his life. For most it was the kind of heartbreak that made the rest of their lives meaningless.

The old fairs in time would set their own agendas, becoming known for the product of their geographical area or identified principally with the collection of one kind of livestock or commodity: wool, glass, cheese, hops, ironware, timberware, cloth and so on. Bury St Edmunds' so-called London fair, it is said, was already living up to its name by the eleventh century as the capital's merchants flocked to buy its cloth. The great fairs were something else: their appeal was cosmopolitan and they created their own all-pervasive charisma. For Stourbridge, merchants travelled from as far as Iceland, Arabia and even Africa as well as eastern Europe; with them they brought the fabled merchandise of the sophisticated world for the lord's lady, or his mistress: the enchantment of fine silks, satins, damasks and jewels, such luxuries as seduced the soul.

There is argument still about which of the mammoth fairs was the greater: Bartholomew's or Stourbridge? The first was an affair of such licentiousness in London's Smithfield that finally it had to be suppressed; the latter, on Cambridge's academic skirts, was little better, though its demise, more honourable, was so lingering as to demean a once-great event. Scarborough, with its 45-day spree – although its memory would live on in the haunting lament of a folk song – went the way of most fairs and faded out under the cloud of its own scandalous behaviour; it too had become a travesty of that once-great trading event to which the French had brought their finest wines, the Italians their glass and silver and gold, the Spaniards their wines and iron.

The mop fairs, the hiring fairs of Old England, would grow out of a tragic past – the time of the Black Death – to become decidedly merrier, even bacchanalian, causing widespread social concern; they, more than most, would maintain the thread of the fair's history up to our own time. Yet the old fairs, whatever depths they would later sink to, opened amid scenes of solemn ritual and declamation. Proclamations – sometimes three or four days in advance – were made by the town-criers, loudly and clamorously at appointed places in the town and around the rim of the fair site. Often the start of the fair followed a celebratory mass in the cathedral or in the principal church of the town and brought out the civic dignitaries in their robes to process through the streets and hand over their everyday authority to the Clerk of the Fair. (Much of that old ritual is revived today in ceremonies that attempt to breathe believable life into redundant charter fairs.) Further processing followed as they tailed the fair's patron to the ground. Welcoming speeches were made – usually by the patron, buoyed up by the hope of good business – whose appeal would be for honesty in the transactions and seemly behaviour from all. Then the opening bell would ring its strident peal, or, more historically, a leather glove would be hoisted on a tall pole, signalling the same message.

For the opening of the celebrated St Ethelbert's Fair at Hereford the bishop's bailiff – with mace carried before him – rode out with his steward to the city's three gates to post porters, who were then sworn to levy tolls on all who visited the fair. This done, the bailiff, now assuming the role of chief magistrate, would ride with his retinue to the city's High Cross to hear the fair proclaimed by the town-crier. Thereafter he would tour the fair, himself tasting the ale or the butter

Merchants brought fabled merchandise of the world for the lord's lady and his mistress

THE FAIR.

Off to the Fair.	Harry Galloping to it.	Receiving a Fairing.	Going to Spend it.
Fine Salmon !	A Blow Up !	Punch & his Wife.	Conjuring.
Players.	Wonderful Doings.	A Merry Dance.	Only Twopence !
Tyger.	Master & Servant.	Bear & Monkey.	Funny Jaques.
Odd Fellows.	Masquerade.	Get Home !	The Flogging.

Peep at London.

Horsemanship.

The Mountebank.

Printed and sold by J. and C. EVANS, 42, Long-Lane, West Smithfield, London.

to determine whether the fair's customers were being honestly treated. At Ovingham's goose fair, the proclamation ritual was known as 'riding the fair' and the procession was from a local inn, headed by the powerful nobleman Percy's pipers. Even today, in its enactment of the past, Alnwick's June fair begins solemnly with a church service in the market-place and is proclaimed at the market cross by a herald on horseback, suitably costumed, as the fair queen and her retinue look on. In the subsequent procession through the town, led by the herald, the town bellman and a piper, her carriage is a humble dray. Thus, as we near the millennium, is reborn yearly a fair chartered in 1297 by Edward I but actually in existence long before that time.

Bread was tasted and ale drunk by men appointed to pass through the fair

The early fairs tended to be three-day affairs, though subsequent charters could extend their duration until almost all the major ones were in full swing for at least a fortnight and the likes of Winchester's St Giles Hill went on officially for twenty-four days before being cut back to sixteen. St Ives, in Huntingdonshire, once spanning eight days, at its peak continued for a frenetic forty. At this level, planning the fair became a demanding problem. The logistics were overwhelming and the crowds truly enormous. For the peasant masses a visit might mean sleeping rough in the woods or in the lee of some hedgerow; for those with coin in their pockets there could be comparative comfort and a bed of sorts at one of the inns in town. But not always, and surrounding farmers turned an opportunistic penny or two by letting people lay their heads in their barns. There was the matter of stabling and of refreshment, neither ever quite adequate: one was augmented by ostlers who indicated a willingness to stall mounts by putting a wisp of hay above their stable doors, while nearby cottagers were allowed to sell their home-brewed ale, provided they put the branch of a tree or a shrub over their doors. There were the beasts and folk of the fair itself to be accommodated and here, too, was a chance to profit. The lord of the manor himself took on this responsibility – and the money. Pens to take livestock had to be built, booths and tents erected. Platoons of labourers took over the site in advance. The activity would be frenzied. Town-criers would be busy for a week beforehand crying the fair in every corner of town – as though anyone could be unaware of it. Crowds would gather for days ahead, and the work in the surrounding countryside came virtually to a halt until it was all over. Whatever its ancient start, the big fair was no longer a haphazard affair.

It might have its own central buildings as well as 'streets' of booths, belonging to the patron. Occasionally these were permanently on site. The grander edifices, rented to the wealthier merchants, had their own sleeping quarters, perhaps a necessary safeguard even where the fair did maintain its own strict security. Alnwick, in its return to the past and when that year's theme makes it appropriate, features a ducking pool and stocks, either or both the fate of the trader who tried to get away with something less than fair-dealing. Weights and measures might have been subject to slight regional variation but the local standard was firmly enforced; a stall-holder giving short measure would find himself in the village stocks as evening came on. Bread was tasted and ale drunk by men appointed to pass through the fair; at Stourbridge in the late 1700s an

(Opposite) the hurdy-gurdy man. His music accompanied all occasions of joy and carousal and especially fair revelry. The painter is unknown, but his subject's reign in the fair would be eclipsed by the arrival of the strident steam organ

Trading place. A booth typical of the many that lined the 'streets' and 'rows' of Stourbridge's great fair in its heyday

official, aptly titled the lord of the tap, was appointed to circulate among the booths, sampling their liquors. Thus experienced palates guaranteed fair standards, and a man found to have adulterated his wares would be borne boisterously to the stocks or lodged in the pillory, there to be pelted with putrid fruit and exposed to the crowd's derision. Bakers who transgressed – selling short weight or inferior loaves, perhaps – might come in for special treatment by being paraded round the fair with one of the offending loaves hung round their neck. Butchers too, like beer-sellers, were never above suspicion. Those guilty of more serious offences such as handling stolen goods would have their merchandise impounded by the patron, in addition to paying compensation to the true owner of the goods. The fines inflicted in a fair's summary court – which would usurp the local magistrates' jurisdiction for the duration of the fair – would conveniently line the manorial pocket. This was, however, the kind of nice little earner that a monarch might covet for himself, sometimes giving only a cut to his liegeman.

So the fair grew, a mechanism for wheeling and dealing that would become increasingly sophisticated, its toll-houses ringing the fair site. The arrangement at

Taunton's St Botolph's and St Thomas's fairs was probably typical. There the onerous duty fell on the town beadles, who manned the fair's four entrances and were expected to show a high level of dedication in safeguarding the income of the lord of the manor. Their mandate was compelling: 'You shall diligently, faithfully and truly keep watch and ward at the fair aforesaid and you, for that purpose, during the continuance of the fair for horses and cattle shall not through fear, profit, favour or affection permit or suffer any horse or bullock beast to graze or be driven through your ward without permission to be signified by me by some ticket or tickets and you shall not quit or leave your said wards without being therefrom ordered by me . . . so be with you God.' A tariff was taken on all merchandise entering the fair, its special court dealing with disputes or claims for exemption. In leaving the fair all had to show proof of their purchases to the gate-ward. There was, too, the kind of policing that would have done credit to a modern football derby, with much the same surveillance of the shifty and troublesome. Free trade there wasn't, but there was instead a strict protection for both merchant and goods under the sign of the glove – the king's emblematic pledge to protect those who traded with integrity and kept the conditions of the fair's charter. The glove, after all, had a long history as a token of honour, like the handshake that would legally seal a deal in the fair. It remained aloft until it was time to cease selling. The rule on trading was likely to be rigid: from ten in the morning until sunset, with special days set aside in the fair sequence for specific dealing, particularly in the livestock sections, which might be located on the fringe of the fair for the obvious reason. Anyone ignoring the regulations, who traded unlawfully outside those limits (and perhaps was guilty of forestalling), was liable to have his stock seized and forfeited.

Champion knights travelled from the Continent to find challengers worthy of their mettle

Yet for all its striving for dignity, the fair soon sunk to something less solemn, and frequently outrageous. Their duties done by the community, bailiffs were apt to take themselves with a few friends or fellow dignitaries to the privacy of their tents for something to slacken the sinews of authority and beguile the magisterial stomach: the ceremonial party that adjourned to the bailiff's booth at Bury St Edmunds, for instance, did so to feast on Suffolk sausages. And even as the deals were being clinched and toasts in fine wine were being drunk in the rich merchants' booths, there was the kind of spectacle taking place that the *hoi polloi* had come to see. The jousting, for instance, gave the hard-pressed underclass a chance to judge the worth of their betters. For it wasn't just the merchandise that had come far to the fair. Champion knights travelled from the Continent to find challengers who would be worthy of their mettle. Bowmen whose skill was a byword in their own English shires came to add lustre to their name – or tarnish what turned out, in the event, to be an inflated reputation. Like the knightly contests in the tournament, these competitions would run for the duration of the fair, reaching their climax on the last day. A profusion of prizes kept the interest at fever pitch – the patrons of the old fairs, one feels, needed few lessons in promotional skills. For those who liked their sport even bloodier in tooth and claw there was the bloodlust of bull-baiting (setting, say, four mastiffs on a bull) along with bear-baiting and cock-fighting. And when the fair closed its stalls and booths and the merchants shut their pocket-books for the day, jollity finally took over as the strolling players, the jugglers, the tumblers and the wandering minstrels, mingling with the throng, made the fair their own.

For centuries the old fairs, so deeply ingrained in our social history, were the important markets, the vital focus of trade. Sometimes they even made a significant impact on the shaping of the landscape; the fair, claiming the site, as at St Ives and Marlborough, became the settlement. With their groupings and rows of booths there is no reason to doubt that the old fairs deeply influenced early town planning, even foreshadowing today's shopping malls. Although they have been oddly neglected since they ceased to be meaningful occasions, their former central role in the social fabric is confirmed by the fact that the country's new laws were proclaimed there.

And they had a further, crucial purpose. They provided the great meeting point, a place to make contacts, a chance to assess one's peers in the market, to weigh the worth of their commodities against one's own products; above all, a chance – to use a modish word of our own time – to network. Fortunes, doubtless, were made and lost in the fair. Behind the clamour of its carnival atmosphere serious men did serious business. The dealing was intense, across frontiers and in a babel of tongues. It was an occasion that could enhance one's status – or sadly diminish it. A man could come to grief that day. But that was in the fair of the trading *bourgeoisie*, among whom the real wealth circulated, a fair far different from that the rural masses came to see. For them the occasion had its own, more earthy, diversions.

CHAPTER THREE

TRADING AMONG THE TOMBS

The early Church's feasts and festivals, and the crowds they brought together to celebrate them within the city walls, drew the dusty-footed pedlars of the old ridgeways like moths to a flame. They set up their stalls and spread out their wares in and around the cathedral, in the churchyard – and even in the church itself – for the saints' day fairs that throve in its holy shadow and blithely mingled the spiritual with the profane. Tented 'villages' sprang up among the graves so that worshippers emerging from the martyr's commemorative service stumbled out to the sunlight, straight into the secular fun of the fair. Who can say but that many, after their piety and promise of fire and brimstone, were not glad of the diversion and the excitement of haggling among the tombs.

They did so at first with the Church's connivance. Or at least without being burdened by its displeasure. As the fair's patron its attitude, if ambivalent, was understandable and those wandering chapmen fell in willingly with the religious calendar, bending their steps from the shrine of one saint to the next. Down the old pilgrims' roads of England fairs sprouted – or were unashamedly amended – to coincide with the tide of penitents that passed that way to their respective meccas. Around Canterbury there were so many they became known as the Becket fairs, after the unfortunate Thomas. Those once held in homage to some heathen hero were as summarily appropriated (and circumspectly chartered for the collection of tolls) and appended to the name of a convenient martyr whose font would draw wanderers off their beaten tracks. With the saint's blessing, the pagan past was itself sanctified – and besides, matching the fair to a saint's day was a good way of fixing the date on the country memory in a calendar more flexible than our own. But there was the even more compelling reason that these were the days when the country labourer took his ease from the mattock and the plough – by order, for his flouting of the custom would have brought him a fine, or a dire penance, in the church court.

For centuries to come there would be fairs that clung to the skirts of the Church. St Stephen's in Norwich held a horse market in its churchyard. Wells, granted a charter in 1180, held its fairs in the cathedral precincts and continued to do so for the next hundred years or so. In an age that has lacerated itself over the question of Sunday shopping, it is curious and salutary to reflect that in the Middle Ages Sunday was the preferred and most profitable day for markets – with the churchyard always a favoured venue! In spite of protest and legislation some markets would continue to be held there until at least the eighteenth century. Earlier the relationship had been even closer: traders had set up their stalls in the nave, without accusation of sacrilege, moving reluctantly on appeal only as far as the church porch before there came final ejectment into the churchyard. In the sepulchral gloom of St Paul's itself, in sixteenth-century London, cheek by jowl with the great market of Cheapside, hawkers traded their wares, lawyers rendezvoused with clients in the porch, city merchants – Cheapside's mercers and haberdashers – met in the main aisle to do business while whores and cut-purses lingered hopefully in the deep shadows of the side-chapels. Deals were even done around the font as God and Mammon amiably co-existed.

England's cathedrals – and the Church generally – grew exceedingly rich from their fairs and the trade of the pilgrims processing to the relics of their favourite saints. Dunstable gained its three-day St Frehemund fair on the saint's day of 11 May after King John had made a pilgrimage to Dunstable Priory to see the saint's bones. St Frehemund was murdered in 866 after defeating the Danes at Ware; he was said to be the son of Offa, Saxon king of Mercia, who had a palace at Offley and, in 793, founded a Benedictine abbey on the site of St Alban's martyrdom. St Frehemund, it is said, drew many pilgrims and reportedly worked many miracles. Monastic houses, assuming an increasingly important role from the mid-twelfth century, sprang up the length and breadth of the land, with the Benedictine monks claiming the richer regions of the south and east, while the Cistercians, with their simple-life creed, colonised the bleaker landscape in the north, draining and ploughing and planting a more hostile soil. More lay brothers were enrolled as the monasteries became the great wealth creators. Some, it is believed, were not above giving a boost to trade by the felicitous discovery of the remains of an obscure martyr whose ancient bones would then be displayed to the unworthy. Chaucer thought many of the relics on show were pig bones. One thing is certain: the saints' day fairs provided the monasteries with flourishing and rewarding outlets for their produce at a time when many of them, particularly those of the Cistercians, were pursuing a highly progressive agriculture far ahead of that of the surrounding peasantry. Abbots lavished the money on their shrines and appointed bailiffs to run their multiplicity of manors even more effectively. Christ Church Priory at Canterbury had 21 manors in Kent alone, with others round the country. Fountains in Yorkshire had an interest in 150; Bury St Edmunds encompassed 170; while Glastonbury, considered the richest of all at one time, rivalled Canterbury. In Henry II's reign, it is estimated, the Church held one-third of England's wealth.

Whether or not Chaucer's suspicions were well founded there is no question but that the saints themselves were unmercifully manipulated and exploited. Bury's great fair was chartered in 1135 by Henry I to help the abbot erect the then Church of St James, later to become the cathedral. The fair, however, suffered a convenient date-change when it was found that St James's Day fell right in the middle of harvest, hardly the best time for a profitable fair. Henry III (who else) soon rectified this oversight by a shift in favour of St Matthew, whose

Whores and cut-purses lingered hopefully in the shadows of St Paul's side-chapels

China run. Road trains like this one were once common in England's summer countryside as the fair traders took their gleaming traction engines, caravans and living vans from one venue to the next. This trim turnout of 1900 was shifting crockery, always a fair commodity

September saint's day fell more sympathetically into the farming calendar. It was a realignment in everyone's interest, not least that of the king himself. The fair was one of his favourites and some shopping was usually done there on his behalf. In 1231, William Addison tells us in his delightful *English Fairs and Markets*, '. . . fur-trimmed robes of scarlet and black burnet [a fine dark cloth of the Middle Ages], with tunics, over-tunics and mantles from cloth woven on the looms of Ghent and Ypres were bought for him there by William, the royal taylor'. That was the kind of recognition that could do a fair's reputation no harm and Bury Fair was one of the most prosperous in eastern England, a region then very much more advantaged trade-wise by its closeness to the Continent when communications were more difficult.

Bury had other advantages though, with all the classic elements that composed themselves into an important occasion. A martyr's bones – almost certainly those of the former East Anglian king, Edmund – had been brought from Hoxne in 903 AD, thus diverting a steady stream of pilgrims to a market that had been in operation long before the Conquest. It would be lucky in having the consistent support of the Crown: King John forbade competitors except with the abbot's consent, always an unlikely concession, and even more magnificent was the patronage of Mary Tudor, sister of Henry VIII, by then married to her second husband the Duke of Suffolk and living at Westhorpe Hall. She had an impressive pavilion built for her use during the fair of St Matthew and the duke,

Evening performance. After the wheeling and dealing of the day the old-time commodity and livestock fair wound down to an evening of (frequently drunken) revelry and the stage dramas presented by strolling players – as in this work from the brush of Cornelis Beelt (1660–1702)

too, was an ardent devotee, staging knightly tournaments and pageantry of great splendour for the entertainment of the many nobles who attended. The duke himself was a notable challenger in these martial contests. The evenings were graced with equally glittering assemblies and the fair continued on this high note for fifty years or more. Alongside, there continued the usual business of the fair with the customary booths but also with the 'shops' of the London merchants, who shipped much of their stock up to the fair, enabling the gracious ladies of the region, on their promenades, to inspect the latest silks available from the capital's mercers and weavers.

Northampton's fair, held in All Saints' and its adjoining churchyard, was equally fortunate in enjoying royal esteem: here, too, at the height of the fair's importance and popularity in the thirteenth century, the royal tailors were being ordered to buy for the king's household. Ely, in the Fens, drew pilgrims – and trade – with the remains of St Ethelreda, the daughter of a prince, who founded a monastery there and became its first abbess. To its impressive cathedral church they came, swelling the crowd at the charter fair granted by Henry I, to be held on her feast day, 17 October. The saint was also known as St Audrey, and her fair would become famous, among other things, for the form of a lace pattern known as St Audrey's Chains, a 'fairing' bought there up until the First World War. Sadly for the saint, it would give the corruption of its name, 'tawdry', to the cheapjack junk of the fair and the market-place. St Ethelreda's seems to have suffered more than most from infidels, and found its reputation blighted by an embarrassingly large and regular attendance of ne'er-do-wells. So fraught was the situation that the fair was forced in its proclamation to make the message clear: beggars, rogues and vagabonds were bluntly advised to move on immediately or accept the consequences.

In the fairs calendar some saints were more popular than others; there were in the old Roman calendar no fewer than ninety-five saints' days to be kept as holy-days. Bartholomew (24 August) was freely invoked in the name of lay and ecclesiastical commerce, particularly of course for that Smithfield occasion that can have given him nothing but heartbreak. Another, more seemly, was granted

Small family. The fair was the natural refuge for those whose oddity became their livelihood. Of those who courted the gawps and embarrassed stares of the crowd few were more famous than 'General Tom Thumb' (here with wife and daughter). His real name was Charles Sherwood Stratton

by King John in 1215 to Newbury in Berkshire; the proceeds are still divided charitably among those living in King John's Almhouses. Ubley in Somerset favoured the saint, to whom its church was dedicated, in its fair granted in 1318 for 'cattle, hogs and cheese'. But one at least, it seems, impressed nobody: Bartholomew-tide was the time of Rye's Beggars' Fair, which so singularly failed to excite the peripatetic Celia Fiennes. It was, she said, 'the saddest fair I ever saw, ragged tatter'd booths and people'. For a fair there could hardly be a more humiliating commendation. In what became Nottingham's giant Goose Fair, Edward I's charter of 1284 honoured St Matthew. It was a fair by then already well established.

Increasingly, however, there would grow a disquiet at the closeness of God and Mammon. The fairs chartered to Holy Church had become too unseemly for the churchyard, occasions indeed of slobbering drunkenness and debauchery. Besides the fairs, there were the wakes, so-called, though it might have been difficult to distinguish one type of event from the other. Both in principle honoured the local saint – but this in no way prevented the wake from becoming a thorough-going disgrace as 'the grossest indulgence in pleasures of various kinds, not to say in brutal and licentious practices'. People who flocked to the watch services – or feasts of dedication – and their devotions, ere the day was out, according to one observer, had fallen 'to lecherie and songs, dances, harping, piping, and also to glotony and sinne, and so turned holiness to cursydness'. The Church's involvement in such scenes had an odd ambivalence. Many of England's medieval inns were attached to the monasteries – places where the pilgrim after arduous bouts of piety could find physical solace and the refreshment of the monastery-brewed ales. Considering the profits to be made from the ale, the monks may have been inclined to a certain leniency. The church 'ales' were no less ambiguous. They were part of the social fabric: gifts of malt would be bought (or donated) to the churchwardens, the resultant sales funding the parish poor and needy. Whitsun ales, particularly, were given over to feasting and merry-making and sports; held in some suitable barn their debauchery quite shocked the Puritans. Church ales declined after the Reformation.

It was a situation, long endured, that caused the bishops themselves some concern. It also touched that crusader king and indefatigable 'Hammer of the Scots', Edward I, who, offended by the reports reaching him, in 1285 passed a law, the Statute of Winton, which decreed that markets and fairs should no longer be held in the country's churchyards. The time had come for the fair to move away from the church's door, though that custom long persisted. Wells decanted its fairs into the surrounding streets. Most places chose to move to the market-place where the situation was no more tolerable but at least did not defile sacred ground. Reluctantly the traders moved their stalls – to ring the churchyard and line its approach roads, in the process probably also outlining the future growth of the town, as happened at St Albans.

Sometimes the fair moved out of town, away from the cramping, medieval streets to the pastoral fringe where the clergy could turn a blind eye to the unsavoury goings-on – and where their grossness no longer impinged on the

Fairs chartered to Holy Church became occasions of drunkenness and debauchery

Crowned heads. The wonderful hats and bonnets of Oxford's St Giles in 1909. Today the two-day, early September event is one of England's few big street fairs. Sans charter, sans space, the fair expanded out of Walton parish's annual wake. Anciently, the showmen's vans lined one side of the street while the shows and menageries occupied the other; there were the ever-popular puppet shows, performing dogs and monkeys, boxing booths and Bible groups. Like many fairs, St Giles incorporates a service of worship in its opening ritual with a Sunday evening sermon preached from one of the fair's rides (usually the gallopers) and the hymn music from the ride's central organ

Behaving wildly. Here are
all the classic elements, and
the doltish near-anarchy, of
the purely 'fun' fair
caricatured in paint and
most vividly so in the style
of Charles Altamont Doyle
(1832–1893). It was
undoubtedly not an
occasion for the churchyard
or cathedral precincts

Starting the year.
Traditionally the fair season
began here, with the
opening ceremony of King's
Lynn Mart (shown here in
1933) on St Valentine's Day
(14 February). It was a
fitting tribute to the East
Anglian town's famous son
and one-time mayor
Frederick Savage, whose
engineering genius
pioneered that perennial
fair favourite, the gallopers

words of prayer. Which is not to say that the Church relinquished its strong interest; this it would continue until the sixteenth century. A saint's day, after all, was a fine day for doing business; it was still a day when the peasantry took a holiday and came to cleanse their souls – and hopefully empty their pockets. The festivals of Easter, Whitsuntide and Michaelmas were favourite times, as they still are. The combination of the spiritual with the secular was encouraged, but it was a heady mix. Things got so out of hand that in 1448 Henry VI, disgusted by the scandalous behaviour that marred the Christian feasts, forbade the fair on holy days, unhappy about the 'abominable injuries and offences done to almighty God and to his saints'. The royal command seems to have fallen on deaf ears, however, and Elizabeth I in the sixteenth century would be compelled to enact further curbs. Meanwhile, the fair would continue to reflect its traditional association with the Church in 'the peace of the fair', that truce in the affairs of men that meant they were unlikely to be arrested during fair-times for crimes committed elsewhere, though the Church was prepared to make an exception for outlaws and traitors. The amnesty, many felt, was a charter, an invitation, to those who had learned their light-fingered skills well and believed they could practise them with impunity. The whole raffish scene is brought vividly to life in Ben Johnson's play *Bartholmew Fair* (sic), a parade of the louche, the loitering and the profane.

The Church's grip on the fair, all the same, was usually deeply resented and its monopoly would not long go unchallenged. York, Ripon and Beverley fairs all belonged to the Archbishop of York – until the townsfolk of Ripon decided to declare one of their own. The Archbishop, furious at the intrusion, responded with a show of force that made the town's fair into a war zone as irate townsmen battled it out with two hundred mercenaries (Scots and Borderers) hired by the prelate to resist the takeover of his tolls. Similar unholy scenes were enacted at Bury St Edmunds, where the abbey was sacked by the mob. The townspeople there were still dominated by the Church, the independence enjoyed by the inhabitants of not-so-distant Norwich and Yarmouth still being denied to them. Several times they had challenged the monastery's rule but to no avail. Riot was followed by the monks' armed retaliation while they worshipped in their parish church. There was counter-riot as the town-dwellers descended on the monastery and all but destroyed it, kidnapping the prior and abducting him to Flanders. So highly confrontational was the mood of the town that in Wat Tyler's rebellion the abbey officials' quarters were looted. The then luckless abbot, having managed to escape, was later caught near Newmarket. The following dawn showed that the rebels had beheaded him on Mildenhall Heath. His head was borne back to Bury and, in the barbarous manner of the time, was placed in the public pillory; his body, it is reported, lay for days on the heath since the monks were surrounded and no doubt too terrified to go and claim it for a decent burial. It may well have been because of its cassock-versus-town dissension that Bury found itself one of the more violent centres of the peasants' uprising. Certainly Tyler's mobs in 1381 saw the monks as a particular focus for their fury. Elsewhere, too, the rebels viciously sacked monasteries and their manors, burning their charters and other documents, the symbols – as they saw it – of privileges and their own slavery. At Barnwell also, not far from Cambridge, the long-standing hatred of the local citizens for both the monastery and the university erupted as the rebellion presented an opportunity to wreak vengeance against the prior. In Norwich the aptly titled Tombland Fair – the site was cheek by jowl with the cathedral – had also led to friction between town and cassock, which fortunately stopped short of desperate injury in a compromise that divided the fairground equally between the warring factions. There was general disquiet also about the customary handover of civic power to the fair-owner during a fair's duration. There came a time when the citizens of Hereford, like those elsewhere, felt they should be free to run their own town and here the king, Henry III, he of the almost-instant charters, stepped in to redress the balance by granting the town-dwellers a fair of their own.

Increasingly the Church, with its huge domination of the country's economic affairs, would find it necessary to draw in its skirts. It had run its fairs to make money and for disparate reasons, some grandiose, some highly commendable, some less so. Horncastle's horse fair, later to acquire such international fame, was granted to the Bishop of Lincoln to raise the expenses that would let his lordship live in some style and keep up appearances by maintaining a fine residence in town. The notoriety of the great Bartholomew Fair began blamelessly with Henry I's 1133 charter to the priory of St Bartholomew the Great to fund good works. At Cambridge the Garlic Fair, held on the Feast of the Assumption,

The Archbishop hired Scots mercenaries to resist the take-over of his tolls

belonged to the abbess and nuns of St Radigund and continued to support the order into the nineteenth century – in spite of the fact that the behaviour of the nunnery's inmates had once badly shocked the Bishop of Ely. The sickly benefited to a commendable degree: London's infamous St James's Fair was originally granted by Edward I to St James's hospital 'for maidens that are leprous'. Henry VIII, whose charity to maidens was less evident, would later build a palace of the same name where the hospital stood. Edward III, on the other hand, seems to have been as sympathetic to the clergy as his warrior namesake, granting Tower Hill Fair to 'the master, brothers, chaplain and sisters of St Katharine's', a nunnery for female lepers.

That time was passing when the Church's power as lord of the manor was absolute; when its organisational flair had put the fair on its feet, so to speak. Its mistake – the cause of disruption and riot – was to cling to the purse-strings for too long. But the Dissolution, when it came, would cure all that, often with disastrous consequences. As the country's monastic houses were closed down and the monks dispersed, the hospitals and colleges with which they were associated were also shut. Many of the old fairs, likewise, passed out of monastic hands into the more fragile control of the laity. The old social structure was in disarray and the Church, finally, was breaking its link with an occasion which, with the loss of its influence, would only grow more scandalous. Soon, too, the fairs would begin to unshackle themselves from the hallowed saints' days which they had so assiduously observed. There were those who would see in this the further erosion of the Church's authority, though the preacher John Wesley, for one, was unrelentingly active in promoting the breakaway of commerce from the sacred days of the year. Just as relevant perhaps in effecting change was the fact that the saints' day fairs were thrown into some confusion with the switch-over from the Julian to the Gregorian calendar in 1752 and that the saints' days themselves, while still 'holy days', were no longer holidays for the peasant and thus lost their significance in country lives.

CHAPTER FOUR

WINES AND WOOL, HOPS AND HABERDASHERY

Wool gave England wealth, and not only wealth but status for the first time in Europe. 'Wool,' say Croome and Hammond, piquantly analogous in *An Economic History of Britain*, 'was to 13th-century England what coffee is to Brazil'. Without it she would have been just another 'backward' nation and the great fairs of Old England such as St Giles Hill might never have become internationally acclaimed. Wool was intertwined with royal ambition; monarchs shamelessly manipulated it to finance their territorial conquests. Alongside grain, wool was the country's main export out of the east coast ports until cloth manufacture edged it off its pedestal in about 1420. But other commodities, too, flowed through the harbours of Boston and King's Lynn and London, the premier port of them all. Into them sailed vessels laden with necessary raw materials such as alum, wool oil, soap and woad and dyestuffs for the cloth-makers, while others brought more exotic cargoes; into the ports' hinterlands these goods filtered via the packhorse trails and the waterways to stock the booths of the country's great fairs.

They are barely remembered now, those tremendous occasions; indeed they are scarcely credible today, so fast is the pace of progress and the speed with which we leave the past behind us. They deserve better, for once they burst like beacons into the year, essential rivets in the country's trading economy. They were a time of reckoning and renewal; occasions of feverish transaction in disparate currencies where, in a pre-banking era, much of the business was done on credit and men had to meet their bonds. Which was the greatest of them all? Stourbridge probably, though the answer hardly matters, for all of them were vital at their own level. It may be difficult now to pinpoint their impact on everyday lives but for the nation they were the arenas in which that fashionable phenomenon 'market forces' first came decisively into play. For the great fairs had everything the soul might crave, however bizarre: for the wealthy and nobly born and the emerging rich middle-class in particular, they offered luxuries not otherwise obtainable, such as silks and satins, carpets and glass, fine linens and silver work, tapestries and Toledo swords, songbirds and parrots, monkeys and amulets. Truly the merchandise was almost beyond one's wildest imaginings.

St Giles Hill Fair, as its hilltop site suggests, was a very old fair, originating in early Saxon times. It claimed a favoured spot where the Tin Way from Cornwall met the Gold Way from Wales on the way to the South Downs; it was near the

Landscape of the fair. An early 1880s wide-angle attempt to present the panorama of the rural fair and the layout of the rides and sideshows (frustratingly foiled by an elegant pole). Making an intriguing backcloth are the always popular ghost and marionette shows

river and not too far from the sea, significant then when so much of the merchandise had to come by the country's waterways. It may once have been the scene of pagan rites, perhaps not, but it was already an old fair when William Rufus, favourite son of the Conqueror, in 1094 – a few years before a stray arrow in the New Forest ended his reign – gave Bishop Walkelin of Winchester its charter, which banned all business during fair time for seven leagues around. The tolls would help the bishop with the building of Winchester Cathedral. William Rufus himself would be buried there.

At St Giles Hill cloth from the wool of the downlands sheep was traded for the iron of Spain, the wine of Gascony, spices from the East and a host of other commodities, including expensive, high-quality cloth and taffetas from the Rhineland and the Low Countries, where the international fair was already established in such famous cloth towns as Ypres, Lille and Bruges. The Flemish cloth-makers drew their main supply from England; at the close of the thirteenth century wool exports were running at an average of 30,000 sacks a year. St Giles Hill was a veritable city of booths. There was, they say, nothing quite like it for variety – bears, apes, all sorts of beasts were for sale; streets were built, each for the sale of a selected commodity. Whatever one's wants, the need could be satisfied at Winchester's September fair.

It began, officially, as a modest affair, the usual three-day saint's day fair – on the 'vigil, the feast and the morrow' – but was soon extended to sixteen days in the reign of Henry I and ultimately to twenty-four days under Edward II. Sixteen days, however, would then become its normal duration.

Perhaps the bishop let it all go to his head. Beyond question he got a little above himself. Banishing the mayor and bailiffs temporarily from office, he had his henchmen haul the city's weighing machine up the hill in order to determine the tolls on fair goods. He had his own Court of Pavilion erected on the site and took unto himself all the powers of the piepowder court and a great deal more, extending its rule over the entire city, whose merchants were ordered, willy-nilly, to shut up shop for the whole period of the fair. Bakers emptied their ovens and were compelled to cart their loaves up the hill to sell them at the fair, where they were subject to the same tight regulations as the other fair goods. The bishop's court even managed to cast the net of its jurisdiction as far as Southampton, while the bishop's men shamelessly widened the circle for the collection of tolls and taxes as far as Redbridge, Romsey and Stockbridge. Understandably, the people of Winchester celebrated the end of the fair and the return of the city to the rule of its mayor and his officials! In time, though, Winchester's long-suffering people would have their revenge when they were granted their own eight-day fair in the mid-fifteenth century, starting from the vigil of St Swithin, and had this later augmented by another. By then, however, the bishop's great fair had already been hit, like the other big fairs of the time, by the start of the Hundred Years War (1337), which would cost it much of its international elan as the travel curbs on Continental merchants seriously reduced its range of the exotic and bizarre.

Seeing things. Naturally all is quiet around Biddall's ghost show of the 1890s, as quiet as the grave. Come spooky night, with its sinister shadows cast by the arclights, it would be a challenge to all who dared to enter this booth of illusions

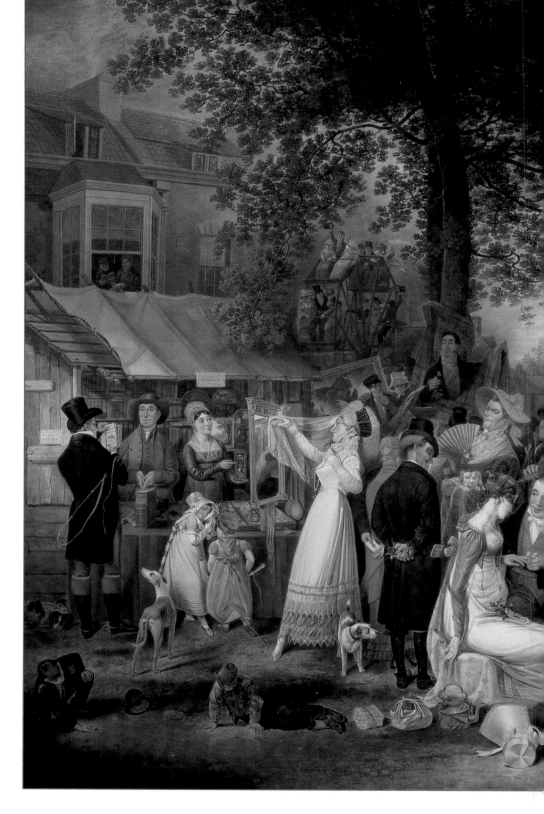

Fair of notoriety. Bristol's St James's Fair at the height of its infamy in the 1820s, when its reputation for crime and dissolute behaviour was second to none. Painted (in 1824) in all its superb detail and with its cast of shifty characters, it emphasises Hogarth's influence on its artist, Samuel Colman (1780–1845). The work is an absolute delight and moral outrage at the fair was at its peak even as the painter worked

Huntingdon's great fair of St Ives – granted for the upkeep of the saint's shrine – did unquestionably give birth to the town that is now the main reminder of its fame. It grew from the river edge where the fair cargoes that came up the Ouse were landed, among them bales of the fine Flemish cloth that would be extensively bought for the royal household. The fair's principal commodities were wool, cloth and hides, and the London skinners regularly beat a path there with their furs in the hope of attracting royal patronage. Henry I had granted the fair's charter – originally to the town of Slepe – ten years into his reign, in 1110, to the powerful Abbot of Ramsey, though the fair was probably a *fait accompli* long before then. The fair crowd, happily, would be swollen by the pilgrims who came to see the saint's relics, which had conveniently been translated there from Ramsey Abbey. The Fair would become, for a time, the largest in the land. At first St Ives Fair lasted for eight days, but soon its popularity was demanding a longer run and, as with any crowd-pulling show, its impresarios had extended it by Henry III's time to four weeks. But even that seems not to have been enough and in the reign of Edward II, about fifty years later, it ran for forty days up to the eve of Pentecost. Up the Ouse in its heyday sailed the merchants of Ghent and Ypres, Amiens, the Brabant and St Omer and Cologne. Row upon row of booths were hired by traders who congregated from all over the country to meet them and do business. Others came too, for like all fairs St Ives drew harlots in great numbers. Just as sure of sweet pickings, came the tricksters and cut-purses.

But if the sin of lust was rife, so also was that of avarice and the great fair of St Ives seems to have fallen foul of it. Clerics vied for a share of the wealth it generated, along with the townspeople, who were in a state of constant dispute over the rights to collect tolls. As always with a good thing, everybody wanted a bigger share. The fair, alas, in the end would disappoint them all for it fared less well than some of the other big occasions. As its fame faded in the trading calendar, so the town took root where the booths had stood. Its bad fortune may simply have been that it was too close to Stourbridge, whose star waxed as St Ives's waned. Defoe visited the Cambridge fair in its heyday and had no doubts. He was not a man to stint praise if praise was due. He said simply and unequivocally that the fair was 'not only the greatest in the whole nation, but in the world, nor, if I may believe those who have seen them all, is the fair at Leipsick in Saxony, the mart at Frankfort on the Main, or the fairs of Neuremberg, or Augsburg, any way to compare'.

Held two miles out from Cambridge's market-place, on a wedge of land between the Cambridge–Newmarket road and the Cam River, Stourbridge, like its venerable neighbour, stood in the mainstream of international trade. Its astonishing success, ultimately, may have rested with its location, even easier to reach by sea and river from the east and from the south via the Icknield Way. Merchants arrived with ease up the Ouse and the Cam by barge, right up to the fair field; its enticing imports poured in through the ports of Blakeney and King's Lynn. Wholesalers came, says Defoe, to meet 'their chapmen from all

As the fair's fame faded the town took root where its booths had stood

Easy riders. For these young women on the gallopers at Birmingham's famous Onion Fair about the turn of the century decorum (and ankle-length skirts) demanded a side-saddle seat but brought admiring glances from the fairhands

parts, make up their accounts, receive money chiefly in bills, and take orders'. Down to the Fenlands in packhorse trains came acres of woven cloth from Wakefield, Huddersfield, Halifax and Leeds, from Rochdale and Bury, and the remote Pennine villages – kerseys, penistones, cottons and fustians. From the West Country arrived druggets and shalloons, cantaloons and further durable kerseys.

Packhorse trains indeed converged from all the compass points of England, bearing lead from Derbyshire, iron from the forges of Sussex and tin for the pewter trade from Cornwall, knives and sharp-edged tools from Sheffield, glass from Nottingham, hosiery from Leicester, brass and iron from Birmingham, as well as that special wealth, wool. The scene that met the eye must have seemed like something out of the *Arabian Nights*. In his *History of Agriculture and Prices in England* Thorold Rogers describes its cosmopolitan mêlée:

'Going to the Fair'. The painter E.V. Rippingville (1798–1859) here superbly captures the holiday mood and air of anticipation as country society, high and low, hies itself to the fair. It was a day for best clothes, best bonnets and general bonhomie

The Venetian and Genoese merchant came with his precious stock of Eastern produce, his Italian silks and velvets, his store of delicate glass. The Flemish weaver was present with his linens of Liège and Ghent. The Spaniard came with his stock of iron, the Norwegian with his tar and pitch. The Gascon wine-grower was ready to trade in the produce of his vineyard, and more rarely, the richer growths of Spain; and, still more rarely, the vintages of Greece were also supplied. The Hanse towns sent furs and amber, and probably were the channel by which the precious stones of the East were supplied through the markets of Moscow and Novgorod.

There, also, G.M. Trevelyan assures us in his *Illustrated English Social History*, 'were many of the farmers and half the bailiffs of East Anglia'.

But there were the geegaws, too, that would delight the poor and curious, brought there to Cheapside 'street' by the London shopkeepers whose merchandise was the ephemera of the fair. Defoe assures us: 'Scarce any trades are omitted, goldsmiths, toyshops, braziers, turners, milliners, haberdashers, hatters, mercers, drapers, pewterers, china-warehouses.' And for all its seductive luxuries, the fair had its staples from nearer home: the north brought its wool and went home with the hops of the south and the year's prices of both were set by the fair's trading. Dealers who took cheese round the fairs brought it from as far as Cheddar, claiming it to be 'the best in England' and finding a ready sale. And from the seventeenth century onwards, Suffolk's progressive dairying farmers found buyers at Stourbridge for their butter. Wool sales alone were said to be worth £50,000 to £60,000. As at St Giles Hill, there was practically nothing that could not be bought at Stourbridge. Surrounding roads would be clogged by the fair-bound carriages of the gentry as well as by gently jogging hackneys – some with their occupants deeply engrossed – and in Defoe's time, to cope with the crowds, wherries plied ceaselessly with their passenger cargoes between the town and the fair. The world had romance then!

There had been a Cambridge fair, however, long, long before Stourbridge got its charter from King John in 1211, probably for a thousand years before, since tradition credits the self-proclaimed Roman Emperor of Britain Marcus Carausius with founding it in around 290 AD. The king's charter was granted to the lepers of the Hospital of St Mary Magdalene for the vigil, feast and morrow of the Roman

Monkey business. His assistants are obviously stealing the show from this peripatetic organ-grinder as he tours the summer lanes taking his music to the fair or any other country event that might enjoy it. This 1842 painting of the man and his instrument is by Edouard Klieber (1803–1879)

Country comes to town. The interlocking of an earlier country economy is perfectly illustrated as the mingling of man and beast chokes the streets at West Sussex's East Grinstead Fair in April 1896

Catholic festival of Holy Cross. Given its long pedigree, Stourbridge was not the kind of occasion to have doubts about its place in the hierarchy of fairs. Its opening accorded handsomely with its reputation. It was clamorously proclaimed and trumpeted through the streets under the grand marshal on St Bartholomew's Day. Musicians played at the mayor's booth for the entertainment of his VIP guests, whom he further delighted with performances by a dancing horse and similar spectacles during the feast that followed. Even so, Stourbridge seems never to have forgotten its country roots: it invariably closed with a horse fair and in an explosion of colour and high jinks that delighted the *hoi polloi*. It is hardly coincidence that the great fair said to be the original for John Bunyan's 'Vanity Fair' in *The Pilgrim's Progress* was a favourite also with Cambridge's undergraduates for the sport it provided. The schism that came with the Dissolution, when both town and university strove to lay hands on the fair's revenues, was finally healed in 1589 when Elizabeth I astutely brokered a compromise that gave the town control of the fair and the university the assize for bread, wine, ale, beer, weights and measures and – some may have thought unwisely – a decree to seek out and punish the fair's vagabonds and common women.

Stourbridge would continue to steal the limelight from neighbouring occasions. It would prosper on the back of the other fairs' decline, notably that of its old rival St Ives. It was perhaps over-optimistic to expect two such important fairs to continue to exist in such close proximity. Stourbridge was probably at the very peak of its fame when Defoe visited it in the early eighteenth century, its highpoint before a sad and lingering fall from grace. It was, he tells us, held in a large cornfield about half-a-mile square. The portrait he draws in *A Tour Through the Whole Island of Great Britain*, is of a 'town' that has mushroomed overnight. It had 'all the trades that can be named in London; with taverns, coffee-houses, drinking-houses, eating houses, cook-shops, etc, and all in tents too'. The fair's 'main street' ran north from the road to the bank of the Cam at Chesterton; at its centre stood the vast 'formal great square' with its large tents and booths and horse traffic, called the Duddery. 'This place is separated and peculiar to the wholesale dealers in the woollen manufacture,' Defoe says, adding that £100,000 of goods could change hands in less than a week – and that was to say nothing of the heady deals done by agents and traders who preferred to conduct business clandestinely, out of their pocket-books. Here, for the first time, Defoe was to see that most amazing of sights, the transporting of a so-called pocket of wool, something still to be met with on England's country roads a century and more later. He says: 'This seems to be first called so in mockery, the pocket being so big, that it loads a whole waggon, and reaches beyond the most extreme parts of it, hanging over both before and behind, and these ordinarily weigh a ton or 25 hundredweight of wool, all in one bag.'

Defoe was highly complimentary about the conduct of the fair: 'there is the least disorder and confusion (I believe) that can be seen any where, with so great a concourse of people'. Here, though, the good order of the fair was not in the usual hands; there was 'a court of justice always open, and held every day in a shed built on purpose in the fair; this is for keeping the peace, and deciding controversies in matters deriving from the business of the fair. The magistrates of the town of Cambridge are judges in the court . . . Here they determine matters in a summary way as is practised in those they call Pie Powder Courts in other places, or as a court of conscience, and they have a final authority without appeal.' And he reveals that uncompromising rigidity with which even a fair as famous as Stourbridge had to fit itself into the countryman's calendar. 'If the husbandmen who rent the land, do not get their corn off before a certain day in August, the fair-keepers may trample it underfoot and spoil it to build their booths and tents; for all the fair is kept in tents and booths. On the other hand, to balance the severity, if the fair-keepers have not done their business of the fair and removed and cleared the field by another certain day in September, the ploughmen may come in again with plough and cart, and overthrow all and trample it into the dirt; and as for filth, dung, straw, etc, necessarily left by the fair-keepers, the quantity of which is great, it is the farmers' fees and makes them full amends for the trampling, riding, and carting upon, and hardening of the ground.' The dung left behind was as good as 'summer's fallow'.

There were other fairs in that older England that would lay claim to greatness, then or later, though none might shine so brightly. Among the big fairs in the north was Durham's St Cuthbert's, held even before the Conquest in that tough

Even famous Stourbridge Fair had to fit itself in with the countryman's calendar

May Day, 1812. This was a time of hiring fairs and a focal point of the year; it looked back to the old feast of Beltane and a pastoral England when the village youths and young maidens headed for the greenwood and returned the morning after . . . Here the occasion is genteelly commemorated by the landscape painter William Collins (1788–1847), father of the more famous Wilkie

and disputatious borderland where the Percy earls of Northumberland – until they fell from grace in 1403 by opposing Henry IV – held such sway; it was noted for its wool and its hides as well as its hardy livestock, and drew dealers from far and wide. Chester was another, great in the time of Edward I, with the Welsh, at last numbed into submission by the tyrant king, bringing their mountain sheep and their fleeces to trade for sophisticated goods from the Continent. Bury St Edmunds in its heyday must have come close and Hereford's St Ethelbert's, they said, was also something to see. Others would seek similar recognition in their time for Horncastle or Weyhill, Brough Hill, Appleby, Barnet, or for that splendid occasion, unique of its kind, the Yarmouth Herring Fair.

It would be easy to find advocates for Boston's St Botolph's, already important in 1200. Boston was a medieval boom-town, a port second only at one time to London, reaching into its wool- and corn-producing hinterland along a network of rivers. Traders came from all over England and from the Continent for its big annual fair. Here fish was bought in some quantity for the king's table; here the wool-rich abbeys and priories, in their prime time, bartered that commodity for more worldly wines. The long wool off Lincoln flocks went down the Witham to meet the demand of the Hanseatic merchants as well as those from Cologne, Ostend and Ypres. Northern noblemen brought their wives to view the cloth, which was said to be of a rare quality. The town was also to become a haven for many religious orders, including the Franciscans, Dominicans, Carmelites and Augustinians. Alas, the great wool-exporting port would lose its standing with the collapse of that trade as cloth took over as England's main export. It would suffer a fate as sad as that of St Ives, falling into a slow decline by about 1570 – though history has somehow much exaggerated the downward spiral and for a long time afterwards vessels would put in to the east coast port with cargoes of Norwegian deal, Brazilian wood, as well as French wines and spices. They would sail on the tide well laden with leather and woollen goods, linseed and hempseed and glue. Scots ships docked with that medieval dietary necessity salt, and vessels of the port would set off with a favourable wind for France, with anything from butter to goose quills.

Men would speak with awe of Scarborough Fair – granted its charter by Henry III in 1253 – which ran from mid-August until the end of September and attracted the international traders to a mart for their silks, wines, furs, spices, amber and perfumes and to bid for return cargoes of grain and leather and cloth. It had mummers and jesters – all those who followed the fair – and there the country folk might come just to hear the babel of strange tongues and gawp at the smooth, olive-skinned faces from the Levant. The fair opened yearly with a proclamation and procession, staged with a panache that rivalled that of Stourbridge, but its commercial significance dwindled disastrously in the early eighteenth century and it lapsed first into a disreputable, purely pleasure affair and then finally, in about 1790, into oblivion. Time was already running out for those grand occasions, the great international fairs, that chequered England's year and had once so heavily underpinned the nation's economy. Their importance, however, would be assumed by fairs that functioned even closer to the core of the nation's prosperity.

CHAPTER FIVE

GATHERINGS OF THE GOLDEN FLEECE

The great sheep fairs of Old England were truly established when the cloth-makers of Flanders and Florence, wearied of scouring the Low Countries, finally crossed the Channel to trade in the wool markets of East Anglia and the West Country – the areas producing the country's best wool – and buying up almost everything these regions could produce. English wool was then the best in Europe. Truly it was the time of the golden fleece. Men would become rich beyond their dreams. Monarchy's debt to the wandering ewe would be immense. Wool wealth helped to raise a king's ransom in 1193, when Richard I, four years on the throne and on his way home from the crusades, found himself languishing in a secret prison after being captured by the Duke of Austria and then 'sold on' to the Emperor Henry VI. That warrior king Edward I had no compunction about commandeering the wool clip from the merchants to subsidise his numerous wars, and in 1338 his third namesake, in an only slightly subtler scam, financed his war against France by persuading parliament to allow him to become the broker in the purchase of 20,000 sacks of wool, the flockmaster-producers getting £3 a sack, the king £10, while the merchants realised £20 in the markets of the Brabant.

By the early twelfth century the country was exporting fine wool along with the meat and fat cattle it sent to Germany. The monks, with their hundreds of thousands of acres of pastoral land, would pioneer the development of sheep-farming. And, coincidentally, since the subsequent manufacture of cloth would not, unlike the other crafts of the time, be a self-sufficient activity, effectively trigger the start of capitalism. That momentous milestone, which so fortuitously heralded the improved status of a near-bankrupt England, was truly reached as Edward III brought over Flemish weavers to make rough woollen cloth for the export market. It would mark a road at times bleaker than many might then have supposed. For centuries to come the country's wealth would ride on the back of the downlands ewe, on the hardy uplands breeds, and on those flocks that nibbled the rich pastures of East Anglia and the sweet green grass of the Yorkshire dales and the Border marches. Increasingly the sheep fairs of Old England would assume a central role in the country's financial well-being.

For the first time, in the thirteenth century, speculative finance entered the frequently untidy, fragmented manorial system. With it, the more intensive sheep-farming would bring the first exercises in enclosure and tentative steps

Small-town drama. A moment of critical appraisal as bowlered buyers inspect a pen of ewes at an end-of-harvest Cornish sheep fair in the 1890s. Prices would have been just as important to farmers and graziers as on the big occasion

towards that agrarian movement that would so alter the English landscape. From about the mid-fifteenth century sheep fever would spread; landlords, gripped by greed, took to evicting their farmer tenants to make way for their own flocks, depopulating large tracts of the countryside and bringing cries of rural outrage. Merchants and staplers – with a monopoly the Crown connived at, for its own good reasons – would run their own flocks on the West Country sheep-runs, with their own sheep-reeves; the farming abbots – at abbeys like Fountains and Bolton – would number their flocks by the thousand, even the tens of thousands. In a social upheaval that foreshadowed the later disaster of the Highland Clearances, the impact was far-reaching. The changes, wiping out at a stroke vast acreages of tillage, and with their heartless evictions casting adrift large numbers of the rural population, drew the anger of that obdurate statesman Sir Thomas More, among others. 'Your shepe,' he protested, 'that were wont to be so meke and tame, and so smal eaters, now . . . become so great devowerers and so wylde, that they eat up and swallowe downe the very men them selfs. They consume, distroye, and devoure whole fieldes, howses, and cities. For look in what partes of the realme doth growe the fynest, and therefore dearest woll, these noblemen and gentlemen: yea and certayn Abbottes, holy men no doubt, not contenting them selfes with the yearely revenues and profytes, that were wont to grow to their forefathers and predecessours of their landes, nor beynge content that they live in rest and pleasure nothinge profiting, yea much noyinge the weale publique: leave no grounde for tillage, thei inclose al into pastures: thei throw downe houses: they plucke downe townes, and leave nothing standynge, but only the churche to be made a shepe-howse.' It seemed, for a time, that the English must become a nation of flockmasters. By the early eighteenth century, according to Defoe, some three million fleeces yearly were coming off the horned downland breeds alone.

Nowhere more than in the West Country would the economic dominance of the wandering ewe be felt. If we should ever doubt it, the number and setting – not to say rivalry – of the region's superfluity of fairs provides evidence enough. They came mostly near the end of the year in an intricate and integrated geographical spread that brought turmoil again, briefly, to the tor-camps of earlier men. Yarnborough Castle's annual October fair, on its hilltop site on the Wiltshire Downs, would become one of the most famous. W.H. Hudson in his classic *A Shepherd's Life* describes its bleak location, a vast prehistoric earthwork on the high down at Wylye, between Warminster and Amesbury: 'There is no village there and no house near; it is nothing but an immense circular wall and trench, inside of which the fair is held.' The downs had a host of such fairs, claiming lonely hilltops, including the ancient Tan Hill, convenient places where the downland flocks could converge. Hudson was writing his downland shepherd Caleb Bawcombe's story in the early years of this century. The Castle fair, he says, was 'formerly one of the most important sheep-fairs in the country', but it had by the time he came to write his now famous account of the shepherding life 'for the last two or three decades been falling off and is now of little account'.

The country writer Ralph Whitlock in his study *The Folklore of Wiltshire* believes the old hill-forts of the region were anciently corrals where the livestock were gathered in for the autumn slaughtering and mating and that such occasions would naturally have a fair-like atmosphere and give way to scenes of revelry as the stockmen met their fellows from far and wide. Right up to the outbreak of the First World War, he tells us, fairs were still being held at three of the county's hilltop sites: Yarnbury (Yarnborough in Hudson's book); Westbury Hill and Cold Berwick Hill, near Fonthill. Though mainly sheep fairs, these occasions might also see some desultory trading in horses and cattle – and dogs. And for all their bleak setting, they had their following of cheapjacks and wandering jesters.

The sheep fairs brought turmoil again to the lonely tor-camps of earlier men

Westbury Hill Fair, in Whitlock's view, was held on the brow of a windy crest above the outline of the hill's white horse; it might, he believes, have had an earlier home in Bratton Castle earthwork, just a little way along the ridge. Cold Berwick Hill, near Hindon, in November, undoubtedly was just that, since it had no protecting earthwork. Tan Hill was a large Lammastide (August) affair in the eighteenth century, drawing people from all over Wiltshire and from adjoining counties. It had all the attractions of a big fair and a large turnout of horses as

Charting the fairs. A Wiltshire map of 1742 lists and dates the fairs and market days of the county at that time, many of them still with a resonance in the showmen's calendar

well as its massed sheep flocks. Its charter, granted initially to the Abbess of Nunnaminster in 1499, permitted a fair on Chalborough Down, near the Wansdyke, on St Anne's Day and the day after (26/27 July). The Down confusingly became known as St Anne's Hill, from which the fair's phonetically curtailed name is derived. There is no indication that the fair was ever a market for hides and leather.

Westbury, as a village, brought out the facetious streak in that post-Cobbett traveller Alexander Somerville, who none the less conceded that it 'had the appearance of a respectable, open, full-sized village, and looked upon as a village, it is

Penned in. People and livestock get caught up in a Cumbrian crush as they hear the proclamation read for the start of Kirkby Stephen's St Luke's Fair

not to be found fault with'. It had a 'handsome town hall, a market on Friday, and three fairs'. Camden was kinder. He passed on the thought that the name was Saxon and derived from the settlement being one of the 'considerable towns of the west'. The borough had a yearly fair by 1252, granted to the lord of Westbury manor, one Walter Pavely, for the vigil, feast and morrow of All Saints (1 November). Later the lord of the manor was given a further fair on the vigil and feast of the Translation of St Benedict (11 July) and the five days following, though this would later be moved, perhaps for agricultural convenience, to the feast of St John (6 May). Some adjustment followed – as so often – so that by 1460 we know of the borough's three fairs now being held on the vigil, day and morrow of St George (23 April), on Whitmonday, Tuesday and Wednesday, and on the vigil, day and morrow of the Exaltation of the Holy Cross (14 September). Not content with that, Westbury would add to its calendar with fairs for the Monday before the Trinity of St John the Baptist (24 June), the day of the Translation of Edward the Confessor (13 October) and the Friday prior to the start of Lent, each with its piepowder court. Later still, in the early nineteenth century, it would also have an Easter fair. Close by, Bratton Down in the late nineteenth century had a considerable sheep fair, still selling 20,000 animals into the present century. Berwick Fair, held on St Leonard's Day (6 November), had been part of that old landscape since at least the late thirteenth century but by 1822 had sought greater comfort in permanent buildings close to Cold Berwick Farm.

But the Wiltshire downlands, with their sheep and corn farming, also had their valley fairs – Wilton and Britford, both just outside Salisbury, for example – where the dealing was more congenial than in the blustery exposure of the hilltop occasions. The flockmasters came to favour them. Of the Lammas Day

Britford Fair the diarist John Aubrey said: "'Tis an eminent fair for sheep and wool.' The numbers sold at Marlborough's fairs, among the greatest in southern England, were prodigious; it still had not one but three (July, August and November) in the nineteenth century, with the animal pens cramming the extraordinarily broad High Street. Marlborough's 'great sheep fair' of August was the lineal descendant of the eight-day affair granted to the burgesses by King John in 1204 for the eve of the Assumption (14 August) and held almost certainly on the Green. Marlborough was indeed a place fond of fairs: in 1229 Henry III granted a four-day event for the eve of St Martin (10 November) and in the later eighteenth century it was still usually held on the Green. The same monarch followed this up in 1246 with a further four-day fair for the eve of St Peter and St Paul (28 June) – to be held in the churchyard of St Peter's – after suppressing a fair at Little Wittenham in case it should provide unwanted competition. Such, again, was the power of royal favour. In later times, Marlborough's famous Michaelmas mop fairs would also crowd the town.

Lammastide indeed unleashed a yearly flood. Britford Fair, held about mid-August and entirely for sheep, in the early years of the century was still one of the biggest in the south, with a bobbing, weaving mass of sheep and demented, stick-waving shepherds – one drove at the tail of another – threading their way through the eerie pre-dawn streets of Salisbury to the fair site a mile or so beyond the city. Warminster, Highworth and Trowbridge (three days), Bradford-on-Avon and Cricklade (with wrestling, boxing, bull-baiting and cock-fighting as well as the more menacing hack-swording, kickshins, and cudgel-fighting) crowded the August calendar with their own sheep sales, with Swindon's following close behind in mid-September.

Warminster's yearly fair on the vigil, day and morrow of the feast of St Laurence (9–11 August) had been granted to the local lord of the manor, William Mauduit in 1253. A further fair, running from 22–29 October, would be granted to a Henry Greene in 1447 and yet a third, from 10–12 April, in 1679, to Thomas Thynne. The August fair was known more memorably as the Hang Fair after some executions had been added to the fair days' attractions on Sutton Common in 1783. About then the fairs were for cattle, sheep, pigs and cheese, with only the sheep, apparently, sold at the October one, which was by far the largest. Throughout the nineteenth century it maintained its importance, with 20,000 sheep changing hands. The fair through the years had been something of a movable feast, in the eighteenth century being long accommodated in the town's enclosure (complete with hurdle house), known rather uninvitingly as Carrion Close, before later in the century being found a new venue in a field north of what is now George Street. It had two further moves before coming to rest, in 1856, in a field suitably close to the station.

Among the county's quite extraordinary calendar of occasions, Highworth's hilltop fair honoured St Peter ad Vincula on the saint's vigil and feast and morrow, and received its charter in 1257. Under a special right of its patron, as lord of the Highworth Hundred, a thief could be hanged there without further ado. In the mid-sixteenth century, Highworth's fairs belonged to Thomas, Lord Seymour, later Lord High Admiral of England, and, even more importantly, brother to Jane,

On Sutton Common some executions were added to the fair days' attractions

Henry VIII's third wife. Later Seymour married Catherine Parr, the much-married monarch's widow and together they brought up the young Princess Elizabeth before he met an unfortunate end on the block when rumours of his bed-romps with the young princess scandalised courtly society (or more likely gave it the chance to be rid of him). By 1645 Highworth had two yearly fairs for livestock, both of them important; both, with the weekly fatstock market, were particularly hit by the plague and the town's occupation in turn by both royalists and parliamentarians, calamities that turned away dealers and graziers for a time to the safety of Swindon. Cricklade of the many spectacles and seemingly dangerous amusements also had considerable cattle and corn markets. It had three yearly fairs in the early eighteenth century (one fewer than a century earlier) held on the third Wednesdays of April and July and on the ever-popular equinoctial eve, feast and morrow of St Matthew (21 September) – a fair kept since 1257. The April occasion (later amended to the second Thursday of the month) was for sheep, cows and calves, while the emphasis of the latter was on 'chapman's goods'.

Yet the overwhelming focus in the West Country was Wilton's great autumn fair in September, still selling about 100,000 sheep in the 1860s. There are those who believe that sheep have been gathered together at Wilton for as long as they have been gathered anywhere in England. Certainly Wessex's ancient capital was always a vital trading centre with many markets and fairs. Though sheep were never the exclusive concern of the latter, they were nevertheless the mainstay of most of them. Timothy Woolley, writing in 1977 in *Wiltshire Folklife*, put it succinctly: 'Today there are four sheep fairs a year at Wilton, in August, September, October and November. The fairs are held on the second Thursday of each month. The August fair was formerly held at Britford.' The October fair was a late-comer, introduced in 1938.

The Great Fair was traditionally held on St Giles's Day (1 September), a saint's day much favoured in the medieval fair calendar; in comparison, the November event was a kind of clearance sale of small consequence. Back in the seventeenth century the town had also honoured St George with an April fair. Just past the mid-point of the eighteenth century (with the adoption of the new-style calendar) Wilton's sheep fairs had moved their dates to 4 May and 12 September, and by 1775 the site had moved to Fugglestone, a fair field of about 12½ acres alongside the Salisbury–Warminster road. This would remain their venue. Something like 40,000 sheep were sold at each of the two fairs, and in the nineteenth century that number vastly increased until the September fair was considered 'the largest in the West of England'. The figures would fluctuate but even as the century turned, Edward Slow claimed in his *Wilton Chronology*, the Great Fair still had 60,000 or so sheep for sale. They converged in the fair's heyday – and even up to the Second World War – along the old drovers' tracks, some 90 ft wide in places, from as far away as Exeter, lodging overnight in 'pennings' – fields that could be rented on the way, sometimes for a matter of pence.

Wilton, like Marlborough, had a positive penchant for fairs, one might almost say an obsession, rooted perhaps in its need to compensate for its diminished standing against its great rival, Salisbury. Wilton was probably a market town in

Lord Seymour's bed-romps with the young Princess Elizabeth led him to the block

A fair for St Giles. Wilton's Great Fair is traditionally linked with the popular saint and sheep have long been Wilton's concern; the ancient capital of Wessex from its earliest time has been locked into Wiltshire's sheep-and-corn economy. It has had to fight hard for its survival

Anglo-Saxon times and relations with its neighbour were seldom less than acrimonious. The two were in simmering conflict as early as 1240 when Wilton accused New Salisbury of infringing the rules of its charter by holding markets every day. Violence erupted seriously when Salisbury's traders lodged complaints about Wilton's bailiffs ambushing itinerant merchants and forcibly making them trade in the latter's market. Wilton in turn railed at New Salisbury's alleged trading to the detriment not only of its own market but of others in the region. The situation was such that the king's will was proclaimed, banning the cathedral city from trading on Wilton's market days. Much good it seems to have done. Soon, in their incandescent fury, Wilton's bailiffs were laying a charge that '10 butchers, 18 fishmongers, 7 cloth merchants, 5 merchants dealing in wax and other merchandise, 6 skinners, 5 sellers of hides, 4 men dealing in oxen and other animals, 6 ironmongers and 31 grain dealers . . . had marketed their goods in Salisbury on the prohibited days'. And so through the years 1306 and 1307 it went on, with the king intervening only to have his writ of command flagrantly flouted. The truth is that Salisbury had meanwhile grown into an important centre of trading. It was where the itinerant traders wanted to be. Wilton's status and its market days, inevitably, were diminished and became fewer in number.

The charter of Wilton's early fair – an eight-day occasion and already a *fait accompli* by 1212 – was granted to the Abbess of Wilton, but with lesser rights belonging to the lord of the borough, a not untypical arrangement where the fair was shared. In the year 1300, the fair was held in September, taking place from the 14th to the 21st. The abbess administered the piepowder court. By 1414 the mayor and burgesses of the town were given a fair of their own, a two-day event, by Henry V, which was extended a year later to run from 19–22 July. This time the piepowder court remained in town hands. In 1433, underlining the wealth now vested in the downland fleece, the town was given the right to stage its first two sheep fairs in May and September, subsequently revised in 1496 by Henry VII to allow the one for St George's Day and the other on St Giles's. Both were three-day affairs and were still commemorating their respective saints on the appropriate days well through the seventeenth century. Although the abbess's September fair of St Matthew vanished with the Dissolution, Wilton in the eighteenth century was still playing host to three or four fairs. There seems, however, to have been a slight re-ordering in the early nineteenth century with the main fairs revised to 5 May (for cattle as well as sheep) and 12 September (the big sale for sheep only). The latter would be Wilton's saviour.

It is easy to understand the carpet town's envy of its larger neighbour – it sometimes blocked the roads to the Salisbury fairs! – and to sympathise with the damaging impact it felt to its own position. When that 'Whistler at the Plough' Alexander Somerville turned his steps in its direction, in the mid-nineteenth century, he found that 'Salisbury robs it [Wilton] even of the value of its markets and fairs'. The cathedral city's Lady Day fair, with its big turnout of cloth-sellers, had become by the sixteenth century a mecca for London's merchants and drapers. Both its Epiphany and Lady Day fairs were important cloth sales: in the late seventeenth century Aubrey mentions 'a very great fair for cloth at Twelf-tyde called Twelfe Market'. When an attempt was made in the eighteenth century to switch the Epiphany fair to August, leaving the early fair for cattle and cheese, it failed completely and by 1770 the city's four fairs had a settled pattern that would prevail with only minor variations until 1831: the Tuesday after 6 January for woollen cloth and cattle; the Monday before Old Lady Day (5 April) for woollen cloth; the Whitmonday and Tuesday for pedlary and horses; the Tuesday after 10 October for hops, cheese and onions.

With its atmosphere of culture and its several coffee-houses, including, most fashionably, the Parade in Blue Boar Row, the Salisbury of that time was a pleasant place to do business. It had been a market town from the Middle Ages with a Market House used weekly for corn, once a month for cheese, and once yearly for wool. To the three fairs granted to the Bishop of Salisbury, there was added a fourth, given to the Dean and Chapter and held in the Close, which had its own court of piepowder by 1457 and fifty years later took a definite step in defining its future character – and awakening Wilton's wrath – when a sacristan of the Chapter got leave to erect sheep pens in a meadow in the Close for the fair of Whitmonday, Tuesday and Wednesday. In 1565 the Chapter ruled that the meadow be set aside permanently for the fairs. By 1572 there is mention of a Michaelmas sheep fair being held on the Greencroft of the city. By the eighteenth century this had its own hurdle house, indicating an established event. Soon two fairs a year were being staged on the Greencroft, with Wilton vying strenuously the while to have them banned. As late as 1853, the city countered Wilton's opposition with two new sheep fairs in mid-July and mid-October, both held at the Butts. By 1860 they were well established and both would continue down to our own time. Such bitter

Wilton, in its envy, closed the roads leading to rival Salisbury's fairs

The grand occasion. Lewes Great Sheep Fair in 1850 with some 30,000 sheep in the pens. It was a good year, with business generally up on the year before against a sagging market and good ewes getting 30s-plus. Lambs were brisk at 23s; rams at 15 guineas

rivalry, undoubtedly, was typical of that which existed between the fairs of many other English counties. Such, too – exampled in some detail – was the complex geographical pattern and history of one county's fairs – exceptional perhaps but a pattern repeated to a lesser degree in every shire of the land.

Elsewhere, too, the shepherds of Old England herded their flocks to the great meeting points on long-appointed days of the year. On the South Downs, Findon's Great Fair on Nepcote Green, held there since 1796 on the second Saturday of September, continued a tradition: there had been Findon sheep fairs since medieval times. The largest of Sussex's sheep fairs – there were others at Lindfield and Lewes as well as lamb sales on the local St John's Common and at Horsham – Findon was still an occasion about 1930, with 10,000 sheep and lambs being sold. Flocks then were still being 'droved' to the fair: one Burpham shepherd would rise at two in the morning to have his animals penned by six. There that day, almost certainly, somewhere in the milling crowd, would be that remarkable recorder of South Downs shepherding life, Barclay Wills, a Worthing grocer who regularly forsook the sale of lentils and tea and sugar for the company of sheepmen, and whose accounts are as evocative as Hudson's in their portrayal of a vanished lifestyle.

The solitary men of the downs would make the most of such an occasion. From an old shepherd Barclay Wills heard an account of a light-hearted eve-of-the-fair ritual in an earlier era: 'Mr Trigwell told me of the old days at the fairs, when flocks were taken thither a day in advance. Shepherds met at an inn at night, a room being reserved for them. On these occasions there was plenty of merriment, and "colt-shoeing" was performed. "Colts" were young men whose experience of shearing was limited to one or two seasons. The man appointed caught each one as he entered, lifting one of his feet and pretending to shoe him. The "colt" was then expected to stand treat for the rest by buying half a gallon of beer.' It was a ritual that had its parallels at fairs elsewhere when shepherds met, and sometimes with an added vigour. It may have been considerably less respectable in earlier times. Wilton Great Fair had its own eve-of-fair event, when the shepherds of Salisbury Plain met at the town's Wheatsheaf Inn to vie for the title of 'King of the Shepherds'. Shepherding skill had nothing to do with it. It was straightforwardly vicious: cudgels, kicking and wrestling were all allowed. Almost nothing was barred. But when a victor had been declared enmity faded and the shepherds would retire to sleep it off in some barn, or on the floor of the inn, in a circle with their heads at the centre, pillowed on their dogs.

The shepherds would 'sleep it off' with their heads pillowed on their dogs

Such customs emphasise the loneliness of the shepherding life. The sheep fair was where the men of the downs met their friends – fellow shepherds not seen since the previous year. It was on the day of the fair that the shepherd took his bow, so to speak, before the wider farming community and, if his flock were in fine condition, received the public due of its respect. For Hudson's Shepherd Bawcombe the day of Yarnborough Castle Fair was one that conferred prestige. 'When Bawcombe was shepherd at Doveton it [the fair] was still great, and when he first went there as Mr Ellerby's head-shepherd he found himself regarded as a person of considerable importance at the Castle. Before setting out with the sheep he asked his master's instructions and was told that when he got to the ground he would be directed by the persons in charge to the proper place. The Ellerbys, he said, had exhibited and sold their sheep there for a period of eighty-eight years, without missing a year, and always at the same spot. Every person visiting the fair on business knew just where to find the Ellerbys' sheep, and he added with pride, they expected them to be the best sheep at the Castle.'

Dorset too – staging over sixty fairs as the eighteenth century started – had its big sheep fairs, including one held near yet another ancient earthwork, Poundsbury. This was Hardy country and it was Hardy who would write the requiem for all those rowdy and sometimes sodden occasions, 'A Sheep Fair':

> Time has trailed lengthily since met
>   at Pummery Fair
> Those panting thousands in their wet
>   and woolly wear:
> And every flock long since has bled,
> And all the dripping buyers have sped
> And the hoarse auctioneer is dead.
> Who 'Going–going!' so often said,
> As he consigned to doom each meek, mewed band
>   at Pummery Fair.

So Poundsbury, a relative upstart among fairs, first held on the banks of the Frome River in 1848, acquired its moiety of fame. A lesser pen, in the *Dorset County Chronicle*, would wax more lyrical in 1904. 'From sunrise to sunset the regnant orb of the sun shone steadily,' reported its correspondent, launching into full flow on the September fair: 'At an early hour flocks began to arrive from all quarters . . . fretting the surface of the roads. . . . Upwards of 12,000 sheep were brought together and penned in streets of hurdles pitched on the grassy plateau. Brakes and other vehicles were continually plying between the railway stations and the camp. The gathering was large and representative of various types of an agricultural population, with a sprinkling of the parasitical element always attracted by such fairs.' Though mainly a sheep fair, Poundsbury had 'a good number of horses and some cattle were also offered for sale . . . The pleasure fair has now quite disappeared.' The stalls selling hard liquor remained, however, as did the 'coffee barrow'.

Fair-goers could lodge for the night, laying weary bones on beds of hides

Dorchester's early fairs in the 1330s honoured the feasts of Holy Trinity and the Nativity of St John the Baptist and the memory of St James – with a late-comer for Candlemas Day. The city's fairs were for corn as well as sheep, with the main occasion for the latter being held in the city's Pease Lane until 1757, when it came to be considered a danger to citizens and on the corporation's orders was transferred to the Walks. But Hardy's favourite above all was September's Woodbury Hill Fair, again held in an old earthwork near Bere Regis, and granted its charter by Henry III in 1216. It was the most popular of all the old Wessex fairs, continuing for several days, and passed as a date into the social and manorial, and even legal, calendar of the region. Day four was the important sheep day, for the fair had cattle as well as its sheep pens. Horses, too, were sold, along with the usual fair commodities of cloth (of course), cheese, butter, hops and haberdashery, lace and leatherwork. Chapmen peddled trinkets to the unwary and tents served meals and ale. A 'bower' was erected on the hill, where fair-goers could lodge for the night, laying weary bones on 'beds' of hides. Poole oysters were the gastronomic highlight of the fair, which Hardy brought to life in *Far from the Madding Crowd* as his 1840s Greenhill Fair.

Yet the most historic of them all was Weyhill, in Hampshire, held in October near the junction of several of the ancient tracks at a lonely village three miles beyond Andover and once the largest sheep fair ever held in England. In 1683 30,000 sheep were being sold; by late in the eighteenth century it was turning over sheep sales worth £300,000 at a time when the price of a ewe was about 12 shillings. Defoe in the early half of the eighteenth century, describing Weyhill as the 'greatest fair for sheep . . . that this nation can show', reckoned 500,000 animals changed hands at it. As many as 140,000 might be sold in a single day. The fair was the wandering Cobbett's favourite; he bought his hunting whips there, made by one of the home-workers who came to sell their goods at the fair. The rector of Fyfield, the Revd H. White, brother of the more famous Gilbert, bought his cheeses there, brought up from Cheddar by the factors who took its sought-after taste round so many of the fairs. In 1822, however, it was the quality of the fair's hops that much occupied the critical Cobbett, who found fairs ideal for taking stock of the countryside and its affairs.

*Weyhill flourished
near the spot where
the old gold and tin
trails met*

His visit, a century after Defoe's, would find the fair in decline and reflecting the then depressed state of farming, the sheep fair's sales figure diminished to just £70,000. 'The countenances of the farmers were descriptive of their ruinous state. I never, in all my life, beheld a more mournful scene.' Not only that, but the bottom seems to have temporarily dropped out of both the horse and the hops market. The gloom, however, appears not to have soured the old boy unduly. He was back at Weyhill four years later, telling us in diarist style: 'To Weyhill, which is a village of half a dozen houses on a down, just above Appleshaw, they bring from the down-farms in Wiltshire and Hampshire, where they are bred, the Southdown sheep; ewes go away into the pasture and turnip countries to have lambs, wethers are fatted and killed, and lambs (nine months old) to be kept to be sheep.' With a sheep sale the previous day at Appleshaw, the fair had (as they say in farming circles) 200,000 sheep forward. 'The prices were just about one-half what they were last year.' The grief is genuine, never doubt it: 'There were Dorsetshire ewes that sold last year for 50s a head. We could hear of none this year that exceeded 25s. In 1812 these ewes were from 55s to 72s each at this same Appleshaw fair; and in that year I bought South-Down ewes at 45s each, just such as were, yesterday, sold for 18s. Yet, the sheep and the grass and all things are the same in real value. What a false, what a deceptious, what an infamous thing, this paper-money system is!' He continues: 'How many, many farmers' families are now just preparing the way for their entrance into the poor-house . . . certainly many a score farmers did I see at Weyhill, yesterday, who came there to know their fate; and who are gone home thoroughly convinced, that they shall, as farmers, never see Weyhill fair again!' A few days later, though, nothing loath, Cobbett was back to see the cheese and hops sections of the fair.

Like its near neighbour, the ancient fair of Winchester, Weyhill perched on a hilltop, one that bordered three parishes. It dated at least from the eleventh century, though its charter, from Elizabeth I only in 1599 might suggest otherwise. It flourished close to that spot where the old gold and tin trails met and maybe more than most of the hill fairs it carried the tenuous thread of history from that earlier time when men had met there to do homage to some forgotten hero; when some entrepreneurial soul perhaps had first seen the chance to put down a marker for trade. Its fame was incontestable. It was held on Old Michaelmas Day and continued its remarkable reign into the present century, diminished in stature it is true but rich still with lore and legend. Like so many of the sheep fairs it, too, had its initiation ceremony for young shepherds, the Horning Ceremony, part of the Horn Supper, in which the novitiate was required to stand with an ale-filled metal cup, set between a ram's horns, on his head while his fellow shepherds set up the customary chant:

> Swift is the hare; cunning is the fox;
> Why should not this little calf grow up to be an ox!
> To get his own living among the briars and thorns,
> And die like his daddy, with a great pair of horns.

Flock festival. A genial air pervades Bicester's gathering of the golden fleece back in 1908, a day for boaters and bowlers and, like all country fairs, for standing gossiping in the sun

Having drained his cup, the young candidate was required to fill the ale cups of the others – the prime purpose, one suspects, of all such occasions, whether they were meetings of the Society of the Horseman's Word or secret associations of shepherds. Or was the ritual, as some have suggested, perhaps a sinister remnant from the pagan past?

Dealers and their droving men moved from one West Country sheep fair to the next, bargaining, persuading, taking a fast profit on the animals they bought at one fair and then sold at the next; some purchased the downland horns for droving down the old green roads to the Home Counties farmers, who would fatten them for London's Christmas market. The scene was frenetic – as it was up and down England at each of the autumn's plethora of sheep fairs, many of them of vital significance, some of them, admittedly, less so. Yet large or small, each in its way and for its own region would be an economic indicator, an occasion at which farmer and flockmaster could measure their own viability, or prepare themselves for a failure in their fortunes.

Northumberland's Stagshawbank was the north's great sheep gathering, drawing Border flocks and those of Scotland's south-west and selling 100,000 head at the end of the eighteenth century when the fair was at its height. Near Corbridge and close to the Roman wall, it may have seemed a bit remote to survive, something it had managed to do, however, since at least the thirteenth century. Keswick's fair was for the disposal of the hardy Herdwick breed. Skipton (meaning sheep town) in Yorkshire had two fairs, honouring the feasts of St Martin and St James. Scunthorpe's was important and of ancient lineage while the famous Brigg Fair, an occasion that later came to be synonymous with the horse, in its earlier years was mainly for sheep. The Midlands, perhaps less recognisably sheep country, none the less had fairs of some size at Leicester and Nottingham and Bicester, and at Market Ilsley on the Oxford–Southampton road.

Corby Glen, claimed to be England's oldest sheep fair, even now keeps its October date, although the fair like the village itself has been in slow decline since the late eighteenth century. Its charter (to one Hammo Pecche in 1238) gave the right to hold several fairs but Corby Glen settled for the autumn date, held down the centuries until the 1930s on the first Monday before 10 October. Sheep have been the main interest, penned (as they still are) while horses and cattle were tethered by the roadside. For Corby Fair Monday the streets would be swarming with shepherds and their flocks, the inns seething with dealers. Right up to the Thirties, the dealing was in the traditional way, hallowed by custom, sealed by a handclasp.

There was a blip of revival for the old fair through the nineteenth century. The 1863 fair, it was reported, was 'the largest show of sheep, beasts and horses that has ever been seen on the ground'. There was a case, some felt, for making it a two-day affair. The following year the fair sent off ninety-three truckloads of livestock by rail alone. Alas, it proved a false dawn: the 12,000 animals in the pens by 1876 had dipped dramatically by 1877 to only 7,400. In 1882, in the words of one local commentator, the fair was 'the poorest I have ever seen' with the number down to 5,000. Yet there is a certain fair-day air still in the Woodhouse Arms as buyers and farmers wait for the sheep to be trucked in, or for auctioning to begin. With its sideshows and shooting galleries, swings and gingerbread stalls and boxing booths cramming the market-place, it was always a convivial kind of occasion, a day for reunion, but now more for the locals than for the shepherds.

Kettlewell would give that committed Dalesman Halliwell Sutcliffe the chance, in his book *Striding Dales*, to summon indelibly before the eyes the typical, timeless scene: '. . . a fair in keeping with the grim, limestone crags that shield the narrow meadows and the pastures on either side of the Wharfe River. It is a gathering not to be missed by any lover of the Dale. The first glimpse of it is the story of bygone days that live on among us. Constant to types inbred by the generations, the thickset farmers gather, and the wise sheep-dogs, and the ewes bleating with a sorrow that will not be quiet. Above them are the ancient hills that know no change, save in winter's cold and summer's heat. The men and the bleating ewes, the bright-eyed dogs, seem as old as the hills, and as young.'

The streets would be swarming with shepherds, the inns seething with dealers

Wool wealth had once made Norwich the third city in the kingdom and East Anglia's sheep fairs long reflected that. Norfolk, eventually to be more renowned for its cattle fairs, had its share, with sales at Swaffham, Diss and East Harling, to mention but three of the most important of the 1800s. Lincoln staged ram sales of some note and at Boston's May Fair sheep were considered the main business in that region with its reputation for fine wool. On London's northern

Wall-to-wall wool. Boston's May Sheep Fair, about 1850, in the vast market square, in a wonderfully luminous lithograph by George Northouse and dedicated by him to 'the gentry, farmers, graziers, dealers, tradesmen etc of Lincolnshire'. Behind the fair is the Fenland landmark of the Boston Stump (St Botolph's Church), whose fretted tower soars 272 feet above the scene

fringe, Barnet Fair, a mecca for the country's horse-copers, would have a goodly offering in its sheep field. Dorking, whose prime poultry was the main attraction for London's Leadenhall dealers, adequately managed a lamb fair on Holy Thursday (Ascension Day).

Launceston's fair was once one of the largest in Cornwall; another in the region and one of the biggest in the 1830s was Summercourt alongside the A30, still selling 6,000 head as the century closed. In August each year the sheep fair atmosphere of old still grips the old wool town of South Molton in Devon, with as many as 12,000 sheep being auctioned, and even that fair of high insobriety Widecombe – now for ponies – began life innocently in the mid-nineteenth century as a sheep occasion that drew in its flocks from the lonely silences of Dartmoor. Bampton Fair, long before it became the great ingathering for Exmoor ponies, had a role as one of the West Country's sizeable sheep fairs, selling up to 14,000 animals.

Somerset's sturdy flocks were driven to gatherings such as Woolavington, Wiveliscombe and Bridgwater. Its South Petherton yearly fair became so popular as far back as 1448 that its three days had to be lengthened to six. By the eighteenth century it was famous equally for cattle and sheep, and a century later was still congesting the village with pens containing 'eight and twenty thousand

Hallowed Priddy. The centuries-old sheep fair, still riven by controversy, marches on. It will continue, claims local superstition, for as long as its ancient pen hurdles remain stacked in their thatched hut (centre, right) on the village green. Before the Second World War it was a mecca for Irish horse-dealers, sharply dressed and carrying their ready cash in bags of chamois leather

lambs'. But Somerset's pride is Priddy. Today the Mendips hilltop village's sheep fair, now over 600 years old, is probably the nearest thing we have to the wonder that was Weyhill or Woodbury or those countless other occasions that once dotted the autumn calendar. Sheep have been Priddy's concern since Roman times, and its ancient fair takes place on a Wednesday in the second half of August on the village green, where its old pen hurdles stand hutted and thatched through the rest of the year.

Initially it was held, until at least 1785, on 10 August (St Laurence's Day) in the old calendar. The Somerset historian J. Collinson describes it as 'a large fair for horses, sheep and horned cattle' and while it had, for many years, a day given over to the sale of horses, by 1936 it had assumed its present traditional character as a sheep fair on the village green. Yet it is a fair 'stolen' from Wells, where it was the 'midsummer fair': in 1348, the worst year of the Black Death, the cathedral city's narrow streets presented a contagious threat and the August fair was transferred temporarily to the hill village. Wells would have the rest of its fairs restored when times improved, but by then Priddy had made the August one its own. It still has something of the atmosphere of the original occasion, with its bleating lambs drawn off the surrounding hills or even the Somerset Levels but with pedigree stock also brought in. The auction imposes a strict order: first the lambs, then the ewes with lambs, and finally the rams and wethers. Several thousand animals change hands in a fair that links Priddy with England's green and pastoral heyday and that time when the wool clip made her a nation to be reckoned with. It is part of the past, a time when men believed that 'the first rain after Priddy fair is the first rain of winter'; it will endure, say Priddy folk, despite recent controversy, for as long as the fair's hurdles continue to be stacked on the village green!

CHAPTER SIX

BEEF ON THE SLITHERING HOOF

The long drove to Smithfield began in the dawn mist of a late-summer morning by some quiet loch on Skye as the island's small farmers and crofters gathered to trade their ill-nourished beasts to the dealers and their herdsmen. It crossed Kyle Rhea to gather its momentum and merge with other droves from points north and east – Strath Halladale and Assynt, Strath Carron and Muir of Ord, Craigellachie and Aikey Brae, that great fair of Scotland's eastern shelf. It became a great, slow-moving black drift of beasts through the Lowlands to the meeting points of Crieff and Falkirk, where all the green tracks converged on Scotland's two principal trysts. It would have been something to see, one of those great gatherings, an endless, undulating mass of men and beasts, a cacophony of bellows and shouts and ever and incessantly the yap of drovers' collies. A man would have had to be dead in his soul to see it and not be moved. And that was but the beginning, for the big drove would be swollen by animals from the south-west and the fairs at Dumfries and the road led on by Annan and Esk, Lockerbie and Langholm, to Carlisle and to Brough Hill or Northallerton and after that, south to the greatest goal of all, Norfolk's fair of St Faith's, the last stop and long pause on the marathon drive to the capital's meat market.

Gathering the drove. The collection of beasts at a remote cattle fair in the Isle of Skye, dramatically portrayed by the artist Richard Ansdell (1815–1885). It all ended long weeks and weary miles later at the massive Norfolk fair of St Faith's

Point of departure. In 'The Highland Drover's Departure for the South', England's celebrated animal painter Sir Edwin Landseer (1802–1873) has not lost the chance to sentiment-alise. The leave-taking, the lonely glen, the shaggy beasts – it was a scene his romantic brush could not resist. All the same, it never fails to delight the eye

North of the Border, Falkirk – Scotland's largest cattle fair – and Dumfries became the main gathering points as Crieff's standing began to decline. At Falkirk up to 40,000 head would be paraded in the two days of the October fair on the scrub-covered, 200-acre 'field' in Larbert parish, two miles to the west of the town, to which it had moved in 1785. Here northern and Highland beef, shaggy-coated kyloes from the west and norlands, equally lean, conveniently met speculative wallets anxious to buy beef that would taste all the sweeter when it had been fed up on rich English pasture. One reporter, from the middle of last century, has left his excitable yet indelible account of the main occasion. On Falkirk moor, he claims, visitors will 'witness a scene to which certainly Great Britain, perhaps even the whole world, does not afford a parallel . . . No stranger accustomed to the bustle and the crowd, the handling and the haggling of an English fair, would suspect transactions of a magnitude to which Barnet, St Faith's, and Wey Hill afford no parallel . . . The scene, seen from horseback, from a cart, or some erection, is particularly imposing. All is animation, bustle, business and activity; servants running about shouting to the cattle, keeping them together in their particular lots and ever and anon cudgels are at work upon the horns and rumps of the restless animals that attempt to wander in search of grass or water . . .'. In fields all around were more beasts, waiting to be driven into this vast arena, seeking to swell its sweating activity.

There are faint if incongruous echoes even of the great beef-drives of the American West: 'The cattle-dealers of all descriptions chiefly on horse-back are scouring the field in search of the lots they require. The Scottish drovers are for the most part mounted on small, shaggy, spirited ponies that are obviously quite at home among the cattle; and they carry their riders through the throngest groups with astonishing alacrity . . .'. The English graziers – they have come north from Yorkshire and beyond – are stolider men, mounted on stouter horses, cautious and considerous, asking prices, haggling. But the closing of the deal has that familiar ritual and certainty of all fair transactions: 'the purchaser claps a penny of arles into the hand of the stockholder, observing at the same time "It's a bargain".' The protagonists then repair into one of the many drinking booths to finalise the negotiation, for Falkirk, for all its high seriousness, never forgot that it was a fair. Mingling through the dealers, the drovers and their restless beasts were the pedlars, gamblers, ballad-singers and jugglers. Says our deafened reporter: '. . . a person hears the uncouth Cumberland jargon and the prevailing Gaelic, along with the innumerable provincial dialects, in their genuine purity, mingled with the astonishing roar . . . When cattle dealers are in the way of their business, their conversation is full of animation.' Our correspondent, one feels, may have had a talent for understatement. Falkirk at such a time was like Babylon on an overcrowded holiday: every room in town and for a long way round would be taken – as Dorothy Wordsworth found in 1803, when her visit coincided with the September fair.

The Scottish trysts would become closely bound to the English fairs. London in particular, with its taverns and coffee-houses, was an insatiable market. But it had all started tentatively enough in the later sixteenth century, a statute of 1587 noting that there had recently begun 'the transporting of nolt [cattle] and sheip to England in grite nowmeris'. Such droving was frowned on, as further statutes make clear, and was to the detriment of Scotland's own needs. It was at first a precarious trade, at the mercy of the fickle relationship between the two countries, to say nothing of the fiery skirmishes that engulfed the Borderlands from time to time. It was only after the union of the crowns in 1603 that the cross-Border droves began to swell and became an accepted part of the Scottish economy. Even then, the Scots beasts, miserably lean through the overstocking of pastures and the lack of winter feed in that northern climate, were eclipsed both in quality and numbers by the Irish steers – 61,000 head in 1663 – then making heavy inroads into the English market, and would have to wait for the restrictive measure of 1666, the Irish Cattle Act, before they really commanded the attention of the English graziers. Welsh and north of England beef-rearing areas would feel a similar benefit from the ban on the Irish cattle. Dramatic reductions on the once-punitive Border customs duty – and its subsequent abolition after the union of parliaments in 1707 – would also give Scottish droving a fresh impetus. As the Treaty of Union was signed the official tally of beasts coming south was some 30,000 annually.

The trading of beef on the slithering hoof was certainly well into its stride as the peripatetic John Macky was passing through the region of the main Scottish

London, with its taverns and coffee-houses, was an insatiable market

fairs. In *A Journey Through Scotland*, published in 1723 at about the time Defoe was discursing on the wonder of St Faith's, he tells us: 'The Highland Fair at Criff happening when I was in Stirling, I had the curiosity to go to see it. There were at least thirty thousand cattle sold there, most of them to English Drovers.' By the mid-nineteenth century the more convenient venue, Falkirk, would be sending south 150,000 black beasts yearly. Not everyone was happy, especially not English farmers. As early as 1665 a protest to the House of Commons had railed against the inroads of the Scots and Irish trade and the deprivation experienced by southern farmers, who felt that the cattle trade had not only passed into the hands of strangers but strangers, at that, who took their ill-gotten gains home with them – out of the English economy.

Lairds and noblemen had an interest in the droving, and sometimes, like the Galloway landowners, a close involvement. Before the end of the eighteenth century the south-west – including the counties of Dumfries, Wigtown and Kirkcudbright – were adding perhaps 20,000 to the Falkirk total. In most districts by 1800 the new mode of turnip-feeding had lifted the condition of the beasts being sent to market and with it, their price: now around £10 a head against the £2 of a century or so earlier. A four-year-old Galloway bullock, recognised even then as prime beef, might make £12. Scotland's south-west indeed had moved strongly into stock-rearing, badly neglecting, so some thought, the other exciting developments in agriculture. As Kelton's then minister put it when he came to present his cameo for that most fascinating of records, the late eighteenth-century *Old Statistical Account*, the trade was 'the staple commodity' of Galloway, and even in the highly arable parishes of Wigtown, substantial earnings were pinned to the black cattle trade. In Kirkcudbright its place was beyond doubt: it provided the chief farming income.

It might all have seemed random and arbitrary in its organisation but in fact the droving involved a network of trails and fairs that interlinked with meticulous timing. Each venue gathered and dispersed to another and the green roads spread a tracery over the landscape the entire length of Britain. Dumfries's three autumn fairs on the White Sands at the mouth of the Nith were the most important in that region. That other perambulator Pococke, passing through the landscape in 1675, claimed that some 20,000–30,000 beasts from Galloway (we may take it he meant the entire south-west) were that year sent to 'a Fair near Norwich'. (Like all such chroniclers, with their passion for round numbers, it is possible that he slightly exaggerated.) The biggest sales were those in September, linking the movement of beasts to the big Brough Hill Fair later in the month – and just as keenly to the October fair at St Faith's in East Anglia. Usually a composite Dumfries drove would be formed for the drive through England; it was known as the 'St Faith's Drove'. To be economically viable a drove would have to be at least 200 strong – requiring at least four men to manage it – though most droves leaving Scotland would be much larger. (The reckoning on ratio was one drover to every sixty or so beasts.) In one year, 1794, the four main drovers between them accounted for 20,000 head worth £130,000; later still, in 1830, the number of beasts sold in a single week in September would total 6,000.

Lords and noblemen had an interest in the droving, sometimes a close involvement

South of the Border. Carlisle stood at the convergence of the old cattle drovers' routes, an important gathering-point in the flow of beasts to stock southern tables. Here on the Sands, in a pleasing watercolour of 1864 by William Henry Nutter (1819–1872), and with the city's distant townscape and cathedral as a backcloth, dealers and buyers haggle over prices

Dumfries's later mid-October, mid-week tryst also embedded the name of a distant landscape in the local folklore, for then the beasts would be bought for a long drove that would end at the November fair at Hempton Green in West Norfolk. So central was that occasion to the northern region's economy that it was locally dubbed 'Hempton Wednesday'. For all that, if he feared a glut and low prices there a drover man, at the last, might well turn his herd's heads towards the lesser fairs at Bungay or Hallisworth or Harleston.

With Falkirk behind them the droves went south in a surging tide that might thread through the tryst at Hawick and roll on to Carlisle, or St Luke's at Newcastle. Horses, too, joined the dark throng. One route led via Gretna, sometimes cutting across the Solway Sands; its beasts would congregate with the other droves on the way to Carlisle. Even in 1663, 18,574 head paid toll there. The Carel (or Carlisle) autumn fair would later send 60,000–80,000 head onward on the trail. And that trail led on – to Brough Hill, a bleak, wind-scoured expanse close to the Bowes–Appleby road on the border of Yorkshire and Westmorland, a fair probably of Roman origin whose charter was granted by Edward III to Roger de Clifford in 1330. Over the Stainmore Pass, the main crossing point of the Pennines, poured cattle, beasts and geese to the famous fair at one of the main coaching crossroads of the north and a stopping place for travellers coming and going all over the country. It was where the Romans had built their fort to secure their military road from Carlisle to York. The village and its fair were at their peak in the eighteenth and nineteenth centuries as the south-bound drovers made use of the route the Romans had left them. Over the old hump-backed bridge of Market Brough poured the beasts bound for London's tables. The congestion was horrendous.

From Carlisle the drovers' trail might have taken them down the old Penrith coach road to High Hesket (Broadfield), then via Penrith, over into the Eden Valley and then by Hilton and Dufton. But the Scots beasts arrived also by two other main routes, one through Gilsland, the other down the line of the Great North Road heading for Scotch Corner. Before enclosure, many preferred to pick their own way over the moors. If the journey was wearisome and the drove tardy, one of the droving crew might get out his bagpipes and step to the front to blow a lively tune in the hope of increasing the pace. At the end-of-September fair, in the late eighteenth century, 10,000 beasts would find buyers; most would march on to satisfy the capital's palates.

The fair was the focus of their year; it could bring them profit or ruin

Under its early charter Brough held four important cattle markets a year in addition to its famous four-day fair. Besides the cattle and geese, it gathered thousands of sheep and turkeys – and, of course, horses. There had been an earlier fair, from 1280, which may or may not have been the one chartered by the king. Given the opportunity it later presented, more than a few of the district's farmers were involved with the droving trade, either as graziers or in letting pasture to graziers. Local breeders crossed the Galloway and Irish cattle bought at the fair to create strains that fared well on the northern hill ground. Others bought young animals for over-wintering, or even for fattening over a longer period, before selling them back to the drovers. Many were themselves unashamedly dealers for whom the fair was the focus of their year and could bring them high profit – and doubtless, at times, ruin as well.

The fair was a great gathering point also for fell and dale ponies – and for gypsies who, at the end of the fair, would light great bonfires and dance into the dawn. The poet Thomas Gray (of 'Elegy' fame) was there for the fair in 1759, while the Scottish droving trade was still growing yearly and was astonished at the sight that met his gaze: 'myriads of horses and cattle on the road itself and in all the fields around one . . . thousands of clean healthy people in their best party-color'd apparel, farmers and their families, esquires and their daughters, hastening up from the dales and down the fells on every side, glittering in the sun and pressing forward to join the throng.' Conjure the commotion if you will with the further evidence of William Addison, as he looked back nostalgically in the Fifties in *English Fairs and Markets*:

For days before the fair was held, strings of ponies were to be seen along every road and green track – the old drove roads – from the fells of Yorkshire, Westmorland, and Cumberland, trotting towards Brough as well as great herds of Scots cattle drifting slowly down from the Highlands. On the lonely tracks now used only by hikers these herds and droves passed year by year through the centuries, and at cottage doors where ice-cream is sold today, or where a board is hung out in the summer months to announce that teas are served indoors, stalls would be set up before and after Brough Hill Fair and spread out with the real old country meat and drink – home-brewed ale, or jugs of tea, and enormous game pies with crusts the like of which we haven't seen since we became a Welfare State.

The Scots drovers in their kilts – and sometimes knitting as they walked – caused amusement in England's gently rolling countryside. But folk gave them a wide berth not because of their sometimes fierce appearance but owing to the ferocity of their dogs. Both were oddities in the landscape and one who noted their progress was the unfortunate pastoral poet John Clare, whose *The Shepherd's Calendar* is not entirely complimentary to either the beasts or their drovers:

> Scotch droves of beast a little breed
> In sweltered weary mood proceed . . .
> Followed by slowly pacing swains
> Wild to our rushy flats and plains
> At whom the shepherd's dog will rise
> And shake himself and in surprise
> Draw back and waffle in afright
> Barking the traveller out of sight
> And mowers o'er their scythes will bear
> Upon their uncooth dress to stare
> And shepherds as they trample bye
> Leaves o'er their hooks a wondering eye
> To witness men so oddly clad
> In petticoats of banded plad
> With blankets o'er their shoulders slung
> To camp at night the fields among
> When they for rest on commons stop
> And blue cap like a stocking top
> Cockt o'er their faces summer brown
> Wi scarlet tazzeles on the crown
> Rude patterns of the thistle flower
> Untrickd and open to the shower
> And honest faces fresh and free
> That breathe of mountain liberty.

The drovers' road to St Faith's led south by Northallerton, Boroughbridge, Doncaster, Gainsborough and Newark to Grantham and Peterborough, then east to Spalding and Wisbech before entering Norfolk at Setchey just south of King's Lynn; the memory of it would live long in the names of the wayside inns where the drover men slaked their thirsts. One of the last 'stances' or stops on the route was at Holt; the following day the road to the fair's Bullock Hill would be through the by-lanes of Horsford. The pace, as Addison suggests, was ponderous, perhaps no more than 10 to 12 miles a day, as the beasts straggled and nibbled their way through the English landscape, the drover sometimes at their head, his wise old dog mounting a rearguard action a mile back and managing, just, to keep the caravan moving – although in the last few days the rate might be increased to 15 or 20 miles in order to claim a good pitch at the fair. Too much haste earlier, however, and the animals would lose condition, something they did at the best of times. Night stops were in some fold or rented field where the drover slept wrapped in his plaid – the 'blanket' of Clare's poem – under the stars. There would be other stops perhaps, points of dispersal, along the way: at Malham Tarn, in Upper Wharfedale, one English dealer, a man named Birtwhistle, gathered drove beasts on to a limestone pasture of over 700 acres – maybe 5,000 head at a time – fattening them into prime condition before holding his own 'fair'. He alone, it is said, was selling 20,000 animals a year, besides managing a considerable sideline in horses and sheep.

For any long drove the bullocks might be shod with lightweight metal, crescent-shaped shoes (two to each cloven hoof, with each shoe secured by three nails) to prevent deterioration of the animals' feet over stony tracks: one Boroughbridge blacksmith reckoned to make some 30,000 ox-shoes each droving season. To be shod a beast would have to be thrown on to its side and its legs roped together. A skilled blacksmith could shoe sixty animals a day. Smithies along the route would

The end of the road. Only this sign of old times remains as a reminder of the once frenetic scenes that ended the long drove south to Norfolk's famous fair of St Faith's from the Isles and Highland glens

In remembrance. A scarlet poppy tosses in the wind and the barley stirs gently across the peaceful acres of Norfolk's Bullock Hill where once the Scottish drovers brought their black 'runts' to meet southern graziers' purses

refit or repair loose shoes, but the head drover would himself carry 'spares' for emergencies, along with the necessary nails, which would be encased in a lump of fat to prevent them rusting and perhaps causing infection when driven into a hoof.

To the big autumn fairs of East Anglia the drove from Falkirk or Dumfries would take a month – perhaps even longer – with long rests at midday as well as the overnight respite in the 'accommodation' fields. Such pauses may have been irksome to the drover but he well understood their necessity; his reputation at the fair, and his success in their eventual sale, depended on the animals' appearance. A beast, it was estimated, lost 20 lb for every 100 miles, and the distance on the drove road, say from Dumfries, was much longer and more tortuous than today's 300 or so motorway miles. Sometimes the black beasts of 'prodigious quality' and the 'large noble breed of oxen' that went south from Northallerton's fairs would be sent only as far as the fens of Lincolnshire and the Isle of Ely rather than Norfolk, but they, too, would be fattened for Smithfield.

The old drovers were tough, durable men, most of them (alas, not all) acutely aware of their responsibility, adroit at avoiding the toll-bars en route; one claimed that he could take a herd from Sutherland to Falkirk paying only once, at the bridge at Stirling. Some of them were men of substance, cattle dealers rather than drovers, but employing bands of droving men. In business they were robust and astute, early exponents of the 'hard sell'. Often they would act as couriers. Theirs was a hazardous calling. Walter Scott called them 'princes among herds', saying of them:

It affords exercise for all their habits of patient endurance and active exertion. They are required to know perfectly the drove roads, which lie over the wildest

A drover in his fashion. Suitably badged and licensed, this is what the well-dressed Smithfield herdsman was wearing when William Henry Pyne (1769–1843) came to do this aquatint for his *Costume of Great Britain* in 1808

parts of the country, and to avoid as much as possible the highways, which destroy the feet of the bullocks, and the turnpikes, which annoy the spirit of the drover; whereas, in the broad green or gray track which leads across the pathless moor, the herd not only move at ease and without taxation, but if they mind their business may pick up a mouthful of food by the way. At night the drovers usually sleep along with their cattle, let the weather be what it will; and many of these hardy men do not once rest under a roof during a journey on foot from Lochaber to Lincolnshire.

Stevenson, too, knew something of the drover's life and was plainly fascinated by it. He adds the somewhat less romantic side of the story, an aspect the drover legends seldom mention. His boyhood friend, the ageing Pentlands shepherd John Todd, had once been a long-drove man. In his essay 'Pastoral', written about 1887, with the droving days already fading into history, Stevenson says:

John Todd, when I knew him, was already 'the oldest herd in the Pentlands' and had been all his days faithful to that curlew-scattering, sheep-collecting life. He remembered the droving days, when the drove roads, that now lie green and solitary through the heather, were thronged thoroughfares. He had himself often marched flocks into England, sleeping on the hillsides with his caravan; and by his account it was a rough business not without danger. The drove roads lay apart from habitation; the drovers met in the wilderness as to-day the deep-sea fishers meet off the banks in the solitude of the Atlantic; and in the one as in the other case rough habits and fist-law were the rule. Crimes were committed, sheep were filched, and drovers robbed and beaten; most of which offences had a moorland burial and were never heard of in the courts of justice. John, in those days, was at least once attacked – by two men after his watch – and at least once, betrayed by his habitual anger, fell under the danger of the law and was clapped into some rustic prison-house, the doors of which he burst in the night and was no more heard of in that quarter.

Disaster could strike a drove out of the blue. A man who had started out with dreams of riches might find himself a pauper by the time he approached St Faith's. There was, for instance, the delaying frustration of toll-gates that let through only one beast at a time. Trade could slump badly in times of agricultural depression, or when the Norfolk turnip crop failed. But sometimes it was much worse. As George Williamson, one Scottish drover-dealer – almost certainly one of the renowned and respected droving Williamsons of St Johns Wells in Aberdeenshire, who bought heavily in such northern fairs as Aikey Brae – was passing through Perth with 1,000 beasts the bells pealed out joyously for the victory of Waterloo. For the drover man, however, the clangour was more the knell of doom. The drop in prices that would immediately result, he told the toll-keeper, would cost him £4,000. In 1746, and probably in the following year, St Faith's fell victim to a local outbreak of rinderpest, leaving the drove beasts stranded and dying in the Norfolk lanes and their drovers facing financial ruin. Some, in their despair, simply abandoned their beasts and fled for home. Today there are Scottish drovers of that time lying far from home in Norfolk churchyards, themselves sometimes the victims of disease. The parson-diarist John Woodforde, sitting in his parsonage at Weston Longville to the east of St Faith's, noted of the October fair in 1787: 'St Faith's Fair today. I would not let any of my servants go to it, on Account of a very bad Fever of the putrid kind raging there and of which many have died there already.'

Like the Stock Exchange the livestock fair was always a lottery. The capital involved was the farmer's or possibly a banker's but the player was the drover, who usually took the beasts on credit (sometimes with a low payment and a promissory note for the balance); their disposal was in his hands. His 'dividend' was the profit he hoped to take on their sale. Some drovers, it is true, were simply hired men; others worked on commission. A number were men much-respected and of unimpeachable integrity; many were speculators permanently facing bankruptcy, juggling debt against hoped-for profit, whose accountancy, it has to be said, could be rough and ready. (All the same, their bills of exchange had the value of banknotes; there were times indeed when such drovers' bills – passing happily from hand to hand – constituted almost the entire, if fragile, currency of the Scottish Highlands.) It was a high-risk trade in which the drover-

Disease left the drove beasts stranded and dying in the Norfolk lanes

negotiator, as the central figure, had to gauge the subtleties of the market and judge, to a fine degree, when to tip his hand. Men who had brought beasts from Falkirk or Dumfries, who had invested so much time in their slow progress on the drove road, were willing to invest a little more as they mingled with the crowd and waited to see how the market would run. Long acquaintance would make the best of them shrewd assessors of the atmosphere and the way trade would turn. It was a battle of wits, of nerve: grazier-buyers, knowing more droves were on their way, would stay their hand, leading to a sharp fall in prices as drovers got desperate to clear their beasts before the bottom fell completely out of the fair. But in their turn – and in their own strong interests – the drovers could forestall events by holding back, say, in Lincolnshire, or by diverting their droves to lesser fairs at Harling, Cawston, Swaffham or Kenninghall. Each English region in fact had its arrangement of fairs, one 'feeding' the other, or satellites with a particular function in the local economy. In East Anglia, the principal fairs, usually, for the sale of Scottish cattle droves – once the trade had become well established – were at Harleston in early September; Setchley in early October with St Faith's a week later; Halesworth in early November with Hempton, near Fakenham, mid-month, and Hoxne, near Diss, in early December, an occasion that would continue until Christmas if demand warranted that. Shrewd drovers might even take their droves deep into Essex.

For most of the Scottish drovers, however, their big gamble came at the fair of St Faith's (or St Fay's), held just four miles north-east of Norwich and undoubtedly the greatest sale in England for Scots cattle. Parson Woodforde, living at Weston Longville and a regular attender, in 1777 described it as a 'very large Fair for all Things and lasts for a fortnight, a great concourse of people there'. He found the road as crowded as did Dorothy Wordsworth at Falkirk. In 1783 he notes what had become commonplace, finding a 'good many Scotch Beasts and Scotch Men with them there'. A writer in the *British Archaeological Journal* in 1932, casting back the years, evoked a 'wonderful scene, cattle, horses, highlanders, Norfolk men chaffering, drinking and dancing. Every road and lane in the neighbourhood packed, with cattle and their drovers sleeping together in the fields and lanes.' St Faith's indeed was four fairs rolled into one: pleasure fair, provision fair, horse fair, and, most importantly, the cattle fair. The latter took place on Bullock Hill, which had been under crop during the summer, on the road leading to Old Catton; the horse fair was staged beside the Norwich road; the pleasure fair nearby on a strip of land called the Lond, and the provision market in an adjacent field called Fairstead. A donkey and pony fair took place on waste ground by the side of the road near the White House. There was a sizeable cheese fair where local farmers could buy sufficient quantities to see them through the year, and in the provisions section clothes, crockery and many other kinds of merchandise, not forgetting the ubiquitous gingerbread stalls, and the fair's temporary pubs – the 'bush houses', so-called from the broom or furze pinned above their doors – many of which were also trading posts for rabbit skins and for ferrets, the sleek but savage means of acquiring them; and of course, farm labour could be hired.

'A wonderful scene: cattle, horses, highlanders, Norfolk men chaffering, drinking and dancing'

St Faith's had flourished since the twelfth century and by the eighteenth century it was, too, a social occasion attracting 'the first people in the country' and 'many very pretty women'. They came in every known type of conveyance including carriages, curricles, gigs and phaetons. The fair lasted officially for three weeks – but went on much longer if necessary. Drovers with their beasts, predominantly steers, might arrive up to three weeks beforehand to loiter in the lanes or pre-booked fields waiting for the fair to begin.

Droves of a thousand animals were not uncommon and fortunes fluctuated almost by the minute for the men who brought them there. Much depended on the condition of the beasts and in 1781, as William Marshall reported in his *Rural Economy of Norfolk*, this was as usual variable. Marshall, however, rather contradicts the view that the animals were always in poor condition after their long drive south: 'It is astonishing to see the state and condition of the cattle: they look as fresh and as sleek as if they had not travelled a mile from home: some of them tolerable beef. Even so high as eleven pounds apiece was asked for some bullocks; it was however to choose four out of a large drove; but ten pounds was asked to draw fifteen or twenty.' The option of choice throws light on the manner of dealing at the fair; clearly the drovers were into bulk-selling long before the hypermarket was ever heard of. Heifers had a poorer market that year, down at around £7 a head, and the fair average for cattle that would 'finish' to a weight of 50 stone was between £6 and £9. Buttonholing him at the fair, Marshall was told by the oldest Scots drover there that day that he had seen prices better by 30 shillings.

Marshall gives us an insight not only into how the fair coped with its autumn inundation of beef but into the drovers' considerable overheads on top of the droving costs from Falkirk or Dumfries, which could be anything from 18 to 24 shillings per animal: 'Each drover hires meadows or grazing-grounds in proportion to his quantity of cattle – farmers in the neighbourhood preserving for the purpose a full bite of grass; for which the Scotchmen pay very amply. The charges on sale must run very high. The number of attendants, the high price of grass, the treating of farmers to the amount perhaps of a couple of guineas a day, must lower the neat [net] proceeds very considerably, even of each bullock taken separately.' He is complimentary about the Borderlands beasts: 'The larger bullocks are principally of the Galloway polled breed, and most of them are very handsome; in general, four or five years old; mostly black, some brindled, some dun, and some few red.' The animals from Skye though were far from impressive: 'This morning, I saw ten two-year-old Isle of Skys, drawn out of a lot of two hundred, at two guineas and a half a head. Very small: not larger than ordinary yearling calves of the larger breeds of cattle.'

Most of the beasts sold at St Faith's were four or five years old, with the exception of oxen that had been pulling the plough. They would generally be twice as old. But fattened on turnips and Norfolk's lush pasture, even a lean, 'neat' Highland beast would soon make up the weight it might have lost on the drove and come into prime condition for Smithfield, the capital's livestock market, where the beef was still driven in on the skittering hoof. Or as Defoe

Droves of a thousand were not uncommon, fortunes fluctuated by the minute

Dealing on the fringe. Welsh drovers favoured Barnet Fair and liked to take their beef droves there. This scene of 1849 shows the fair still as one of the most important, selling 40,000 head of cattle (as well as other livestock), before the railway blighted its future. It was also called the Welsh Fair – the Welsh drovers even brought their preachers!

puts it: 'These Scots runts, so they call them, coming out of the cold and barren mountains of the Highlands in Scotland, feed so eagerly on the rich pasture in these marshes, that they thrive in an unusual manner, and grow monstrously fat; and the beef is so delicious for taste, that the inhabitants prefer 'em to the English cattle.' He estimated that at any one time about 40,000 beasts were being fed up on the marshland pastures between Norwich, Beccles and Yarmouth. They would be fattened for six months before being gathered for the hundred-mile or so drive into Smithfield. Then, an East Anglian farmer who had paid £10 in October for a good Galloway bullock would expect in April to get £15 – even £17; a smaller Skye beast bought for two and a half guineas might be lucky to make four.

The convergence of droves on St Faith's, of course, was not only from the north. They came in from the west, with Welshmen clogging the green arteries of the land as they brought in beasts from such gatherings as that beside the Anchor Inn on the western boundary slopes of Clun Forest – though the Welsh preference was for England's industrial heartland and the pasture fields of Leicestershire and Northamptonshire, where their animals would be fattened for sale at the region's spring and autumn fairs. During the fairs season as many as 400 cattle might be found waiting at any hour of the day to cross on the Chepstow–Bristol ferry, before meandering their way through the southern counties of England. A considerable number would be bound for Barnet, on the capital's northern fringe and once one of the country's largest cattle gatherings. There the September fair was sometimes dubbed the Welsh Fair, an indicator of the high number of Welsh beasts and ponies brought there. The fair traditionally ended with the Welsh Drovers' Race in which the drovers raced the ponies on which they had marshalled the drove. They competed for the prize of a saddle and bridle (bought by public subscription), riding shirt-sleeved and with handkerchiefs round their heads. The riders, one commentator observed, 'sometimes have saddles, sometimes none, and occasionally rode their mounts on halters only. The shouting and jabbering in Welsh at the start was something terrific, there generally being about ten or a dozen riders, and as they came into the straight run to the winning post, the cattle-dealers followed immediately on their horses, galloping up the course as hard as they could go, all shouting. The dealers then used to start for a race upon their own account, shouting and yelling at the top of their voices as they pushed their unaccustomed animals along the stretch to the winning post.' The old affinity had been further cemented in 1746 when Islington's fair for the sale of Welsh beasts was transferred to Barnet after a 'distemper' had struck the horned cattle breeds round the outskirts of the capital. It is likely that the Welsh were as possessive about Barnet as the Scots were about St Faith's. Perhaps fearful of the moral contagion of the big city, they even brought their preachers with them!

That Barnet was an 'event' is beyond question. From the hill fairground there would be a raucous overspill on to the adjoining commons, where the drovers would 'lodge' and graze their livestock for weeks beforehand, with separate fields designated for the different types of livestock. The turmoil was unimaginable. Barnet's residents became resigned to dodging the horses and cattle droves as they blundered through the main street to the site on the skirts of the village. Men maddened by the dust of a long cattle drive tethered their animals to anything that offered a reasonable anchor, obstructing the pavements while they slaked unquenchable thirsts in the village's innumerable inns – or set the seal on the deal they had just done.

Some of the black Welsh beasts, however, would find their way to Smithfield off the fattening pastures of Wiltshire. Others took their droves to South Somerset's Whitedown Hill Fair, between Chard and Crewkerne, where the sheep pens of earlier fairs were eclipsed by 1640 by the cattle dealing. From Farnborough's village school, remembers George Sturt in *A Farmer's Life*, the boys liked to look out on the Welsh droves passing on their way to Blackwater Fair in November; there was the chance to see them again, those unsold anyway, as they passed again to Farnham Fair a couple of days later. The road at other times of the year was deserted. The Welsh drovers, like the Scots, avoided the turnpike roads and the tolls, slowly working their way via the commons and the green roads. Though the droves were small – each numbering perhaps only 150 – they would stretch drove-to-drove across the countryside. It could take them four days to pass by on the road to Blackwater.

The Welshmen's main market, Sturt asserts, was at the coast. As the droves neared London they veered south to the sea. After Farnborough, in Hampshire,

Fearful of the capital's contagion, the Welsh drovers brought their preachers

they would head for Horsham and Brighton, watering their animals at ponds along the route – knowing where the ponds were and the time it would take to reach them was part of the drover's expertise. Night stops would be in 'accommodation' fields and, to get their money's worth, the droving men would be in no great hurry to move on in the morning. Some, it is said, left their departure almost until nightfall. The Welsh were considered particularly close-fisted by the renting farmers; they bargained in English but squabbled among themselves in Welsh. Four or five men handled each drove, usually mounted – sometimes two to a horse! Like the Scots, they shod their animals for the drive. Inns along the green roads they favoured catered for their insatiable appetite for fried liver and bacon!

Inns along the green roads catered for an appetite for fried liver and bacon

The Welsh had been droving for as long as the Scots, and maybe longer. In 1312, 700 beasts were dispatched from the Welsh pastures for the king's kitchen at Windsor to tease the taste-buds of the old warlord Edward's disappointing son. The Welsh indeed, perhaps because of the royal warrant, seem to have seized an early grip on the quality market by supplying many of the country's noble houses. In later centuries, in the high days of the droving, however, the always informative Marshall in his switch of scene in *Rural Economy of Southern Counties* believes that some of the animals brought east by the drovers were only one, two or three years old and intended simply for stocking farms rather than for onward sale to Smithfield. Though they came from all parts of the Principality, Marshall speaks particularly well of those of the Pembrokeshire breed: they made 'handsome cows which are said to milk well and to fat quickly'. The October roads were 'everywhere full of them: some going for the uplands districts, others to the Marshes'. Their route was the one their sheep-droving countrymen and their dogs followed in bringing vast autumn flocks for dispersal on the marshes around Rye.

Somerset, like its neighbour Wiltshire, was rich with fairs – by 1500 it had ninety-four – most with a heavy turnover in livestock. In 1798 the county still had forty-six, more than thirty of them with days for the sale of fat cattle. The legendary but somehow little recorded Whitedown fair, held on the downs and still being staged in the mid-nineteenth century, was at a convenient crossing of the roads that led east–west to and from London. As an earlier, Whit-week fair, Whitedown in its heyday understandably sold more oxen than cattle. The Glamorgan drovers found their way to this 'great fair', increasingly so after the Civil War, getting around £4 in 1640 for a bullock or a cow, an acceptable figure perhaps but not the best price. Local dealers fared better: about that time 'William Leace of St Mary Ottree sold two oxen to Henry Qauntock of Norton under Hamden . . . £10 13 04'. The fair's emphasis would continue strongly on draught oxen but, among other things, it was a favourite with tanners, who gathered to stock its famous market for leather.

Somerset's fat beasts from such fairs, including South Petherton, held in late June on the 'vigil, the feast and the morrow' of the wool merchants' favourite saint, John the Baptist, were by 1800 being driven not just to the main cities of the region but also to London. A drove took nine days to reach the capital –

Drovers' mecca. The smelly, noisy and very messy Smithfield that Dickens knew and so evocatively described in *Oliver Twist* and here marvellously evoked by an aquatint from the peripatetic Thomas Rowlandson (1756–1827). It was the scene of great moments of history and revelry as well as the capital's (and the nation's) greatest livestock market. On the left is St Bartholomew's Hospital; in the background, the towers and spires of City churches and the familiar dome of St Paul's

some 130 miles on the hoof. The drover's charge was 12 shillings a head. Shepton Mallet, like its neighbours a sheep town hit after the eighteenth century by the downturn in wool fortunes, and where once wives were for sale in the market, chose to look west, bringing in butchers from Bristol and Bath to buy sometimes up to 400 fatted calves a day. The calves' privilege – more horrifyingly humane – was to travel deadweight by horse-drawn cart. And there were other venues: Shrewsbury (with its eight fairs), Taunton, and Glastonbury's Tor Fair in September, still a mecca for the sheepskin industry, which combined business – their trading in livestock – with uninhibited pleasure. The west, too, had substantial fairs at Lansdown, a hill village near Bath: its August fair was really a wild pleasure occasion, but it had also a considerable trade in cattle as well as sheep. Cornwall's Summercourt gathered thousands and Hereford's October fair promoted the county's emerging breed. Skipton, that famous Yorkshire sheep town with a golden fleece registered on its coat of arms, for one fair at least gathered in the cattle from Yorkshire's western dales, the East Riding or again those on passage south from Scotland, for on-selling to the graziers of Wharfedale. Its dealers, in their search for beasts to buy, were rumoured to travel even to the Hebrides. Almost every fair of the time, whatever the commodity on which its reputation rested, or however much it had capitulated to the pursuit of pleasure, had a token buying and selling of livestock. Even at fairs like London's naughty Bartholomew's:

> There double beare and bottle ale
> In every corner had good sale:
> Many a pig, and many a sow,
> Many a jade, and many a cow:
> Candle rushes, cloth and leather,
> And many things come in together:
> Many a pound and every penny told,
> Many a bargain bought and sold.

The calves' privilege, more horrifyingly humane, was to travel deadweight by cart

As the feeder fairs had swollen the numbers at the great trysts that mustered the droves, so was the routine of their dispersal round the capital matched by an equally refined structure: a subsidiary 'overspill' system of alternative markets where a dissatisfied drover might take his beasts and hedge his bets, or where a middleman could cut himself in on the profits. Pressed for time or riven by uncertainty about that year's Smithfield, a Norfolk grazier might lay off the risk by trekking his Scots beasts down through Essex to the capital's outskirts and taking the best offer he could get, say, at the fair on Wanstead Flats. Or he might drove the beasts to Barnet, in Dickens's day still capable of shifting 40,000 to 50,000 head on its cattle field. Beasts that did not find a buyer there would be driven east to Harlow Bush Fair. For the tardy who missed the maelstrom of St Faith's altogether there was, as we have seen, yet the compensation of Hempton Green; from there the lean and less-favoured beasts percolated down to Enfield. It was a fascinating, complex but effective network – the droving

A slack day in the market. Two of Smithfield's less important functionaries in the food chain have time for a quiet chat amid the ceaseless drama to feed the capital

tracks drawn thickly across the face of Old England – that linked the trysts of distant Scotland with fairs in the far south, a web at any one time with uplift and movement from the outposts of Skye to the precincts of St Bartholomew the Great. The astonishing thing is how quickly it would all collapse, unravelled by events.

Smithfield had been London's livestock market since 1150; it had a long, turbulent and unsavoury history. By the start of the seventeenth century demand was already necessitating the holding of the market on several days each week. In 1725 the capital was consuming 60,000 head of cattle (a high proportion of them fattened on Norfolk's pastures and therefore mainly from Scotland), 70,000 sheep and 239,000 pigs yearly. Seven years later, 76,000 cattle beasts were being sold yearly; by the end of the century 109,000 head. In 1810 that meat-flow to the city's tables, taverns and coffee shops had risen to account for 140,000 bullocks and 1,000,000 sheep. Eighteen years later the totals were 150,000 and 1,500,000; by 1853 277,000 and 1,600,000. Smithfield was bursting at its seams. Besides the pigs, the cattle and the sheep, it handled horses as well as hay and straw.

The cattle, on the final stage of their journey into the country's premier market, would be taken over in Islington by London drovers, badged and licensed by the City Corporation for the difficult drive down the tortuous length of St John Street. In the market, salesmen working on a commission basis negotiated a deal for the owners, like the drovers at St Faith's hopefully timing their efforts in volatile trading. Afterwards the animals were collected by the

butchers' own drovers for delivery through the streets to the nearby slaughter-houses. The pigs, they say, with their uncanny premonition, were a particular problem.

For its Great Day – its famous Christmas market – 30,000 beasts would be penned into the close confines of Smithfield's market space and spilling willy-nilly into the confusion of adjoining streets. It was pandemonium with drovers, butchers and salesmen running frantically in all directions. A contemporary report describes the scene: 'In one place was a group of brown-coated Devons; in a second a group of bulky Herefords; here and there were the favourite short-horns; a mass of black Scotch cattle diversified the picture at one spot, a cargo of Holsteiners in another . . .'. Indeed, from the middle of the eighteenth century Smithfield was something of an embarrassment: a sweating, stinking livestock market in the middle of a metropolis; 'a braying discord such as the imagination cannot figure,' said Thomas Carlyle as he took in the scene from the top step of an entrance at the edge of the mêlée. In its early days it had been safely outwith the city wall; the capital had expanded to surround it. On market days, as animals were driven in from the outskirts, people in adjacent streets were constantly at risk from the charge of maddened bullocks and children could be seriously trampled underfoot. Dickens, a man who knew his London so well, in *Oliver Twist* conveys comprehensively what people had to endure:

It is market morning. The ground was covered, nearly ankle-deep with filth and mire; a thick steam, perpetually rising from the reeking bodies of the cattle, and mingling with the fog, which seemed to rest upon the chimney tops, hung heavily above. All the pens at the centre of the large area, and as many temporary pens as could be crowded into the vacant space, were filled with sheep; tied up to posts by the gutter side were long lines of beasts and oxen, three or four deep. Countrymen, butchers, drovers, hawkers, boys, thieves, idlers, vagabonds of every low grade, were mingled together in a mass; the whistling of drovers, the barking of dogs, the bellowing and plunging of oxen, the bleating of sheep, the grunting and squealing of pigs, the cries of the hawkers, the shouts, oaths and quarrelling on all sides; the ringing of bells and roar of voices, that issued from every public house; the crowding, pushing, driving, beating, whooping and yelling; the hideous and discordant din that resounded from every corner of the market; and the unwashed, unshaven, squalid, and dirty figures constantly running to and fro, and bursting in and out of the throng, rendered it a stunning and bewildering scene, which confounded the senses.

(*Opposite*) entering the arena. Bewildered beasts being driven into Smithfield's livestock market cause confusion in the street in this painting, full of grim realism, by Thomas Sidney Cooper (1803–1902). A berserk animal, loose and frightened in the adjoining narrow streets, could cause serious injury

CHAPTER SEVEN

SELLING AT A FAST TROT

So, after 700 years, they would run London's livestock market out of town, closing a chapter of colourful history that had begun with an emphasis not on cattle but on horses. The 'smooth field' that would later be the home of the Smithfield Club and the national focus of stock-breeding showed an early concern with equine pedigree. It was at the Friday markets in Henry II's time that the landed gentry bought their mounts at this 'celebrated rendezvous for fine horses', after they had viewed them in the manner that would be perpetuated at horse fairs everywhere – that is, being trotted up and down to demonstrate their action. On show were horses disciplined for the squire, colts of fine breed almost unbroken, elegant chargers 'noble of stature with ears quickly tremulous, necks lifted, haunches plump'. William Fitz-Stephen, twelfth-century monk and clerk to the obdurate and unfortunate Thomas à Becket and an early London historian, foreshadowing Smithfield in yet another, later role, continues: 'In another part of the field stand by themselves the goods proper to rustics, implements of husbandry, swine with long flanks, cows with full udders, oxen of bulk immense, and woolly flocks. There stand mares fit for the plough, dray and cart, some big with foal, and others with their young colts closely following.' That occasion was still a part of the capital's life as Defoe wrote in 1723: 'There is . . . a great market, or rather fair for horses, in Smithfield every Friday in the afternoon, where very great numbers of horses, and those of the highest price, are to be sold weekly.'

The early horse fairs, of course, had more than simply an agricultural relevance; they were of prime importance from the Middle Ages in Yorkshire, where good mounts were bought in large numbers, something that may have reflected an anxiety about the Scots and their activities to the north. Mainly the fairs were held in unison with sheep and cattle sales. One was the great Candlemas fair at Northallerton – lasting as long as a month – one of two granted in 1200 to the Bishop of Durham, Philip de Poitou, by King John, fourth son of Henry II and a man who himself had some trouble with the Church. Horse-dealers came, it is said, from even the far corners of the Continent. The Bishop's other fair was held on the feast of St Bartholomew; that early gadabout William Camden (1551–1623) called it 'the greatest fair of kine and oxen, and of most resort, that ever I saw in my life'. A further two Northallerton fairs were granted to later bishops: St George's Fair (granted by Queen Mary) and St Matthew's Fair (granted by James I). The Candlemas Fair throve until the middle of the nineteenth century, when suddenly and unaccountably it was eclipsed by one at Bedale.

Three in hand.
Characteristically
neckerchiefed, a horse-
coper at Lee Gap's horse
fair shows off the paces of
the animals he has brought
to sell – and, incidentally, a
little of his own form

However, yet another fair granted to the Bishop of Durham – a figure, obviously, of enviable clout in the north – reigned even more gloriously. To Howden, one of the largest horse fairs of Europe in the Middle Ages, came not only dealers from the Continental countries but even representatives from their royal houses. Howden would endure: 4,000 horses a day were said to be sold at the fair in 1807 and into the last quarter of the century it was still going strong. Sometime about 1850, however, the fair did suffer a bout of uncertainty, changing its late September date to the first full week following the Doncaster races so that dealers could come on directly from the meeting – disastrously at first, as it turned out, since many of its regulars seem not to have heard of the change. In 1855 the revised date was Monday 17 September, and for the first time it was rigidly adhered to. A year earlier the dealers had been there aplenty but were being temperamental, holding off in the buying for once and getting their wallets out only towards the latter part of the week. The number of animals brought to the fair that year was fewer than in earlier years. There was a falling off in the trade for 'soldiers' – horses for the military – but there was consolation in the prices being paid for the animals that were in demand, which rocketed to the highest ever known at the fair. Normally the occasion was a mecca for army buyers not only from Britain but from Belgium, France, Germany and Italy.

In a bid at self-promotion, the fair by 1860 was dubbing itself the Great Horse Show, apparently to some effect. The *Goole & Marshland Gazette* reported a bad Monday start because of inclement conditions but was able to record good news for the Tuesday: 'the streets in which the fair is held were crowded by men and horses, so much so in some places as to be almost impassable for foot passengers'. Buyers included 'a number of foreign gentlemen from various parts of the Continent'. The Irish presence was a notably large one and young horses suitable for double harness, broughams, and private carriage work were getting from 65 to 85 guineas; matched pairs of greys or bays from 250 to 300 guineas; high-steppers for the phaeton and single harness going for 85 to 110 guineas. Things were even better the following year – the best fair for twenty years, in fact – or at least better for buyers (and for the innkeepers) but apparently disastrous for sellers. Inns and private houses were crammed with fair folk; boarders slept three to a bed and sometimes wall-to-wall on the floor. The Howden horse fair had come to its highpoint, though nobody as yet realised it.

The supply of animals was enormous, much in excess of any likely demand, and prices plummeted by the day as the fair continued, plunging by 30 per cent. Yet occasionally a seller scored: one coper got £1,700 for nine horses and doubtless was unable to believe his good fortune. In 1863 the pattern was repeated and by the Tuesday evening 'many gentlemen' had to go as far as Selby, and even Hull, to find a bed for the night. The Great Northern railway company ran 'fair specials' that day and on the Wednesday and still found it had to follow that with 'specials' again on the Thursday. Even so, a man with a good hunter for sale might go home with £300 in his pocket. Three years later, again with the fair bursting at the seams, dealers were bemoaning an emerging trend – evident too at Horncastle: there simply weren't enough top-notch animals at the fair. The reason was the growing number of agents resident in the area and acting for the London copers and for dealers in big cities such as Manchester and Birmingham. They no longer waited for the fair before snapping up the available first-class beasts.

By 1871 the dealing had become even more dispersed – anywhere within a 25 mile radius of the town and on a wider time-band. Howden's streets were no longer crammed with 'trotters' for days on end. There were dealers that year from Berne and Milan and Hamburg besides those from nearer home: Fordingbridge, Wells, Stoke, York, Beverley, Birmingham, Newcastle, Newark, Edinburgh and Glasgow as well as Belfast and Dublin. The Irish that year had 300 horses on offer. The year 1872 gave little hope; the supply of animals had dropped considerably. There was a scarcity of riding horses and coach horses and Continental buyers were fewer. The *Goole & Marshland Gazette* at last had the explanation: farmers were breeding fewer beasts and the country was being bled of its best brood mares by the Continentals. 'If not attended to,' it warned, 'English breeding will decline.' The worst falling-off had been in the Cleveland breed – the once-coveted 'blues' of the Scottish farmtouns – in the old-fashioned roadsters, and even in strong horses for farm work. (In 1870, England had 977,707 beasts in this class, in 1872 only 962,548.)

Boarders slept three to a bed and sometimes wall-to-wall on the floor

Power on the land. Many of England's horse fairs were local rendezvous where the country's farmers restocked their stables. The painter John Atkinson (1863–1924) took his brush and palette to this sale of sturdy work breeds, a bleak occasion without the high drama (and high language) of Horncastle or Howden

Forty years earlier, the old-timers recalled, a hundred locally bred animals could come to Howden Fair from just one of the surrounding villages. Now farmers were finding bigger and swifter profits by switching to sheep and cattle, and at such a pace that the country's diminishing horse-power was causing concern in the House of Lords. That year the town cleared overnight on the Wednesday and the Thursday saw only some desultory haggling over the nondescript nags that were left. The fair, for once, had behaved itself and no robberies were reported. Even the pickpockets had stayed at home. One sign of the times was that there were dealers keen to offer for animals suitable 'for railway vans and omnibuses, and one gentleman for black horses for hearse and mourning coach work, for which the prices were as high as £70 each'.

In 1873 the fair's prices ran high for anything that looked stylish and well-bred, especially for riding or coach work, the animals that had once been the fair's particular speciality. Bowman's Hotel had been full since the weekend and on Monday dealers were still arriving on every train. So were the horses; reported the *Goole & Marshland Gazette*: 'Five special trains of horse-boxes came to Howden station on Saturday, one on Sunday, and five on Monday. One of the latter contained 81 boxes, each of which holds three horses. There was

Romany holiday. Piebald ponies have always been the preference of the travelling folk (as they were of the American Indians) who congregated between the wars to do business at Brough Hill's renowned horse fair

difficulty with stabling.' Mr Morley, a job-master, was there to buy for the London Parcels Delivery Company, M. François had come from Brussels with another Belgian, M. Gustave from Germany, Count Valersin from Italy, M. Old was hotfoot from Hamburg – he was a regular – to buy mares and harness horses. That noted London dealer Mr Wimbush bought expansively, as did Mr East and Mr Blackman, both also from the capital, and Irish hunters were selling up to £100. Amid the old-style dealing the new auctioning was stealthily establishing a foothold. And the tables had turned: 'those possessed of any breeding, good fencers and capital goers were speedily disposed of . . . The largely increased call for strong agricultural horses for brewers' vans, rullies, vans, and large town team work has gone comparatively ahead of supply, and they are consequently both scarce and dear.'

But there were other fairs in the calendar of Old England whose names rang with an equal resonance, where slowly the plump chargers for the martial encounter were displaced, as the oxen-team quit the plough, by the stolid draught horses of the new farming. Another of Yorkshire's legendary horse fairs, Lee Gap – still being held after 800 years – was equally international. The region

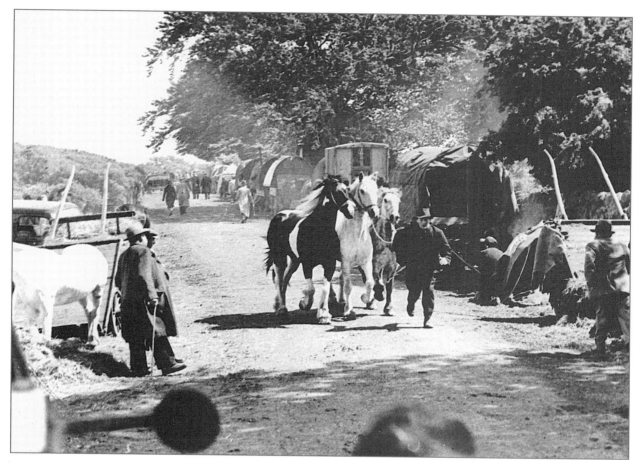

Trotting up and down.
At Appleby in June, as
elsewhere, the potential
buyer wanted to see
horseflesh in motion. This
trio would have had a dip
in the nearby River Eden
before their showing at
what is still one of the
liveliest horse fairs

also had the orchestrally celebrated Brigg Fair. Rothwell, mid-distance between
Pytchley and Market Harborough, was renowned, as was Biggleswade Fair, away
to the south; Penkridge, just south of Stafford, astonished Defoe; Lincoln had
Horncastle as well as the city's own April sale; Burton on Trent's principal fair,
lasting six days, was the premier event for the Lincolnshire Blacks with more of
the breed on sale than in any other fair in the country; East Anglia, that kingdom
of the Horseman's Word, had the famous wool town of Lavenham's horse fair
and Suffolk's Dunningworth occasion in August. Stow-on-the-Wold, reputedly
the highest town in the Cotswolds – where the old stocks still decorate the square
– has its May and October occasions still: it has been drawing dealers from all
over the country since the fifteenth century.

There was always something rogue-ish about the horse fair. It had a dubious
reputation but never in its long history did it cease to exert a raffish fascination.
That long-sung hunting man John Peel, they say, was just leaving for a horse fair
when his wife went into labour. While he waited impatiently the baby was safely
delivered. But at once there came the news that another was imminent. Peel's
frustration could endure no more. Damnt, he said, he cared not gin t'were four,
he was already late for the fair! If it drew composers and artists, it also attracted

more than its share of men who survived by their tongue and their wits. It is not by accident that the term 'horse-trading' has become a part of the political and diplomatic vocabulary of our own time. Horse-dealing was always a risky, devious business. But at the old fairs it could be positively hazardous. There were copers undoubtedly who had the gift of glib and warm goodwill and the knack of persuasion developed to an extraordinary degree – until the deal was done. A man took his life and his pocket-book in his hands.

A tincture of the old excitement and aggressive bonhomie remains, diluted perhaps but detectable in the maelstrom of Ireland's Ballyclare, perhaps at Barnet – and more especially at Appleby, where yearly in June the normally quiet Cumbrian town succumbs to an occasion of dementia that looks for all the world like the start of civil strife. Wheelers, dealers and seemingly all who espouse the nomadic way of life gather in large numbers to give the fair its traditional character and colour. Officially Appleby horse fair is a one-day affair but it lasts at least a week, with the travelling people parked on what was the Gallows Hill but is now more genteelly known as Fair Hill. It is believed to be Britain's biggest gypsy jamboree: you can still find there, parked with the motley of pick-ups, lorries and luxurious caravans of today's travelling classes, a genuine horse-drawn vardo or two, the traditional home of the Romany folk. The dealing starts with their arrival. The town's peaceful Eden River becomes less than idyllic as dusty horseflesh is given a wash and brush-up in its fast-flowing waters. There is a carnival atmosphere, with trotting races in an adjoining meadow as the day's dealing concludes. Some of the town's pubs discreetly close their doors and emphasise the point by also boarding up their windows. Those on holiday are advised to leave their wallets at the hotel.

Something of the kind has been going on in the Cumbrian fastness since James II granted the town's mayor and burgesses in 1685 'a fair or market for the purchase and sale of all manner of goods, cattle, mares and geldings'. He cannot have known the forces he was about to unleash on the loyal citizenry. On Fair Hill there is handslap horse-trading raised to a high art but with more than a nod to the past. For Appleby does not deal in polite cheques. When a colt has been trotted back and forth – dangerously through the crowds – and not found wanting by a potential buyer, the money is dealt straight from the hip or shirt pocket, wadded and soiled, crumpled notes as sweaty as the palm that proffers them, their passage from one to another marked still by that emphatic compacting of flesh that calls a bargain a bargain. It was the way of the old fairs, with a 'luck penny' passed willingly back to the buyer in a gesture of goodwill, and heaven knows, he may often have had need of it! Away from the dealing there are all the elements of the thorough-going fair – glassware, china and saddlery for sale, and of course the fortune-tellers, some of them hotfoot from the Epsom Derby (for such is the occasion); our uncertainty about life – and our endless hope – is their fortune. There are the cheapjack stalls, the entertainers, and caged birds for sale. Even, it is rumoured, a bit of the bare-knuckle stuff, and dogfights . . . if you know where to find them.

Money was dealt from the hip-pocket, wadded and soiled and sweaty in the palm

Lively mover. A spirited grey captures the attention of the crowd at Berkshire's Windsor Horse Fair in 1887. The painting is by the nineteenth-century artist Edward Benjamin Herberte

Barnet has affinities. Its historic September fair is borne with more fortitude, even nonchalance. It is nigh on 800 years old and horseflesh was long the prime interest here on London's fringe on a site that sat conveniently by the Great North Road and, as a great coaching centre, had an abundance of surrounding inns (three of them Red Lions) and adequate stabling. London cabbies came to buy their cobs in the crush. Cattle as well as horses would be brought there, as has been said, to a fair that drew horse-dealers from all over Britain. Local historians claim its origins lie in a charter given by Henry II; more positively the little rural village received another in 1588 from Elizabeth I, recognising its September occasion. Its fame by then was already far-flung. The local market day – that granted by King John in 1199 to the abbot of St Albans – had long had a reputation for a certain bohemian conviviality, as Delavill's play *The English Traveller*, staged in London in 1633, makes abundantly clear:

> This Barnet is a place of great resort,
> And commonly upon the Market Dayes,
> Here all the Country Gentlemen appoint
> A friendly meeting, some about affaires
> Of consequence and Profit, Bargain, Sale,
> And to conferre with Chapmen, some for Pleasure,
> To match their Horses, wager on their Dogs,
> Or try their Hawkes, some to no other end
> But oneley to meet good Company, discourse,
> Dine, Drink and spend their Money.

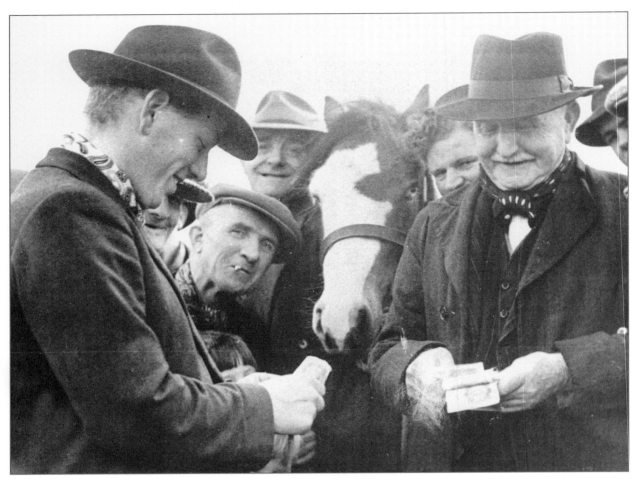

Raw deal. Purchases were made in sweaty, palm-soiled notes at Brough Hill, which has had a fair since Roman times. Payment came at the end of the old palm-thwack bargaining of the true horse fair. Today Brough Hill is a Romany occasion

Barnet races, coinciding with the fair, drew London's riff-raff, opportunists and costermongers. In 1881 the august *Daily Telegraph* described the 'stirring spectacle': 'The high road in the vicinity of Barnet station commands an uninterrupted view of the broad spread of hill and dale where thousands of horned cattle and horses are collected for buyers to pick and choose from, the cattle and horses being separate.' (One detects a cityman's pen.) The horses by then were the undisputed draw: the choice was indeed wide. There were Irish-bred animals, Scottish horses (presumably Clydesdales), Welsh wild ponies off the mountains by their hundreds; not least the ponderous magnificence of the English Shires. There were even foreign breeds of high degree, some of them from Russia.

The big Barnet Fair, indeed, far outshone its Hertfordshire rivals Hemel Hempstead, Bishop's Stortford, Stevenage and the county town's event among others. Local chronicler Father Bampfield in 1899 in his *Early Barnet Recollections* listed its other excitements for the crowd: all kinds of shows, a 'theatre', Aunt Sallies, shooting galleries, minstrels and acrobats as well as the ubiquitous coconut shies. He also noted that the fair engendered rather a lot of

Telling the tooth. At Brough Hill, as at every horse fair, it was an essential precaution to check an animal's age before making an offer. Dealers came a long way to the northern fair just to unload a 'dodgy' animal

unruly behaviour and some petty crime. And the gypsies were there, too, having pottered leisurely down from Appleby, their women threading through the crowd with their baskets, selling lace and ribbons and clothes-pegs and (who can doubt it) white heather. Rowlandson had a field day, sketching feverishly. The fair shed its surplus, its unsold livestock, to Harlow Bush Fair, on Harlow's Bush Common – along with Rowlandson, who diligently followed his subjects into the wilds of Essex. But then, the horse fair always attracted artists. Another much captivated by its colour and movement and its gallery of characters was Sir Alfred Munnings, whose painting of Suffolk's Lavenham horse fair dwells with affection on the robust stature of man and beast.

Munnings was fascinated by the solid strength of the cart horses standing in rows and by the 'manes and tails plaited with straw and braided with blue, yellow and scarlet ribbons'. Such decoration – admired today in the ornamentation of the heavy horses at the pseudo-ploughing matches and demonstrations of how things once were – is thought to have begun in the old horse fairs as a means of diverting the eye from the animal's faults. Red ribbons were – still are – preferred, though an ugly or ungainly beast with a

Figure of substance. From the brush of a master, Sir Alfred Munnings, this study of a horse fair encounter – at Lavenham in 1904 – memorably depicts the elements of the event and immortalises the horse-coper in oils. Typically, he wears the distinctive jockey-type tapering trousers and the bulky jacket of his trade. Munnings (1878–1959) was Suffolk-born and revered the horse; he loved painting colourful fairs and gypsy encampments

bow on its bum is unlikely to fool the knowledgeable gaze. Another possibility is that decoration was a way of actually hiding some distinctive marking where the animal had been dishonestly acquired and was being illicitly offered for sale. One does not wish to speak ill of the nomadic folk but there was a time when one or two of their number might see a likely beast in a paddock and find that it had accompanied them to some conveniently distant fair. It became a coincidence that embarrassed fair officials. So much so that in 1555 laws were enacted to prevent it. Every fair then had to provide a special open space for horses and a watchman appointed to look after it from ten in the morning until sunset. A later statute of 1588 declared the toll-keeper personally responsible for the seller's credentials and for recording a description of the animal being offered for sale. The toll-book for Wiltshire's Highworth Fair, where dealing took place in the Horse Fair (an area now known as The Green), instructs the recording of purchases and purchasers there, in the fullest possible manner, by the toll-taker or book-keeper, including the distinguishing marks of the animal and the price paid. Nottingham's Goose Fair, which catered for 'all sorts of Cattle, Goods, Wares and Merchandise' also firmly stipulated that 'no Horse, Mare or Gelding shall be sold at the Fair but what shall be duly vouched for and tolled'. And while one, equally, would be unwilling to suggest ill of toll-keepers, a fine of £5 – big money then – was the penalty under these Acts of Parliament for either or both if keeper and coper connived to cheat the system.

Munnings' response, in his book *An Artist's Life*, emphasises the relevance of the horse when genuine horse-power was the main motive power of Old England. It dragged, powered and perpetuated all life, social and commercial: the squire's coach, the carrier's cart, milady's carriage, the master's brougham and of course – as the oxen were finally unharnessed – the plough and the carter's waggon in which the glinting hooves of those heavy draught animals, the Shires and the Suffolks, drew home the golden sheaves of harvest. Without the horse Britain would have been immobilised. Even Stourbridge, that Cambridgeshire efflorescence of trade and transaction, with its international clientele, climaxed with its horse-fair day. In London alone, nearing the end of last century, some 15,000 hansom cab horses clip-clopped the well-to-do through the capital's streets to office and illicit rendezvous. The London General Omnibus Company, which had started buying out its competitors in the 1850s, had 10,000 on the road at any one time and around 22,000 in total, while tram horses in the capital totalled another 14,000. And that was just one aspect of the city's transportational life. The railways owned an estimated 6,000; carriers such as Carter Paterson and Pickfords had 19,000, making 25,000 animals on carrier work and sometimes working a fourteen-hour day. A modest 1,500 were enough to pull the capital's rubbish carts; 3,000 drew its brewers' waggons; 8,000 were employed by coal merchants and 700 were needed for final departures – those elegant, high-stepping but sometimes frisky beasts that pulled the hearses. Count the private carriages, milk carts, grocers' delivery vans, removal vehicles and so on and the capital's working-horse population alone was probably around 300,000. Horse dung had to be ferried down the Thames by the bargeful. The capital's horse-copers were kept constantly on the move, trying to sustain a seemingly insatiable demand. Their net went far and wide – wherever there was a horse fair and an inn, for it was inconceivable to hold one without the other.

The horse fair was a spectacle that made men eloquent; its memorable scene is described by George (Gypsy) Borrow, yet another wanderer, working at times as an itinerant farrier, in *Lavengro*:

I was standing on the castle hill in the midst of a fair of horses . . . of old the scene of many a tournament and feat of Norman chivalry, and now much used as a showplace for cattle, where those who buy and sell beeves and other beasts resort at stated periods. So it came to pass that I stood upon this hill, observing a fair of horses . . . I had long since conceived a passion for the equine race, a passion in which circumstances had of late not permitted me to indulge. I had no horses to ride but I took pleasure in looking at them; and I had already attended more than one of these fairs: the present was lively enough, indeed horse fairs are seldom dull. There was shouting and whooping, neighing and braying; there was galloping and trotting; fellows with highlows [ankle-high shoes fastened in front] and white stockings, and with many a string dangling from the knees of their tight breeches were running desperately holding horses by the halter and in some cases dragging them along; there were long-tailed steeds, and dock-tailed steeds of every degree and breed; there were droves of wild ponies, and long rows of sober cart

Genuine horse-power perpetuated the life of the nation, social and commercial

horses. There were donkeys and even mules: the last rare things to be seen in damp, misty England, for the mule pines in mud and rain, and thrives best with a hot sun above and a burning sand below. There were – oh, the gallant creatures! I hear their neigh upon the wind; there were – goodliest sight of all – certain enormous quadrupeds only seen to perfection in our native isle, led by dapper grooms, their manes ribanded and their tails curiously clubbed and balled.

Thus was the old horse fair comprehensively described. A bold man might bet on the setting as Brough Hill, with its rogue-ish reputation and formidable trade in ponies off the fells and from the dales; it was there that Durham's mine-owners bought their pit ponies, safe in the knowledge that they were as hardy as the men they would work with. In fact, the venue is claimed to be Horncastle in Lincolnshire. More safely one can assume that the 'enormous quadrupeds' Borrow is eulogising were the workhorses of the English landscape – probably Shires, but perhaps Punches, the strongly muscled beasts that drew London's horse-copers in their hundreds to the now forgotten fair at the little village of Dunningworth in Suffolk, known locally as Dunnifer. The renowned August fair was held in front of the farmhouse from which it first took its name – that is, until the farmer objected and kept the fair at some distance. It brought dealers from all over the country to purchase the pulling power of the Punch, a breed never too proud or too temperamental to push the thrust of its hefty shoulders into a horse collar. For city merchants and wholesalers, with their heavy waggons, the Suffolk Punch was ideal. But still the dealers would need proof of an individual animal's soundness in wind and limb. They would test these qualities in a dramatic demonstration of the Punch's strength and willingness. What they wanted to see was the beast sinking practically down on its knees in its determination to shift a fallen tree.

It is conceivable that Chaucer, the son of a vintner with a country estate near Ipswich, may have seen just such a 'drawing match' between Punches – or at least between their earlier East Anglian ancestors – and had it in mind when he wrote:

> The carter thakkett his hors upon the croupe
> And they begonne drawen and to stoupe.

They wanted to see the beast sink to its knees as it tried to shift a fallen tree

That hurdle passed, the Punch would then be yoked into a waggon and 'backed up' for some distance. This was a necessary precaution in the purchase of a city horse – a malt-horse, for instance, that might be pulling a brewer's dray – for such manoeuvres would be an essential part of its everyday routine. Not every beast was biddable in this way: though strong and willing, some jibbed at the feel of the breeching-strap taunt across their haunches.

If they were painstaking, the copers nevertheless took an ample profit for their trouble. Those who came to Horncastle to find animals for the carriage trade would expect to buy, say, at between £35 and £40 each while charging the capital's gentry about double that figure. Like used-car salesmen, horse-copers did not enjoy a good press. George Sturt, that chronicler of country life in

A *Small Boy in the Sixties*, looking down from his window on Farnham's Castle Street Fair, indicates a certain misgiving. He saw 'a shady-looking fellow – a horse-coper – running a frightened horse for sale . . . Anybody with a whip, and there were many – gyp, farmer, half-and-half – was liable to crack it loudly for the fun of frightening the horse into a faster trot. And above the yells, the bleating, the clatter of horsehooves, the loud chatter and other nameless noises, came the toot of toy trumpets bought at a stall, the cries of the showmen, the bang of beetle, driving into the road the stakes for some cockernut shy or unfinished stall.' Sturt, in particular, would remember the old horse dealers as a 'sinister lot, cunning, shifty of eye, loud of speech'.

Horncastle, irritably condemned by Cobbett as 'not remarkable for any thing of particular value or beauty', was a Roman town where the River Bain joined the Waring. It was a corn and wool town in the nineteenth century, but its fame rests now on its yearly August horse fair, by 1820 the 'largest fair for horses in the kingdom' and unquestionably one of the greatest in Europe. By 1825 it was establishing horse prices throughout the country. Huge droves of unbroken colts were driven to it, thundering through the narrow twisting streets at the gallop, thirty or forty at a time, scattering the fair crowd in all directions. Horse dealers and buyers in their thousands thronged its cobbled streets, descending from all

Greatest of them all. Certainly Horncastle's horse fair claimed to be the 'largest and the best-known in the world'. It supplied the cavalry of many nations and it was said that the stability of Europe could be gauged by the yearly strength of its trade in 'soldiers' (mounts of the military)

Character study. All the colour and not a little of the raffish ambience of the horse fair on Southborough Common wonderfully captured by the brush of John Frederick Herring, Sen (1795–1865)

over the kingdom, including Ireland and Wales, many of them travelling up from the capital on the London stage – there was a direct overnight service from the Bell and Crown in Holborn to Horncastle's George Inn – or making the long ride on horseback; they came, too, as they did for Howden, its chief rival, from distant corners of the Continent, from Hungary as well as the Low Countries and Germany. By the later nineteenth century they were even coming from America, Australia and New Zealand. As a versifier of 1846 put it:

> Russia, Spain and France have sent
> Their bearded sons and purses
> Well stor'd with cash that must be spent
> In splendid British horses.
> While members of the mighty States
> Of yonder glowing west
> Have come to buy, at highest rates,
> The middling and the best.

The duration of the fair was decidedly fluid: like St Faith's it lasted as long as it had to and (like Howden) was cavalier as to its starting date, causing confusion at times. Traders and town officials failed miserably to stage the horse fair on the dates that had been arranged for it. Here, too, dealers insisted on coming earlier to try and secure the best animals. A hint of this problem – one that affected all the large fairs to some extent and threw their organisers into a blind fury – is contained in the *Lincolnshire Chronicle*'s report of 1860. The newspaper, confirming that the fair was 'exceedingly large and possessed animals of a high order and quality', also confessed that 'business to a great extent was transacted before the formal opening of the fair' – though as usual there were those who did their best business at the height of the fair: like every such occasion Horncastle drew the riff-raff, more-or-less honest entertainers, it is true, but also card-sharps, pickpockets and, of course, prostitutes.

The Continental buyers and hunting men from all over England came to replenish their studs with high-class bloodstock; the caddies (or cads) hired by the London job-masters and cab-owners departed with strings of animals suitable for all sorts of work. From time to time a war here or there would stimulate demand, and the Prussian cavalry came regularly to restock its squadrons. Lamenting the fair's 'great days', the *Horncastle News*, as the century turned, would look back to that time when 'the fair lasted for three weeks. The first six or seven days were devoted to the selling of hunters and high-class riding horses. The second week was set apart for hackneys and coach horses. The third week was concerned mainly with the sale of cart horses.'

The Prussian cavalry came regularly to Horncastle to restock its squadrons

In 1857, when the fair was in its prime, Horncastle had some 5,000 inhabitants, 50 of them believing they were 'gentry', which they may well have been; others included three tallow-chandlers, a pawnbroker, a bird-stuffer, a town-crier, an unconscionable number of boot and shoe makers and (not surprisingly) a plethora of blacksmiths. The town, strangely, was not itself a centre for horse-breeding though its annual event certainly spurred breeding elsewhere in the county. As a result of its illustrious fair Lincolnshire became a notable horse-breeding area, selling its fen ponies from the sixteenth century to the coalminers of Nottingham and the lead mines of Derby. But it was in the heavier league that the county acquired lasting fame with the solid Lincolnshire Blacks, progenitors of the later, better-known Shires. It became the home of the carthorse and countless thousands would be traded down the years in the throng of Horncastle's fair. By the close of the eighteenth century the farmers of Holland Fen were bringing in three-year-olds knowing that any likely looking animal would get £25.

In 1813, in his *General View of the Agriculture of the County of Lincolnshire* the Board of Agriculture Secretary Arthur Young notes in his curious shorthand style: 'Every farmer in Holland Fen keeps mares for breeding, and the numbers are very great; a very good four-year-old cart horse sells at £30 and is a common price; £25 for a very good three-year-old.' He also indicates an alternative practice: 'Mr Thacker of Langrike-Ferry, buys in Yorkshire at three years old in autumn, winters on straw, works a little in the spring, and sells at Horncastle fair in August, one of the greatest fairs in the kingdom.' He adds: 'About Normansby, Burton, etc many bred for saddle and coach: sell at two, three and four years old; get from eighty guineas at four years old, as hunter, down to £7 or £8. A good coach-horse at four years old, £30 to £40. Howden in Yorkshire is the fair; also many to Horncastle. Yearlings and two years old, all to Howden . . . All black mares for breeding, and sell colts at two years old, at £12 to £20.'

During Horncastle Fair, the horses for sale would be ranged for over a quarter of a mile on each side, in an enormous string, from Horncastle's Wong, through

A horse at the door. For the residents of Bampton, in Oxfordshire, the town's important horse fair day, pictured just after the First World War before the tractor took over in the fields, brought some heavy traffic to the main street

the Bull Ring (variously and earlier called the Beast Market and also the Corn Market) and out along Horse Fair (since 1867, North Street), fouling the sidewalks and spilling into East Street, Wharfe Road, Willow Row and the High Street. But many deals would be done in the inn yards, particularly if an animal had thoroughbred pretensions. As in all horse-trading a deal might be done instantly – or continue in a battle of nerve and guile over several days. The inn yards would also, by the 1850s, be the scene of the new auction selling. The fair, more than most and with the exception perhaps of Howden and Penkridge, had an enviable turnover in high-class horseflesh: Lottery, the winner of the 1839 Grand National was bought there. About 1817, with the return of Continental buyers, a prime beast for his lordship's racing stable or his carriage could command £300. In the Brocklesbury country of the north Lincolnshire wolds, in the early nineteenth century, Lord Yarnborough's tenants bred hunters for the fair, sending between them some years as many as fifty; one tenant alone in 1832 netted £1,000 for six hunters. The fair's activity could be feverish, sometimes threatening and sometimes sluggish, with tiny jockeys from the region's racing stables incongruous in the crush of burly horse-copers; a mêlée of men and animals and high language, as army men bulk-bought 200 at a time. Afterwards the caddies – those hard-drinking, gambling 'drovers' of the horse-dealing scene – would leave for the capital but also for all the reachable big cities of the land – Liverpool, Manchester, Birmingham and Bristol – or take their charges by the Barton horse-boat to Hull for export to the Continent and destinations east such as St Petersburg.

Borrow, we do know, was in Horncastle for the August fair of 1825. He had brought a horse to sell to meet a pressing debt – a beast he had bought in Staffordshire for £50 – and was staying at the George Inn in a 'two-bedded room in a garret'. He relates the experience in *The Romany Rye*, published in 1857, in a delightful cameo in which the hotel's ostler is not sure that Borrow, though once an articled solicitor and one-time Bible agent, is wise enough in the ways of the fair. He warns him, among other traps, never to let a Yorkshireman get up into the saddle because 'if you do it's three to one that he rides off with the horse'. The fair, Borrow finds, is peopled by sinister characters, one of whom tells the writer that he is neither 'a coward or a screw either, except so far as one who gets his bread by horses may be expected to be'. Borrow's account highlights the rakish nature of the horse fair. Sellers were truly ill-advised to let anyone on to the back of an animal they were offering, in case they simply did ride away never to be seen again. It was commonly done.

Even the clergy were fair game for the wily coper. One vicar, it is said, having sold his own horse for £25, bought another to replace it soon after for £40, only later to discover that it was his own horse with the star on its brow concealed by dye. One Horncastle vicar even sold his mount on a Sunday – in church! Two dealers had been vying earlier for Dr Thomas Loddington's beast, without either managing to persuade him to part with it. Both had offered £35, but there the deal was stalled until one coper bet the other a bottle of wine he could get the chestnut mare at the price offered. Both were in church on the Sunday for morning service and even as the vicar ended his sermon one walked cheekily forward to accost him as he descended the pulpit steps. 'The fair's over – and you haven't sold your mare!' the coper said, reiterating his offer. Astonished, and no doubt a little shocked by such effrontery, the vicar capitulated – and, as he left, found the other dealer waiting to lobby him at the church door! Sunday during fair time, in fact, was far from sacred and over the singing of the hymns would come the high murmur of the dealing going on outside and the sound of horses being trotted over the street cobbles. Nothing could impede the fever of dealing.

Its hunters apart, Horncastle shared in the booms and slumps of horse fairs everywhere. There had been a dramatic fall in prices after 1815: hacks were suddenly half-price; nags and carthorses were down to £10 after being £40 a few years earlier. Many beasts came to the fair but went home again to the stable they had come from. But by the mid-nineteenth century, with the fair at its height, the heady days would return, with cart or dray horses finding a respectable £60, ponies £65, and even hackneys realising £25.

In the last few days of the fair's dealing, as the dross was sold off, the gypsies had the stage almost to themselves. Then, at Horncastle, there appeared the Pepper Gang, a notorious parcel of rogues based in Mareham-le-Fen. They dealt in a breed of small grey horses called Wildmore Tits, reputedly of Arabian

Over the singing of hymns would come the high murmur of horse-dealing

pedigree, and were accomplished masters of the 'sting'. They took their pickings among the most gullible at the close of the fair, ensuring that some likely mark overheard two of them arguing heatedly over the merits of an animal. With the observer's attention assured, the 'bidder' would finally turn away in disgust, confiding in a conspiratorial whisper to the victim in passing that the price of the beast was no more than £10 – and if he could persuade the obdurate seller to part with it at that there was a half-sovereign in it for him. So in turn the farmer/victim entered the fray, listing the animal's failings while the seller railed against the injustice of the price and finally, with a studied reluctance and a strong oath or two, accepted the mediator's money. By then the erstwhile buyer had vanished without trace in the fair – and the mark found himself holding on to a broken-down nag not worth half the price. The deception was so well known at Horncastle that it was called 'peppering' but, by whatever name, it was probably played at a great many of England's old horse fairs.

Horncastle had its generous share of the vagabond folk. George Hall, the clergyman they called 'the Gypsy's Parson', insisted they were 'our best gypsy families' and he came regularly to the fair to meet with them where they parked their caravans, in a high-hedged field behind St Mary's Church, or, in the case of the poorer families, along the lanes or in the yard of the New Inn. Some at least, one ventures to suggest, may have been less than welcome: characters like Hook-nosed Suki, Rabbitskin Bob and Ratcatcher Charley. Not to mention three brothers, Elijah, Master and Swallow, who preyed on lonely taverns, terrifying their keepers into plying them with drinks.

Cobbett, as little enchanted by Brigg as he was by Horncastle, described its livelihood as 'a good trade in corn, coal and timber. Here are also several manufacturers of fur, with tanners and fell-mongers . . . and it is said that more hands are employed here in dressing rabbit-skins than in any other provincial town in the kingdom.' A visit to Brigg Fair, however, inspired the Bradford-born composer Frederick Delius to write his *English Rhapsody: Brigg Fair*, based on a gypsy song associated with the occasion. Initially for cattle and sheep, the August fair even by 1840 had become more of a holiday, though the horse-trading continued, to the hazard of the fair crowds as the animals were galloped along Wrawby Street under the eyes of would-be buyers – before the serious business could be done in one or other of the nearby hostelries. Perversely, it was the trickle of sheep and cattle that were auctioned off in the Horse Fair Paddock and the horse fair – as so often – met its nemesis when it, too, was ordered into the auction market. It was an alien atmosphere for the real horse fair.

Despite the fame of fairs such as Horncastle and Brigg, however, Lincoln's own four-day April event reserved its first two days for the sale of horses and latterly was an important date as the spring farm work got under way. Aylsham's March fair was for cattle but it, too, increasingly became the venue where Norfolk's farmers sought beasts for the tasks of seed-time. Biggleswade in Bedfordshire and Bampton in Oxfordshire, both notable fairs – among many others – did like service for their own county's farmers in providing the power that then pulled the plough. In the Midlands the great gathering for horse-dealers

A visit to Brigg Fair inspired a composer to write his English rhapsody

The power of haunch and sinew. A handsome, finely flecked grey receives a close inspection in a cobbled corner of Smithfield's horse market as a coper assesses its suitablity, probably for harnessing to a brewer's dray. The artist, Swiss-born Jacques Laurent Agasse (1767–1849), who later settled in England, like Munnings had a penchant for painting England's heavy breeds

was Penkridge. Here, too, early and off-site trading, in the surrounding villages and hamlets, was as big a problem as at Horncastle. As early as 1674 the *London Gazette* was printing a rebuke that 'there hath been a disorderly coming to the Horsefair at Penkritch . . . by horse coursers and others before the time of the said fair ought to begin; by reason of which many persons of quality, that have come from remote places, have been frustrated in their intentions in coming to the said fair'. The Staffordshire event had specialised in the horse trade since at least 1522. In fact the village had two fairs (in April and October in 1817) both being described as 'being among the best in England for saddle horses'. Its big September fair on The Marsh to the east of the village took Defoe by surprise for he had anticipated nothing quite like it in that region. He reported wide-eyed on the superior quality of the horseflesh that had been assembled there:

We expected nothing extraordinary; but was I say surprised to see the prodigious number of horses brought hither, and those not ordinary and common draught horses, and such kinds as we generally see at county-fairs remote from London. But here were really incredible numbers of the finest and most beautiful horses that can any where be seen; being brought hither from Yorkshire, the bishopric of Durham, and all the horse-breeding countries. We were told that there were not less than a hundred jockeys and horse-copers, as they call them here, from London, to buy horses for sale. Also an incredible number of gentlemen attending with their grooms to buy gallopers, or race-horses for their Newmarket sport.

In passing Defoe had a good word for northern grooms and was in little doubt about the fair's stature: 'I believe I may mark it for the greatest horse-fair in the world, for horses of value, and especially those we call saddle-horses. There are indeed great fairs for coach-horses and draught-horses . . . But for saddle-horses, for the light saddle, hunters, pads [for road riders], and racers, I do believe the world cannot match this.' He may have been close in the latter claim, for during his visit to the fair several animals were sold for 150 guineas each. More interestingly, he highlights the traditional linkage that existed between the big horse fairs, one that imitated the pattern of the old cattle droves: beasts bought in Newcastle or Preston, even in Ireland, were profitably brought south by the men – and their caddies – who worked the fairs, moving the animals from one to the other. In the early nineteenth century, as Arthur Young rather suggests, it was not at all unusual for the Lincolnshire graziers to take a trip north to buy three-year-old colts at the Yorkshire fairs. These they kept for a year, while they fattened and were 'nicked' and made ready for sale at the next Horncastle Fair to London dealers, who in turn would break them in for six weeks or so to carriage work before offering them to clients.

There were fairs countrywide that confirmed in some degree the classic, chaotic and often unsavoury perception of the horse fair. Tavistock's famous goose fair was once no stranger to horse-trading; there, too, the gypsies turned out in force to encamp on the moor and deal in horses and ponies between fighting and drinking. Those with Dartmoor ponies for sale would cluster their animals around the Abbey garage from an early hour. There, as in the main horse-dealing, a man could buy back the pony he had sold earlier after it had had a 'make-over' from a sharp coper. One man did, not realising it until he had ridden the beast home to his farm, only to find that it headed straight for the stable door! He had given two guineas more than he was paid for it. But there was a better, legal way in which the itinerant horse-coper could turn a fast penny – as a middleman pure and simple, who 'speculated' on an animal at one local fair and took it, pedigree enhanced, to the next.

Taunton's fairs, like most, were the haunt of such men. These dealers followed the fair circuit like travelling judges in a sophisticated operation that took the old horse fair far, far from its rustic roots. The fact that Taunton's own two fairs were only twenty days apart must surely have been a godsend for such opportunists. There was a further reason for the fairs' popularity: to them for sale came the big Shire horses that were bred to the north and east of the town, conditioned by the fine pastures of the Levels and the Quantocks, and usually lightly worked before they were brought to the fair from North Petherton and Bridgwater to be sold as cart or carriage horses to the farmers of the Vale of Taunton Deane. The quality of the colts brought in copers from as far as Cornwall. Breeders disillusioned by the fairs' prices, however, could opt to take their Shires to test demand instead at Winchester's Magdalen Fair.

Beasts were profitably brought south by the caddies who worked the fairs

Exmoor round-up. Ponies off the moor gathered and corralled about the turn of the century for Bampton in Devon's pony fair. Held for nearly 700 years under a charter given by Edward I in 1275, the famous fair sold its last pony in 1985

The palms that thwacked together at Brough Hill Fair sealed horse deals as suspect as those everywhere else – some believed more so. The fair took place, after moving from an earlier date in the month of that calendar-change year of 1752, on the last day of September and the first day of October. The weather was wet, invariably, windy and thoroughly miserable. The fair-goers came to expect it. Horse dealers brought Clydesdales down from as far north as Strathclyde, animals from as far east as Bishop Auckland and as far south as Lincolnshire. Yorkshire beasts crossed Stainmore Pass over Cotherstone Moor; the Romanies came in droves – from the Forest of Dean, Wales, even the Highlands of Scotland – and the dales and fell ponies that had once formed Old England's packhorse trains were driven in through the drizzle. Brough Hill had just about everything, a gallery of characters that included breeders, dealers and gypsies as well as the usual generous sprinkling of ne'er-do-wells and general riff-raff. It was said that a man had to have bought horses with every known fault and ailment before he was fit to trade at Brough Hill. Each fair yearly dispersed thousands of horses. The locals mostly bought elsewhere.

The meeting of wadded notes and sometimes suspect horseflesh occurred where two of the country's major routes crossed and where, through the eighteenth century and later, the long-distance stagecoaches stopped to change horses. It was an eminently suitable place: over Market Brough's hump-backed bridge (first mentioned in 1369) trotted more than sixty carriages a day; among its many inns (crammed with teeming humanity during fair times) were the White Swan from which coaches left for Newcastle, Lancaster, London and Carlisle, and the George Inn, where the

London–Glasgow mail coach stopped at two every morning as it headed north and at 11.30 p.m. nightly as it hurtled south. At the Castle Hotel the horse-drawn coaches from Kirkby Stephen, Barnard Castle and Penrith drew in at their scheduled times for the kind of pit-stop of their era: a change of horses in two minutes flat.

In its heyday when the droves were thronging down the green roads of Cumbria from May to October, Brough Hill (*Broof'eel*, in the local dialect) gathered in from them not only horses (unbroken) but also cattle, sheep, geese and any other type of livestock that might be seeking a market. Suddenly the solitary moors were crowded as folk from the isolated farms hurried to join the mêlée. Woollen cloth was there in quantity, as at nearly every fair. The local women came to restock their linen cupboards (or such as had them), to find an extra blanket for the marital bed or homespun suitings for their menfolk. You could buy owt at Brough Hill: farm tools, scythes, wooden buckets, a new pair of boots or shoes or sturdy northern clogs – and given the usual weather the umbrella-seller, it has been said, did a prodigious trade. Potters met sufficient custom to entice them back again. The unfortunates of that time also returned regularly, for in the Methodist tent, without infliction of a sermon, the deserving would have their hunger stayed.

What the copers were looking for in the horse market were the 'long-haired stags' (unbroken young horses) herded into bunches on the fair hill by the 'catchers' who had that morning driven them wildly through the small village street. Bringing out a particular 'stag' from the pack for a buyer's inspection and putting a halter on it was work for the brave-hearted, demanding more physical agility than mental ability. There was a certain braggadocio about the task, and for the fair-goers who stopped to observe the spectacle, all the morbid fascination of a bullfight. One report, however, discounts the risk: 'To bystanders the work appears full of danger, but accidents seldom occur, and the men, who feel themselves to be the heroes of the hour, seem to enjoy their work. Doubtless they are much aided by the waving of sticks and shoutings of the surrounding crowd, as the horses become cowed and more easily submit than they would have done had the tussle taken place in their native pastures.'

From the start of the century Brough Hill Fair had declined from its ancient stature, though not in its essence, and was almost exclusively given over to horses, hundreds of them. All of them – unlike those of Howden and Horncastle and Penkridge – were work animals. Fell farmers brought in their ponies in droves; there were plough horses – the usually pure-bred Clydesdales from Scotland – carriage horses and 'vanners' (van ponies), crosses between the Clyde and the fell pony, locally called Galloways, that were also capable of pulling the plough. More than previously the fair had become a gypsies' occasion. They would be lying-up in the lanes and in recognised camping spots for up to ten days beforehand. Between the wars, a young constable, sent with ten of his colleagues to keep order in the normally one-cop village watched their arrival on the fair hill: 'we saw a steady stream of caravans, some expensive, some beautifully painted, and others shabby. Flat carts had canvas covers. Each had its retinue of haltered horses, varying in age, size and colour, together with a lurcher that was invariably seen near the rear axle, untethered and always silent. Children were numerous.'

Bringing out a particular stag from the bunch was a task for the brave-hearted

After them came the sideshows, a small circus, the Punch and Judy man, dealers with farm horses, a drove of fell ponies – and finally people. Cheapjacks – from towns safely distant such as Leeds – came to con the gullible with useless gadgets; quacks offered elixirs to cure every complaint; pedlars sold anything from clothes-pegs to unreliable watches; fortune-tellers – 'maybe 30 or 40 of them' – unfairly raised expectations; and besides the big food tent there were beer tents in abundance. There were escapologists – and, as always, the evangelists, who, unlike the Methodists, sought to save the souls of men in that unpropitious setting. The locals flocked to see the fun, promenading up and down Brough Hill, going home for their midday 'dinner' and returning to the Hill in case they should miss one moment of the excitement. The crowd at the time of the First World War would still be numbering about 8,000; most of the locals knew better than to buy anything and the trading took place between 'outsiders'.

'By noon the fair was at its height. The road was crowded with men and horses with complete disregard for vehicular traffic . . .'. The year was 1927. Writing in *Cumbria* magazine fifty years later the young constable would usefully record the ritual of the horse fair, unchanging down the centuries: 'A youth would run a horse through a corridor of critical spectators several times until one would step forward and flick the animal with his whip, which signalled his interest. The owner strolled towards him loudly extolling the excellent qualities of the creature. Soon the two men were haggling, one smacking the other's hand at each offer, the traditional method of bargaining. If there was a stalemate, usually an elderly man would emerge and, standing between them, a hand on the shoulder of each, would narrate the honest, flawless characters of their respective fathers, whom he claimed to have known well. He would end the recital by splitting the difference in the price of the animal which would be accepted by a resounding hand smack.'

At Brough Hill, the auctioning of animals never intruded into the old man-to-man tradition. The agonising prelude to the old hand-smack ritual was portrayed by the *Cumberland Herald*'s reporter at the 1924 fair: 'At the top of the hill are the honester faces of dalesmen and breeders who stand in groups all about, quiet and reserved and cautious; for the dalesman needs all his native caution here at Brough, if he intends to buy. What a mystery is buying! Tongues are quiet and eyes busy up here. The taciturn buyers stand about, watching the movements of likely animals, passing skilled gazes over possible blemishes, and doubting, always doubting.' The reporter is no city-slicker: 'Here is the shy-looking stag in charge of a cunning rascal. Watch his heels as you pass him! Everywhere there are sturdy little fell ponies, bunched together in dozens, with heads at the centre and heels outside . . . These wonderfully hardy creatures have lived all their days on the fells, and can stand almost everything but this noisy, jostling crowd. There is rare fun when one is selected to show his paces, for the whole bunch scatters right into the crowd and maybe heads are broken.'

Brough's old-timers still vividly remember the day of the fair and its impact on the life of the peaceful village. 'It was all horses,' said one ninety-year-old, a retired farmer, talking of his first visit to the fair in about 1910. 'A tremendous number of horses for sale. There was hundreds of bad 'uns. Hundreds of dealers. Local farmers would avoid the gypsies, preferring to buy from a local, known

Cheapjacks came to con the gullible, quacks offered elixirs for every complaint

dealer. There was a man from Bishop Auckland way. He used to go up to Scotland; he would buy animals up there that were a cross between a Clydesdale and a fells pony off the Cumbrian moors. He'd bring those stags down – have them standing on the Hill. They were great general-purpose horses. Some farmers would buy one from him every year and break it in. I had one – best horse I ever had in my life! There was everything you could mention at Brough Hill – the escapologist, tied up, went round his fair audience with his cap in his teeth. Sometimes he might take half an hour to free himself. One man balanced a cartwheel on his chin – he walked around balancing the wheel on his chin!'

The price of a horse at the fair about 1914, he recalled, would be about £23; a really good one twice that. 'You wanted four good legs and four good feet – you never bought a horse till you saw it walk.' Another Brough Hill veteran, a retired farmer/dealer, who liked to have one pony to take to the fair each year, was equally cautious: 'There were always more bad horses at Brough Hill than good ones. Brough Hill was the place to get rid of a dodgy horse. It had a reputation for that. Dealers would come 50 to 60 miles to offload a few duds in an area where their reputation was not important. They'd come from Bradford or Leeds. If you were buying a horse it was important to make him trot up and down to see that he was sound in wind and limb. To see that he was a good mover; that he didn't throw a leg out. You'd have a look in his mouth to see what year he was – at the fair a horse was never older than seven years, because it's almost impossible to tell after that! You'd see that the beast had no bumps on it. That it hadn't a "slack back". And that it hadn't just one eye . . . It has been done! Not so many years ago one man did buy a one-eyed horse. It had been wearing heavy blinkers. And once you've paid, the horse is yours – no comebacks, even if it drops dead on you! And mind you, if you took a horse to the fair to sell, you'd have to keep hold of it. Or it would be gone!'

The raffishness of the horse fair had changed little down the centuries and the gypsies fell under constant suspicion. 'If they'd bought one with a fault they'd do their best to get rid of it. And they wouldn't tell you about the fault! They would be there a week or two beforehand so that their ponies could fatten up on the roadside verges or on waste land.' Or, as was often suspected, in some farmer's field of good grass, the animals being put in there after dark and quietly removed by morning light. Any farmer who protested could find himself unpopular, to say the least; most felt it prudent to turn a blind eye.

In other ways, too, the horse-dealers at Brough Hill Fair between the wars kept faith with the past. Most had a pedigree far more intriguing than the beasts they were selling and Borrow would have recognised them for the distant cousins of the men he had seen at Horncastle and the other horse fairs of his time for they were characters who stood out even on an occasion that was itself a frenzy of colour and noise and movement. Theirs, after all, was an extrovert calling. Most of them favoured that narrowing, almost breeches-like 'horsey' trouser that tightened down the leg from the knee. One or two, with respectable reputations to maintain, were well-suited and wore trilbies and ties and the good boots that have long been the mark of the serious horseman. And, almost invariably, the coper with an eye to his image would wear the

The escapologist, all tied up, went round the crowd with his cap in his teeth

dealer's stock-in-trade, a lengthy jacket with a multitude of pockets. It was even admitted of some of them that they had good horses and were fair men to deal with.

Few, to be sure, would have felt themselves strangers at Cobbett's Weyhill a hundred years earlier or been at a loss mingling with the dealers in the great fair's horse market, for as the rhyme indicates all too plainly, north or south and down the years, the horse fair and the coper's wiles were remarkably unchanging:

Its I hev' been to Weyhill Fair,
An' Oh what sights did I see there,
To hear my tale 'ud make you stare,
An' see the horses shewing.
They cum from East, they cum from West,
They bring their worst, they bring their best,
An' some they lead, and drive the rest,
Unto the Fair at Weyhill.

There are blacks an' bays, an' duns and greys,
An' sorrelled horses, aye an' mares,
An' pyeballed too, I du declare,
An' more than I du know on.
They are blind an' lame, an' windgalled too,
Crib-biters there are not a few,
An' roarers more than one or two.
All at the Fair at Weyhill.

Now some upon the road are shown,
An' others found upon soft ground;
An' up the hill their heads are turned,
An' that's the way to show 'em.
They can gain or lose an inch or two,
Oh yes, they this, and more can do,
To find the sort that will suit you,
At the Fair at Weyhill.

Sometimes though the song of the fair would be a sadder song. If the mops all too frequently sundered the kitchen girl from the hired farmboy she loved, as they each went their separate ways, so too did the boisterous, back-slapping horse fair have its bitter heartbreaks. At Weyhill, Cobbett, unlikeliest of sentimentalists, records another kind of parting: 'I was struck with a young farmer trotting a horse backward and forwards to show him off to a couple of gentlemen, who were bargaining for the horse, one of whom finally purchased him. The gentlemen were two of our "deadweight" and the horse was that on which the farmer had pranced in the Yeomanry Troop! Here is a turn of things! Distress, pressing distress; dread of the bailiffs alone could have made the farmer sell his horse. If he had the firmness to keep the tears out of his eyes, his heart must have paid the penalty.' Cantankerous he may have been, but clearly the old curmudgeon of Kensington could feel for a man driven to such desperate straits.

North or south, and down the years, the horse-coper's wiles were unchanging

CHAPTER EIGHT

A DAY THAT CHANGED DESTINIES

Michaelmas to Martinmas – through October to November – was mainly the time of the mops, the hiring fairs of Old England, with late March Lady Day and May Day less popular options. They were days that changed destinies; days of heartbreak and misery for the vast numbers of young girls in domestic service and the men and boys who made up the labour force of the country's farms. Though they might change the milieu, the yearly statute fair offered them little but the opportunity to continue in the same drudgery that had dogged their days since leaving school. Few would remember the old 'statty' fairs with affection; for most they were the bitterest of memories. They were the days when the farm labourer and the serving girl shed all human dignity and paraded for inspection like livestock in the prize-ring. Highworth's Michaelmas hiring fair petered out after the First World War but one of those who attended it remembered it: 'When a farmer wanted a man – and these used to stand in a line along the edge of the pathway displaying their badges of whipcord – he walked down the street, eyeing them all up and down till he saw one that pleased him; then he went up to him and asked him a series of questions: where he worked, and for how long, whether he was married, the number and age of his children, and what he expected to receive in wages. If the answers were satisfactory, he offered the man a shilling; if the other accepted it the bargain was considered as made; there was no setting the bond aside afterwards.'

Bitter it may have been, yet they flocked – needs must – to the mop fairs in their thousands, looking for the work and the living wage that would carry them through to the next Michaelmas: fresh-faced milkmaids and farmboys, as well as the old-timers with strained, weather-burned faces, aware that youth was no longer on their side and that their experience must one day soon be discounted against doubts about their stamina; slow, bearded men whose legs had gone – who had followed the plough too long – with no pension to look forward to and nowhere else to go.

The day of the mop fair had its inviolable ritual. Attendance today at the Jobcentre may be a dispiriting experience for many. But whatever its cold inhumanity it is as nothing against the humiliation the housemaids and ploughboys of Old England endured, waiting in some chill, small-town street. By long consent they made their stand in one particular thoroughfare or in the market-place and waited for the farmers and the squires' farm bailiffs to arrive. They paraded wearing or carrying the emblems of their trade in hat or lapel – the tokens varied from county to county – in their Sunday suits and best billycocks,

Feast alfresco. Eager fair-goers (doubtless with eager appetites) crowd round the roasting ox in its popular location in the High Street at Stratford's celebrated mop in about 1900. In 1675 the town beadle was earning himself fourpence for 'crying the mop' with the added incentive of sixpence for two dozen pipes and two ounces of tobacco. Proclamation of the hiring fair would be at the High Cross, long demolished

shaven and dapper in their winged and unaccustomed collars some of them, their faces scrubbed and hopeful; some of them, too – the sepia photographs that have become their memorials show us – with that haunted look in their eyes, shepherds perhaps, uncomfortable and strange in the press of people when their natural element was the still and eerie silence of the downs and the song of the skylark. But come they did, all the same; come they must, for their futures and that of their families depended on it.

The hiring fairs were countrywide. Most had their own patterns and customs: the Rig Fair at Wem in Shropshire on Ascension Day was often called the White Apron Fair, since its girl job-seekers would wear spotless aprons instead of carrying the usual mop. At Ulverston's fairs a matchstick or a straw in the hatband was all that was needed to indicate an interest in new employment. But usually, the emblems worn advertised the worker's skills, the nature of his or her calling: the shepherd would have his crook or a tuft of wool in his lapel; the waggoner his whip or a twist of whipcord round his hat; milkmaids wore a tuft of cowhair; grooms a bit of sponge; maids carried their mops, giving that milling market of rootless humanity its too-glamorous name. With them, in battered trunks and boxes, they had brought the pitiful sum of their worldly goods – like the weary dispossessed our own world would become alarmingly used to. Some called it a slave market, and indeed it was scarcely less demeaning. Understandably, the clergy, though they might continue to hire their maidservants at them, were always less than enthusiastic about the mops, and not only because of the loss of dignity for those who lived by them.

Madcap merriment. Where there was a fair there was a fiddler, and that was particularly true of the mops. He stirred the appetite for pleasure. Remembering the occasion, one labourer of the early 1800s recollected (in Roy Palmer's *The Painful Plough*) that around the fiddler there would stand 'a crowd of men and boys who, at intervals, eagerly joined to swell the chorus of song'

The pattern of the mid-nineteenth century hiring fair is observed by the novelist Thomas Hardy in *Far from the Madding Crowd*, when the destitute farmer Gabriel Oak is forced to attend the Candlemas Fair at Casterbridge to seek a position as a bailiff. The Wessex writer conjures the demeanour of those who had to resort to the 'statty'. 'At the end of the street stood two or three hundred blithe and hearty labourers waiting upon Chance – all men of the stamp to whom labour suggests nothing worse than a wrestle with gravitation, and pleasure nothing better than a renunciation of the same. Among these, carters and waggoners were distinguished by having a piece of whipcord twisted round their hats; thatchers wore a fragment of woven straw; shepherds held their crooks in their hands; and thus the situation was known to the hirers at a glance.' Alas Oak, like so many who pinned their hopes on the mop, ended the February day unhired. Like others he had to try his luck again – at another fair, another day, in another town.

The Dorset writer's portrait of the statute fair, alas, is a sanitised version, one that squares ill with the raw reality of such occasions. It was one, apparently, where the sexes were segregated, something that became necessary as much for the sake of common decorum as for the convenience of the farmers and their wives, and had been early adopted in the north at Kendal and Beverley and Bridlington. By 1900 the practice had become more general with local traditions establishing themselves much as they did, say, at Grantham's May Fair, where the men stood along one side of the High Street, near the Angel Hotel, while the women job-seekers aligned themselves on the other. It seems hardly a sufficient safeguard. The badinage must have been ferocious and at times almost certainly bawdy. In 1874 Brigg, in a handbill circulating at its statute fair, urged young girls not to stand in the street but to gather at the town hall where the handbill's distributors promised 'they would do their best to get them situations'.

The badinage must have been ferocious and at times certainly bawdy

Highworth's hirings were held in the market-place. Norwich's were in the ancient Maddermarket, by St John's churchyard, where the local dyers bought their 'madder', the red vegetable dye, to colour the cloth made by local weavers. Marlborough's High Street had two hiring occasions, Big Mop and Little Mop, held in the earlier nineteenth century on the Saturday before Old Michaelmas Day and the Saturday after 10 October. So, too, had Kirkby Stephen, next door to Brough, at Whitsuntide and November. York's thronged the Coppergate and Parliament Street – already jammed with all the attractions of the travelling funfair: roundabouts, shooting galleries, peepshows, menageries, fortune-tellers and gingerbread stalls. Pandemonium reigned in every pub, the beer flowed, song lifted the rafters. There was some boxing, not all of it in the booths. Ulverston's famous hiring fairs, at Whitsun and Martinmas, crowded the market-place and the narrow streets of the town but the engagements, apparently following the Scots model, tended to be only for a six-month. Here as elsewhere a man who had been passed over in the fair could save face by pretending that he preferred to be 'loose-ending' – working as casual labour in the seasonal country tasks.

The hiring fairs masqueraded under many names. Devon, at Holsworthy, Okehampton and South Molton, had its giglet fairs; why remains a mystery. Canterbury's was called a jack-and-jill fair, with a painful accuracy. Some were more famous than others, not always for the best of reasons. Newbury's big Michaelmas mop was said to be 'a great trysting place for friends and relations in farm and domestic service all over the region'. It may have been, but there were those who grudged the farm labourers and the domestics their day of freedom. In Sussex, recorded one grumpy observer, 'the roads are crowded with farm servants leaving their places and hying to the fair. It is a complete holiday: not a team to be seen, or a stroke of work going forward.'

Hardy's fair seems also to have been a modest affair, perhaps reflecting the decline of the 'statty' in his own lifetime. Abingdon's October fair in 1805, by contrast, was drawing 10,000 people, not all of them, it is true, looking for work. That year, it appears, milkmaids could be hired cheaply owing to a dramatic fall in the price of cheese. Taskers, however, were having a good fair: their barn labour was at a premium as farmers strove to get their harvest crops

The Statute Fair. A vividly
real portrayal of the hiring
mop at which the farmboys
and milkmaids, shepherds
and waggoners, taskers and
domestics and all who
worked the land met yearly
to find themselves new
masters. The brush is that
of John Faed (1820–1902).
The 'statty' continues
today, though not for
hirings, and is still a raucous
occasion

quickly threshed to catch high cereal prices. But east or west, wherever it was held, there was a very basic uniformity about the hiring fair. Brawn and muscle offered itself for usually a calendar-year contract of employment. The 'bargaining' that went on had a guarded, cautionary pattern. Overtures were tentatively or brusquely made, concealing strong interest, and were accepted or rejected, if courage and need allowed, in a like manner. Contracts would be agreed and as quickly regretted. For those disillusioned with their agreement, there followed soon after the so-called 'runaway mops' – the hiring fairs that offered the farmboy or girl a second chance to seek something better in the job-market. But mainly, the bargain stuck. The engagement agreed, the traditional hiring penny – or, as it was often more revealingly known, the 'fastening penny' – would be pressed into the ploughman's palm, confirming the bond. The hiring penny, of course, was not literally so: about the start of the century it would be a shilling, rising to half a crown between the wars. But with that, whatever the amount, jingling in the pocket it would be but a short walk to the inn or ale tent, perhaps to sup unwisely, or in honour of the compact, beyond the usual capacity. The consequences then could be catastrophic. For the mop, effectively over by midday, like every other fair had its diversions: that early nineteenth-century year, Abingdon, for example, had a menagerie, the lure of the Grand Turk's Palace, amazing feats by the Little Strong Woman, the Learned Little Horse as well as an equestrian troupe and seductive airs from the Pentonville Organ. A young farmboy's eyes must have misted with the wonder of it all. There were others there that day too, less innocent: pickpockets, ladies of the dusk, and, says a contemporary source, in the evening a number of fine young men were enlisted by the recruiting parties. That indeed was the fate that could befall any careless farmboy at the end of a fair day. Nor did the situation improve. Quite the reverse. At Abingdon thirty years later the number of pickpockets, prostitutes and highwaymen was greater than ever.

In the Midlands particularly, the statute fair was a far from decorous occasion. King's Norton's appears to have given especial offence with its behaviour in the 1870s – an indication perhaps that the mop was already beginning its trans-formation into a purely pleasure affair. 'Shouting hobbledehoys, screaming girls, drunken men and shouting women swarmed from the station in hundreds . . . The public houses were packed, the customers had to fight their way in and out, treading on floors wet with slopped beer . . . The general proceedings offered a spectacle of debauchery, drunkenness, noise and blasphemy.'

Nor was the trouble confined to the industrial heartland. Brigg's 'statty', one of the largest in its county, was held on the Friday before Old May Day (changing with the new calendar to 12 May). Fair-goers were travelling from Hull by the end of the eighteenth century, coming by packet boat up the Ancholme River. In time they would flock by train. As at Newbury it was a day of reunions; long-lost sweethearts found each other again and kissed and made up. Alas, the fair was not without the age-old problems. The *Lincoln, Rutland and Stamford Mercury*, reporting the event in the 1840s, found 'the town was

His engagement agreed, the 'fastening penny' would be pressed into the ploughman's palm

Postures and proposals. A handshake seals a deal in the centre of the throng at this northern hiring fair of the mid-1800s, while the 'domestics' group themselves on the market cross awaiting an approach that will bring them an offer of work and a barely living wage for the year to come

infested with more pickpockets and vagabonds than we can remember to have seen on any former occasion; but not withstanding they had recourse to fighting, wrestling, and other means to gather a crowd round them, their number and obvious design, made persons more cautious than usual'. However, the report continues (note the condemnatory quotes): 'There was no lack of amusement for the honest lads and lasses, after they had succeeded in "selling themselves for another year"; dancing extensively prevailed and shows of every kind studded the streets, particularly representations of "bloody murders", "gallant actions", "wars in China", etc.' Many a servant lass, one imagines, went home to sleep unsoundly in her bed. Thirteen years later in 1857 the newspaper was reporting 'one of the largest gatherings ever seen in the north of Lincolnshire (10,000 or more people present)' and an amazing amount of hirings. English agriculture, still massively labour intensive, was at its high point. The labourer had suddenly become worthy of his hire and wages were again rising, with waggoners commanding up to £20 for their year and boys getting £6 to £8, all with bed and board and 'living either in the household of the farmer, or his farm foreman'. Domestics fared proportionately well.

Yet the mop was causing increasing concern. A decade or two later Francis Heath in his *Peasant Life in the West of England* was distinctly unamused by its goings-on. Of the fairs of his region he observed: 'These fairs, annually held to

Itinerant entrepreneur. For the cheapjack the country fair was a chance to make a fast profit on usually tawdry but invariably colourful 'fairings' and quickly move on. His prime time came at the end of the 'statty'; by then a farmboy's judgement could be seriously clouded. The painting is the work of the nineteenth-century artist Ebenezer Newman Downard

enable servants of both sexes to be hired were, oftentimes, the occasion of the greatest drunkenness and profligacy. Young girls dressed in their finest clothes were exhibited like cattle to be hired by the would-be employers, who came to the fair to seek their services; and the scenes which frequently took place at the close of the day were too disgraceful for description.' Well, we can imagine, though one could wish, for the sake of future social historians, that Heath had been less hasty with his veil of discretion. Yet, if the behaviour appalled him, so obviously did the parade of humans in the manner of camels at a market. His words would have been confirmatory fuel to the middle-class conscience which had long been made uneasy by the 'statty' fair and all that went on there. By 1860 there would be voices clamouring for its suppression.

But the mid-nineteenth century would prove to be the high point of the true mop. The farm labour force peaked about then with something over 1,250,000 male workers and close on 200,000 women, most of them in the arable east and south where a man was needed for every 25 cultivated acres. Against today's trends, the lowest pay was in the south – at that time almost 40 per cent less than for the equivalent worker in the north. In Lincolnshire in 1851 the farm labourer's weekly wage averaged 11 shillings; in the south-west it might be only 8 shillings, with the normal working day then stretching to 10½ hours. By 1876 the yearly rates were: boys, £8–12; waggoners, £25–28; carters, £16–20; cooks, £12–18; domestics, £8–14. It was the peak before the long fall. In 1894 waggoners were down to £16–19; boys to £5–7.

Few of those hired at the mop fairs stayed in one job for more than the year they had contracted themselves for, yet few moved farther than a 10 mile radius.

Challenging situation. Ring fighters bait the fair crowd, heightening expectation of the impending show inside the booth, as they incite the brave and the foolish. Many famous boxers began their careers in the fairground and promoters sometimes dubbed their booths 'academies of boxing'. Maybe it softened the blow for those who unwisely accepted their challenge

The farmboys were always a restless breed, always looking towards the next hiring fair and fresh fields that were no different from the ones they had known. Michaelmas, in the old countryside, was always a milestone, a time of change as we have seen, bringing an end and beginning to all things. It was the time of that saddest of all partings, the old farmer's farewell, finally, to the thing that had been his life. And the statute fair, too, dipped its roots in a long-past sadness, that time when the Black Death had stalked the land, decimating its working population but, with the labour shortage, in the process destroying at last the serfdom of the old manorial ways. The first Statute of Labourers – the first of several which would continue into the fifteenth century – was passed in 1351 to inhibit the movement of scarce labour but it also gave the farm worker the freedom to offer himself for hire in the nearest market town on the day after Michaelmas Day, 30 September, when pay rates and conditions for the coming year were set by the local justices at the Statute Sessions. The sessions were also held at Martinmas and sometimes at Whitsun. Their intent was to implement an early pay restraint in seeking to peg wages and they were deeply resented. Labourers, incensed, in some cases tried to kill the justices imposing them. These early statutes would finally be quashed in Elizabeth's reign, but the sessions continued to be convened and farmers and labourers still gathered to hear the rates that had been fixed. Gloucester's justices were still setting agricultural wages as late as 1732 – though no one paid the slightest attention to their ruling.

Thus were the hiring fairs created. Not all were exclusively mops. Tewkesbury's – one of the largest of the country's street fairs as well as one of the oldest – was the transmutation of a fair granted in 1324 by Edward II. Cornwall's Summercourt astutely assimilated its hiring fair for the region with a sheep sale – the local residents cashing in on the day by letting the farm lads park their bicycles at 3*d* a time!

The end came gradually. Finally, the country's conscience was stirred by the reported behaviour at the mops and the indignities they heaped on those who were forced to live by them. Well-doing employers, sensitive to the mood of the times, began to distance themselves from the statty's disrepute and moved to fill their vacancies for stockmen and ploughmen and shepherds through the job agencies being set up, and via the small-ads columns of the local newspaper. Mainly, the mop fair faded from the English country calendar with the First World War. When that was over many thousands of the nation's farmboys would not return to it. Those who did no longer had the stomach for it.

CHAPTER NINE

BY RIVER AND PACKHORSE TRAIL

The arteries of commerce criss-crossed the map of Old England in a ragged mosaic of trading trails, locking community with community, the output of one region with the needs of another. Goods bought at one fair travelled to stock the booths at the next. Down the drove roads to the capital and the main cities came that gathering avalanche of beef and mutton on the hoof. By hill track and across the wastes of bleak moorland, by almost every navigable waterway, produce moved ponderously to market. The packhorse trains threading through the landscape laden with cheese, that once important dietary necessity salt, butter and wool, like the slowly drifting barges on the Thames, Severn, Trent and Ouse, linked a countrywide and often precarious economy still closely bound to the nation's fairs. In the complex structure that united market and fair, at times blurring the distinction, the pattern is discernible. It is not well documented, however; country transactions seldom were. Yet there is evidence enough to pinpoint the concerns of particular towns and regions – evidence sufficient at least to sketch a portrait of how commodities moved to meet the needs of the country's burgeoning population.

To the livestock droves drifting south or east were added droves of quite a different kind. Squawking geese were marched miles, most notably perhaps in the national network to Nottingham and Tavistock and Smithfield. Big droves from the farms of Norfolk and Suffolk were walked to the London market, their feet often encased in small cloth shoes. Sometimes the 'shoes' would be of pitch and the geese were 'fitted' for their long 80- to 100-mile journey by being driven first through a shallow pool of tar and then into a patch of sand to harden their feet, this treatment being repeated perhaps at intervals during the drive. A little earlier in the year, in August and September, East Anglia might have sent similar droves to Stourbridge's great fair. In both instances the flocks would be about 500-strong but might even be as large as 2,000. Frequently the slow-moving droves, weeks on the road, were in the charge of young goose-herds with their crooks, many of them those bonneted little goose-girls so adored by country painters and sometimes aged as young as ten. In Lincolnshire's West Fen Frithbank and Brothertoft, where one man might own a flock of 2,000, cottagers bred the birds for their feathers, their down being plucked five times a year, their feathers twice. But come the spring they, too, would be rounded up and driven to the London markets – at times getting

A colourful occasion. This was Nottingham's Goose Fair first pictured in colour, in about 1890. Its mindless, milling throng terrified the writer J.B. Priestley in the 1930s. Today it is one of Europe's top jamborees – without a single goose in sight!

chaotically mixed up with the cattle-droves. Enclosure in the early nineteenth century, alas, would put paid to this fenland industry – assisted by the increasing imports of foreign down and foreign quills. Converging from the south for the same capital market would be flocks that had fattened on the heaths around Chobham Ridges and Farnham. There, too, the birds grazed in their thousands.

Devon had several goose fairs, Brent notably sharing the fame with Tavistock. But the most famous of them all was Nottingham's Goose Fair, documented from 1541 but most certainly older, which began on 2 October and – flouting its fifteen-day charter – in its heyday ran for twenty-one days, enduring down the centuries in the Old Market Place, where Queen Victoria's statue gazed sternly on the scene, and spilling out into its side-streets, already choked with the vans of the showmen. Here droves arrived through the Goose Gate from as far as the Lincolnshire Fens as well as elsewhere – geese fattened into condition on the stubble of the newly cut harvest fields. There would be some 20,000 of them, it is said. Hardly secondary was the occasion's reputation as a cheese fair. The fattest, finest geese of all, though, were said to be those that Dorking sent, along with large capons, to the poultry dealers of London's Leadenhall market, the largest of its kind in Europe.

The origins of Nottingham's well-known fair are lost in the mists. The first real mention of such an occasion is in the borough records – a charter granted in 1284 by Edward I, whose will it was that Nottingham's burgesses and men 'besides their fair lasting for eight days at the Feast of St Matthew the Apostle, shall have for ever one other fair in the same town every year to endure for fifteen days; to wit on the eve, the day and the morrow of the Feast of St Edmund the King and Martyr, and for twelve days following'. The designation 'goose fair' came some 300 years later, an acknowledgement obviously of the vast numbers of geese the fair attracted yearly 'in fine flocks from the stubbles for miles around, and also in Brobdingnagian battalions from the Lincolnshire and Cambridgeshire fens'.

'A fine specimen, sir.' This is the real thing: back in the 1870s this is how it would have looked as fair-goers wandered in to choose their Michaelmas goose. A goose supper at the right time could bring you luck

The goose fair, like the main mops, was associated with Michaelmas, and the apparently ready demand may not have been unconnected with the fact that this was the time of year when the tenant farmer might find it useful to cultivate his landlord, as well as his fields, with the gift of a bird. As the old Exmoor song has it:

> At Christmas a capon, at Michaelmas a goose,
> And something else at New Year's Eve for fear the lease fly loose.

Eating a goose on Michaelmas Day was supposed to bring the diner luck:

> Who eats goose on Michaelmas Day,
> Shan't money lack his debts to pay.

The belief no doubt lost nothing by Elizabeth I's widely reported dinner on the night of 29 September 1588, during which the news of the Spanish Armada's defeat was brought to her. She was dining on roast goose and immediately decreed that henceforth the famous victory should be commemorated yearly with goose for dinner.

In the north Ovingham's Goose Fair and Brough Hill gathered in flocks from the vast wastes of Cumberland. Yet none could equal the pedigree of Tavistock's October event. As goose fairs go, its lineage is impeccable, dating from 1105, when the abbot of the local Benedictine abbey was granted a charter by Henry I, third son of the Conqueror, to hold a weekly market. There is a persistent belief that the tenants of the abbey once paid their rents in kind and in geese and that these birds, gathered to be resold, established the 'goosey'. In any case, the customary fair soon followed, in 1116, when the abbot was allowed a three-day event on the January feast of St Rumon, though the goose fair would later opt for Michaelmas Day, the date then on which, traditionally, roast goose was eaten. At Tavistock certainly, goose dinners would be the order of the day, filling every inn in town. There was even an opportunity for less scrupulous operators, who took a day's lease on vacant shops and served 'goose dinners' that were really rabbit dipped in goose fat! Few were fooled but there was the consolation that the improvised dish was cheaper. Yet clearly the town has always had a fondness for the dish: when the Revd Shaw made his *Tour to the West of England* in 1780 he found the local roads crowded and 'this being market day we met numbers of the people flocking hither with grain, a few sheep and an abundance of Michaelmas geese'. The town was once a famous corn market and the fair, despite its name, has always been as much a farming fair – one drawing its livestock off the expanse of Dartmoor – with ponies, sheep and cattle as well as poultry.

Once, on the night before the fair the darkness of the moor would be dotted with the bobbing lanterns of the drovers as they brought in their flocks and herds. The far-off sound of shouts and the barking of their dogs heightened the excitement. All wanted to be first into the market to claim the most prominent pens. Live geese – grazed on the moor by cottagers with goose and gander rights – were driven in for sale in the cattle market. In a later era they would be brought by cart; at times sixty carts could be waiting to unload. The night before, dressed birds would have been brought in for sale in the pannier market – to hotels and anyone else planning a time-honoured fair-day dinner.

Defoe, though not always the most fastidious of reporters, believed there were more turkeys bred in Suffolk and the abutting part of Norfolk than in all the rest of England. With the geese they would join the London droves as the harvest drew to an end, so that they could glean the field stubble on the way. Defoe quotes an eyewitness, the safe journalistic ploy: 'I received an account from a person living on the place, that they had counted 300 droves of turkeys . . . pass in one season over Stratford Bridge on the River Stour, on the road from Ipswich to London. These droves, as they say, generally contain from three hundred to a thousand each drove; so that one may suppose them to contain 500 one with another, which is 150,000 in all; and yet this is one of the least passages, the numbers which travel by New Market-Heath, and the open country and the forest, and also by Sudbury and Clare, being many more.' But the droving of birds was tedious and time-consuming, and by the 1720s, a new way was being found for the faster supply of the London tables: 'they have of late invented a

The darkness of the moor would be dotted with the bobbing lights of the drovers

An eye-watering event. Mounds of the eponymous commodity grace the site of Birmingham's Onion Fair. A seemingly unlikely candidate for 'drunkenness, rowdiness and general debauchery', it nevertheless became so unruly it had to be banished from the Bull Ring in the late 1800s to the outer limits of the city

new method of carriage, being carts formed on purpose, with four stories or stages, to put the creatures in one above the other, by which invention one cart will carry a very great number and for the smoother going, they drive with two horses a-breast, like a coach . . . Changing horses they travel night and day, so that they bring the fowls 70, 80, or 100 miles in two days and one night.' Similarly, a light fast cart could deliver ducks from St Ives in two days.

There were other commodities travelling longer distances to find a market, though some went only into the next parish – perishables such as fruit and fish being obvious examples. Fairs near seaports could see an awesome array of

Straw men. When the Napoleonic wars cut off supplies of Leghorn straw, plait-making became a cottage industry in England's hat-making towns – and here at Yaxley Barracks near Norman Cross, where dealers surreptitiously traded with French prisoners of war, visiting their camp twice a week. They also made bonnets. Trading day is depicted here by A.C. Cooke

goods and merchants, and pedlars would percolate some of that bounty to those that were held inland. Coastal fairs would have commodities like iron, wool and dyestuffs along with timber and of course, fish; those far from the seaboard stocked more of the produce of the land: livestock, butter, hops and cheese and so on – plus cloth and wool, the dominant commodities. Packed and panniered, the stuff of England's wealth lurched and swayed over the old packhorse trails and their hump-backed bridges as the West Country's ponies bore that region's output to the capital; at Norton St Philip in Somerset the important wool and yarn fair there turned the local George Inn into a kind of 'exhibition centre' as it was largely emptied of its normal furnishings to accommodate the packs and bales of the dealers. The Old Inn, near Frome, dating from 1397, is one of the county's most picturesque, half-timbered with bay windows. Here the Duke of Monmouth, come to claim a crown, slept on the night of 26 June 1685 on his way to defeat at Sedgemoor, a man with a price on his head; standing by one of the inn's fine windows, doubtless contemplating the battle to come, he barely escaped death when a bounty-hunter's bullet whistled past his cheek.

Cloth manufacture – established in East Anglia and the southern counties since the Middle Ages – was often the underpinning of a prosperous regional economy and towns showed little compunction about switching allegiance from the commodities that had earlier sustained them. Bales went to Stourbridge via the Waveney, the Stour, the Ouse and the Cam; packhorse trains – dales ponies, perhaps thirty of them, tied head to tail – brought down the fair's Manchester cotton. Defoe in his early eighteenth-century travels found that Basingstoke, while maintaining its considerable corn market, 'is fallen into the manufacture of making druggets and shalloons'. Leominster's wool accompanied its corn into the Wye and thence via the Severn to Bristol, with its manufacture of druggets and cantaloons. There were powerful incentives: in Exeter, a 'serge market held there every week is very worth a stranger's seeing, and next to the Brigg-Market at Leeds in Yorkshire, is the greatest in England'. Weekly sales worth up to £100,000 were not uncommon and the city regularly shipped off vast quantities of woollen goods to Spain, Portugal, Italy and Holland – an output sustained by the wool and yarn, much of it imported from Ireland, that the Exeter cloth-makers, with those of Tiverton, bought in Barnstaple's big fair.

In Salisbury the concentration was on fine flannels and the longcloths they called Salisbury Whites. Shrewsbury, too, was in the way of making flannel, but strengthened its hand with white broadcloth. But the great gathering for that warming material which kept backs warm at the winter plough was Wrexham, where the merchants, alas, seem shamefully to have fleeced the indigent Welsh by buying cheaply – to trade expensively with London. Taunton turned out mainly serges and the widely worn druggets while many of the Somerset wool towns favoured serges and cantaloons, leaving places such as Frome and Norton St Philip to make the finer cloths. Rougher-textured Cotswolds wool went into the making of the heavier cloths and it was there that the East India Company came to purchase much of its worsted. The cloth towns of Somerset, Wiltshire, Dorset and Gloucester, full of rich manufacturers and exporting widely, were for a time insatiable; the demand was staggering. Kentish wool arrived in the fleece from the capital and was promptly returned as cloth. The wool-clip of the Midlands counties such as Leicester, Northampton and Lincoln was brought down to such important wool markets as Cirencester and Tetbury. The quantity sold was 'so great, that it almost exceeds belief'. Yet it was by no means enough. Stroud alone, in the mid-eighteenth century, needed an astonishing two million to three million fleeces, a demand that necessitated imports of a fine texture from both Spain and Germany.

To the north, Chester's famous cloth halls, in the fairs of July and October – probably the most nationally important of their kind – became a focus for Irish linen, the cloths of Yorkshire and the cotton of Manchester and it was left to Newbury to put its linings into the nation's menswear, a humble consideration that made quiet fortunes for those in the old clothing town who had the sense to stay with shalloons, 'a kind of stuff, which, though it be used only for the lining and inside of men's clothes, for women use but little of it, nor the men for anything but the above, yet it becomes so generally worn, both at home and abroad, that it is increased to a manufacture . . . more considerable than any single manufacture of stuffs in the nation'. Our informant again is Defoe.

Down the Rivers Aire and Calder the output of the northern wool towns was already flooding in that inexorable tide that would eventually eclipse the southern and West Country clothiers; down to the sea at Hull it went to satisfy the markets of America – particularly the British colonies – as well as those of

Down the Rivers Aire and Calder flooded the cloth output in an inexorable tide

Quaint event. Wiltshire's Cuckoo Fair at the Domesday village of Downton on Hampshire's border, frozen in motion for this early photographic record and, on the evidence, not a boisterous occasion. It was held in April

such international centres of trade as Leipzig, Vienna and St Petersburg. But much of it would also find its way to almost every fair in the country through Leeds's focal market, once held on the bridge that linked the two parts of that city but now so big that it stretched right up the High Street. Here again was a scene that astonished the much-travelled Defoe: 'For the home consumption; their goods being, as I may say, every where made use of, for the clothing the ordinary people, who cannot go to the price of the fine medley cloths made . . . in the western counties of England. There are for this purpose a set of travelling merchants in Leeds, who go all over England with droves of pack horses, and to all the fairs and market towns over the whole island, I think I may say none excepted. Here they supply not the common people by retail, which would denominate them pedlars indeed, but they supply the shops by wholesale or whole pieces; and not only so, but give large credit too . . . and as such they sell a very great quantity of goods.'

Round the circuit of these same country fairs, the cheese jobbers moved their quotas like the pieces on a chequerboard and with the kind of guile that would not have shamed a horse-coper. Cheese, too, was a commodity that travelled far; next to livestock and cloth it was probably the most mobile commodity in the land. It came to St Faith's by the cartload – from Suffolk – and the folk of the surrounding countryside hied there to lay in their winter supplies. Burton-on-Trent's famous five-day horse fair for the Blacks, the 'best fair in the kingdom' for the Lincolnshire breed, had a sixth day kept sacrosanct for the sale of cheese. Beaminster and that Hardy favourite, Woodbury Hill, were among the many Dorset fairs that would see local farmers keenly restocking their supplies of a dietary essential for their men. Cheshire cheese – made not only in the county itself but in neighbouring Shropshire, Staffordshire and Lancashire – was favouring the London market in considerable quantities, reportedly some 14,000 tons yearly, by the early eighteenth century, as well as providing plentiful supplies as river cargo on the Severn and Trent to Bristol and York, and was even being exported to Scotland and Ireland. Somerset's cheese markets – at Highbridge and Wells as well as Cheddar itself – brought jobbers whose intention was to stock fair stalls at Reading or St Giles Hill, or even more profitably to unload cheese with such a worthy reputation on to the capital's cheesemongers.

Defoe found the cheese-making village and promptly gave away its secrets

Defoe found the cheese-making village nestling behind the Mendips and promptly gave away the secret of its enviable success: '. . . before the village is a large green, or common, a piece of ground, in which the whole herd of the cows, belonging to the town, do feed; the ground is exceeding rich, and as the whole village are cowkeepers, they take care to keep up the goodness of the soil, by agreeing to lay on large quantities of dung for manuring, and enriching the land.' In an age when the management of commons was always a matter of some contention, the communal will was doubtless relevant, but the cheese-making routine, too, was a strict one. 'The milk of all the town cows, is brought together every day in a common room, where the persons appointed, or trusted for the management, measure every man's quantity, and set it down in a book; when the quantities are adjusted, the milk is all put together, and every meal's milk makes one cheese, and no more; so that the cheese is bigger, or less, as the cows yield more, or less, milk. By this method the goodness of the cheese is preserved and, without all dispute, it is the best cheese that England affords, if not that the whole world affords.'

As always, Defoe is not the man to scruple when it comes to praise of England. Yet there was no question about the peculiar skill of the region's cheese-makers – it was one that supported further markets at Tetbury, Wincanton, Frome, Yeovil and Marlborough, which the diarist John Aubrey believed to be 'one of the greatest markets for cheese in the west of England. Here doe reside factors for the cheesemongers of London.' The north-west area of Wiltshire was a strong cheese-making enclave with an output of some 5,000 tons yearly in 1798, with Marlborough as its marketing hub supplying not only the capital but selling in substantial bulk to the Bath factors. Its cheese was 'esteemed by genteel people'. In Somerset the jobbers would also buy Cheddars straight off the farms for sending to such big fairs as Reading, St Giles and Weyhill as well as the London market.

In adjoining Gloucester Defoe also found dairying and cheese-making 'excellent good of its kind', a vast proportion of the products being shipped by barge down the Thames, and sent also by land routes, to London. At Chipping Norton, 'a place of note for nothing I saw', he stumbled on 'the greatest cheese market in all of that part of England; or perhaps any other, except Atherstone, in

Cheese spread. Waggons and jobbers crowd round the portals of Chippenham's cheese market in the mid-1800s as the cheese-dealers load their supplies for distant fairs. This commodity was almost as mobile as the country's livestock herds

Warwickshire'. At Atherstone's cheese fair the factors bought for reselling at Stourbridge. And the jobbers would have other dates in their diaries. In Yorkshire's North Riding, Yarm's October cheese fair, granted by King John, extended over three days. In Northumberland's Whittingham Fair, whose principal trade was in livestock, mainly cattle, the cheese factors also did brisk business. In the mêlée of Weyhill they vied with each other to buy cheeses that had come over the boundary from Wiltshire.

Doubtless they took a tumble at times, these commodity speculators, for the distribution was wide and complex, the prices constantly in flux. Cobbett's visit to Weyhill Fair in October 1826 coincided with a downturn. He was there to assess the hops as well as the cheese, 'for after the sheep these are the principal articles'. He was not comforted by what he found: 'As to the cheese, the price, considering the quantity, has been not one half so high as it was last year. The fall in the positive price has been about 20 per cent, and the quantity made in 1826 has not been above two-thirds as great as that made in 1825. So that, here is a fall of one-half in real relative price; that is to say, the farmer, while he has the same rent to pay that he paid last year, has only half as much money to receive for cheese, as he received for cheese last year; and observe, on some farms, cheese is almost the only saleable produce.'

Storeyed elegance. The galleried magnificence of Southwark's Hop and Malt Exchange (architect: R.H. Moore) with its airy interior and glass roof so that buyers could inspect supplies by natural light. The area had a large brewing industry, making good beer from the water of the Thames

Hops, however, were a different story, and arguably just as important a one, for then they were part of the farm labourer's sustenance. 'The crop . . . has been, in parts where they are grown, unusually large and of super-excellent quality. The average price of the Farnham hops has been as nearly as I can ascertain seven pounds for a hundred weight; that of Kentish hops, five pounds, and that of the Hampshire and Surrey hops (other than those of Farnham), about five pounds also. The prices are, considering the great weight of the crop, very good' – a fact he explains as due to the country being at the time 'almost wholly without hops'. His specific mention of Farnham we may take as home-town pride. Hops were perhaps less volatile, yet Reading, in trying to establish itself as a big venue for their sale failed miserably to do so and its Michaelmas fair settled instead for being one of the country's biggest 'exchanges' for cheese, with the jobbers bringing up their supplies from the West Country – 1,200 tons in 1795 – to meet merchants' purses from the Midlands and London. Even this success, however, would be tempered by the arrival of the railway, when supplies would be offloaded and left at the railhead while the fair's trading proceeded by sample. Reading Fair would slip slowly into decline – part of that inexplicable history of fairs which saw one venerable occasion sink even as another grew and prospered.

But whether their stars rose or dimmed in the country calendar, most fairs were ultimately local in their resonance, existing mainly for a regional need; the copers and jobbers found it no hardship to stay away. Baldock's organisers showed a shrewd understanding of compatibility with a cheese and onion fair that combined the district's own cheeses with the onions of neighbouring Buckinghamshire. Lincolnshire's Swineshead had an October fair that had seen better times but as late as 1826 was also thriving on the sale of cheese and onions. At Newton Abbot the September cheese and onion fair dated from the sixteenth century; again the onions were grown mainly locally.

Taunton gave the first day of its old three-day fairs on the North Bridge and in the North Town to the sale of 'considerable quantities of garlick from barges'. Chertsey, in Surrey, with unusual panache, coupled crop and flock with its goose and onion fair, also in September. And there are other fairs that have raised eyebrows (literally sometimes) and given cause for confusion. Egremont Crab Fair is not the grand crustacean occasion you might expect from its name, which actually alludes to the tart apple variety thrown as largesse to onlookers in the street. The Michaelmas fair, however, retains its cachet by hosting the world championship of 'gurning' – an exercise in facial distortion raised to a truly horrendous art. Chichester's Sloe Fair, too, is a deceiver: the event takes its title from the field in which the fair was anciently held, which had a sloe tree at its gate. Haywards Heath's Dolphin Fair in its day must have sounded intriguing but was unusual only in being one of the few pig fairs and one where you could watch that now extinct species, the fellmonger, at work fashioning the tanned sheepskins he had brought with him into leggings, hedging gloves, and even 'bootlegs' – long leggings that fastened thigh-high with brass buttons.

One of the fairs that brought tanners to its lonely site on the downs was Whitedown, as important for its leather as for its livestock. Whitedown sat at one of the great crossroads of commerce on the road west from London (now roughly the line of the A30), where, after servicing Crewkerne it claimed the Windwhistle ridge to Cricket St Thomas and at Saint White Down lurched south

Whitedown sat at one of the great crossroads of commerce on the road from London

to the Fosse Way and Axminster and the hinterlands beyond. All routes converged on the low-rising 700 ft Down, making it a natural meeting point for a fair that received its two-day charter (later extended) in 1361. In the early seventeenth century dealers were coming from as far as Shaftesbury and Weymouth to buy in quantity hides produced locally and mainly in Somerset itself by long-established tanners. Sales would be by the dicker and half-dicker (ten and five) and in 1637 the total was 368. Skins (calfskins) were also found at the fair. Axbridge's Lady Day Fair was another important event for the fellmonger, and for the town itself as a centre of the tanned hides industry.

Newbury in Berkshire, with its numerous fairs and great Michaelmas mop of country reunion, had a cherry fair, in July. It was not alone. There were cherry fairs – sometimes (tellingly) called merry fairs – in Hampshire and elsewhere in the south where large, lusciously sweet local black cherries were sold. One feast was at Woodgreen, another at Fawley; one was held at Chandler's Ford, one at Odiham. Hertfordshire grew a similar crop and made merry in the Chilterns' Frithsden. Warwickshire celebrated cherry-picking time with 'cherry wakes' held at Shottery, Shipston, Stratford and Welford, among other places – summer celebrations that lasted right up to the twentieth century. Chertsey held its black cherry fair in early August. Bedford and Harpenden, not to be outdone, had fairs that offered 'hot baked wardens' – less macabre than one might suppose. The fruit was a variety of pear grown presumably in the shadow of the local Warden Hills. Bedford's Michaelmas Fair in particular was renowned for its luscious pears, baked and sold hot. And there were other fairs, all round the country, of equally odd provenance, all of them part of the vast and unifying quilt of commerce that covered the length and breadth of Old England.

Down the muddy, rutted slough of the roads that led into London there passed a ceaseless cavalcade of waggons and their cursing drivers carrying grain to the hungry mouths and ever-increasing population of the capital. Until the late nineteenth century 'the Eastern Road to London, from the great junction at Stratford, was quite inadequate to its growing use as a posting and mail-coach route; and heavy wagon traffic could only be conducted by double teams and with many halts and hazards. Four days was a common time for waggoners from Epping and Abridge; the packman's ride to Romford was often two days, even when the route-blocks and quarrels were avoided . . . In dry weather the great droves of cattle, sheep, pigs, poultry, meandered wearily up to market amid clouds of dust and suffocating atmosphere. In the wet season of 1860 large lengths of the Bow Road and Mile End Road were nothing better than bogs.'

Heavily laden waggons lumbered in from the corn markets ringing the city, Croydon, Farnham and Bedford among them. Bedford's Michaelmas – with its 'hot wardens' – was reckoned by some to be the best fair in the south Midlands. Defoe, as always, has the details: 'Here is the biggest market for all sorts of provisions that is to be seen at any county town in all these parts of England, and this occasions, that tho' it is so far from London, yet the higglers [dealers] or carriers buy great quantities of provisions here for the London market . . . Here is also a great corn market, and great quantities of corn are bought here, and

Down the muddy, rutted roads to London passed a ceaseless cavalcade of waggons

carry'd down by barges and other boats to the Lynn, where it is again shipped, and carry'd by sea to Holland: the soil hereabouts is exceeding rich and fertile, and particularly produces great quantities of the best wheat in England, which is carry'd by waggons from hence, and from the north part of the county twenty miles and beyond this, and to the markets of Hitchin and Hertford, and bought again there, and ground and carry'd in meal (still by land) to London.'

Never, as we have said, a man of faint praise, Defoe, in like terms, said of Cobbett's birthplace Farnham that it was 'without exception the greatest corn-market in England, London excepted'. The grain markets specialised – barley, wheat or oats – the dealers of the small corn markets forming a network that sold on to the bigger merchants. Corn to support the northern cloth towns flowed in, with beef and mutton, 'in great quantities' from Lincolnshire and Nottingham and the East and North Ridings. Croydon's considerable market sold mainly to the millers for the London trade; cornmills clung to the banks of the Lea, the Wandle, and of course the Thames itself, producing the city's flour. Down the Lea came Hertfordshire's grain for milling in Bromley. At Blackfriars stood the famous Albion mills, designed by John Rennie, the Scot who would also give the capital its Waterloo and Southwark bridges, the first flour mills in the world to harness steam (burned down in 1791), and Wandsworth's were no less notable, powered by both water and steam. Into the borough of Southwark, a noted centre, clattered hop pockets from Kent and Worcester and Hereford – even from abroad – to be gathered into the warehouses of the hop merchants before being sold on to the local brewers. In 1866, in furtherance of its trade, the borough would build its magnificent Hop and Malt Exchange, its glass roof – a not unusual feature of such buildings – designed to allow inspection of the hops by natural light.

Whether or not one believes Defoe's hyperbole is unimportant. What his words eloquently convey is the frantic interactivity of dealers and the endless movement of commodities. They also indicate the incredible pull of the capital as an almost insatiable market. Always it had been a traders' city. Always it was the mecca! It was a capital in thrall to market forces. The whole kingdom in Defoe's view was concerned primarily 'to supply the city . . . with provisions; corn, flesh, fish, butter, cheese, salt, fewel, timber, etc, and cloths also . . . It stayed true to Tacitus's description as a settlement filled with traders and a celebrated centre of commerce.' Bede in 730 called it vividly 'the mart of many nations'. It was the great importing/exporting hub: into it was drawn most of the country's best produce in livestock, crop and manufactured goods. From it radiated the national economy. Its markets were legendary: Leadenhall was for poultry but also for hides; Newgate and Farringdon markets were for dead meat, Smithfield for the livestock trade. Southwark was the centre of the leather trade – in Tanner, Morocco and Leathermarket streets – one tannery alone taking 350,000 skins a year. The Old Corn Exchange handled grain and flour, the New Corn Exchange's concern was agricultural seeds. The capital had four main hay markets, including the eponymous Haymarket, which also had a twice-weekly sheep and cattle market. Round Blackfriars were congregated the feather-traders, and to nearby

Always it was the mecca; it was a capital in thrall to market forces

(*Opposite*) perennial Punch (and Judy), always a favourite at the fair. Pepys admitted to being partial. The artist Thomas Smythe (1825–1906) has caught the evergreen attraction of the puppets and an enthralled young audience

Christmas Eve in the market, 1845. Londoners cram the capital's main poultry arena. Leadenhall Market (taking its name from a lead-roofed mansion that once stood on the site) was razed in the Great Fire but was rebuilt with three market courtyards

Basinghall Street, to Blackwell Hall, the greatest cloth exchange in the kingdom (burned down in the Fire of London but rebuilt) came the cloth of the West Country in a ceaseless flow.

In the early seventeenth century the clothiers would take their own 'pieces' to the capital to meet and entertain their customers, but by the eighteenth century the London factors at the Hall had become the men at the centre of the trade. Cloth convoys left the West Country even through the Civil War to find their way to the capital, often by the most devious routes. In Stuart times the capital was the main cloth market: Bartholomew's flourished and the London merchants made their own regular pilgrimages to both Salisbury and Bristol; both held important cloth fairs. A considerable quantity, however, would find its market elsewhere; dyed and finished, it found its outlet still at the country fairs. Most clothiers attended the big fairs. Clothiers themselves, indeed, liked to bypass Blackwell Hall and sell direct to merchants – or to their own outlets in the capital. They viewed the Hall's factors with deep suspicion and made persistent moves to be rid of them. The cloth factors, who rented shops and probably storage space in Blackwell Hall, were middlemen; their role was rather like the old drovers': they took the cloth on credit while they found a market for it.

The corn chandlers of the West Country had been sending grain to London since the seventeenth century by land and also down the Thames. Carriers (acting also as couriers) were already connecting the region with the capital and regular services would be inaugurated from Somerset by the mid-century as they emulated the Cambridge carrier Hobson, who in 1568 had taken over the cart and eight horses his father had bequeathed him and proceeded to build a courier and wheeled transport system that reached into the remotest corners of East Anglia. From Southwark's old Tabard Inn in the eighteenth century carriers' carts set off on scheduled services to towns all over the south of England, clattering through the toll-gate on to the turnpike for Kent. Coaches left the nearby George on similar, if faster, journeys. Soon carriers' carts would link the capital with such distant places as Exeter, York and Manchester; by 1705 stagecoaches were leaving London for no fewer than 180 destinations, all of them increasing the fever of the country's horse fairs!

Royston, by the side of the old North Road and with a fair granted in the time of Richard I, had a rich market for corn as well as horn, though here the buyers were more likely to be maltsters from the surrounding areas rather than the millers. Ilsley, tucked away in the Berkshire downs and more noted for its sheep fairs, had a reputation as a corn centre into Queen Victoria's reign. These markets would grow on the tide of cereal expansion, improving rapidly on what had hitherto been the demand. There was for a time a frenetic rivalry among English towns as they threw up their corn exchanges, fine buildings that threatened to outshine the town halls themselves and sometimes did so; they would become the long-enduring monuments to that surge of prosperity that bore English agriculture through the mid-years of the nineteenth century but alas foundered all too soon. Few had foreseen the grain bounty that would flow from the American prairies, where the weather was unfailingly favourable and the enormous acreages would work to usurp the position of Britain's farming.

In England's old landscape there were towns and regions that staked their own unique claims. Chard, as early as 1791, was acknowledged the country's largest potato market, selling some thirty waggonloads each weekly market day at a time when Britons were still suspicious about a root they would sooner have fed to their livestock. Bishop's Lydeard, in Somerset, had a special September fair for toys, and a similar trade would become an unexpected feature of such celebrated fairs as Brigg. Coventry's Crock Fair, rather sadly, is the last survivor of the city's many charter fairs, but even now sticks determinedly to the spirit of the past. York once celebrated St Luke's Day with a Dish Fair granted by Henry VII for the sale of kitchenware. And Norwich's Rush Fair, on the first Monday of August and selling bundles cut from the Broads, once served more than local needs with its candle rushes, cut and peeled and dried. But probably the oddest, most unexpected occasion of them all was Yarmouth's Herring Fair, by far the most colourful along that coast, held at the very height of the herring-fishing season and already an important event in 1611 when the historian and cartographer

Corn exchanges threatened to outshine the town halls themselves and many did so

Beside the quay: 1.
Fairs (it is often forgotten)
were held by the
harbourside almost as the
cargo vessels docked to
land their exotic imports in
an atmosphere of carnival
gaiety. J.G. Moyle reminds
us of this in his 1850
painting 'Quay Fair'

John Speed (?1552–1629) wrote his *Historie of Great Britaine*: 'There is yearly in September the worthiest herring fishery in Europe, which draweth great concourse of people.' Camden in Tudor times, had similarly noted that Yarmouth (Norwich's port) had 'a great and throng fair here at Michaelmas, and what quantities of herring and other fish are landed'. And such indeed must have been the case, for the autumn herring fair would last for forty days, from Michaelmas to Martinmas. The stench must have been stomach-turning. Kent and Sussex as well as North Sea fishermen landed their catches with little or no restriction – not normally the case with a fair. This liberal attitude was also reflected by the fair's court, which was allowed to take tolls and impose fines, but was not permitted to take anything from such people as 'minstrels and women of pleasure frequenting the fair'. During the fair's third week a great banquet was held for all the notable people of the town.

Yarmouth's sandbank from the earliest times – and probably before the Conquest – had been a landing point for the autumn herring harvest, bringing in men from all the coastal ports as they followed the shoals down the English coastline and landed their catches. In improvised shelters along the bank the fish was salted and sold, or more likely bartered, for silks brought over by French merchants, Dutch china, and timber from Scandinavia. The herring fair would

Beside the quay: 2. Yarmouth's colour and bustle during the period of its great herring bonanza attracted the eye of George Vincent (1796–1832), who also, most memorably, put the port's famous carnival of Dutch Sunday on canvas

grow huge and cosmopolitan, internationally important. Control was essential and this, with the rights of the fair, was given to the influential barons of the Cinque Ports. They were, it seems, a touch despotic, sending their bailiffs by rota each year to keep a grip of the occasion and to maintain the peace of the fair. But in time, in 1277, Yarmouth's burgesses would wrest an equal share in the running of the fair, their reward for being helpful to the king, Edward I. (The truth is the soldiering monarch seems to have been particularly partial to a herring: Stirling Castle bought 18,500 of them in 1300 when he was there, harassing the unruly Scots.) By then some 360 vessels were paying toll at the fair.

But there were other, overweening reasons for royal concern and why the herring – and the men who caught them – enjoyed particular favour with the monarchy and the English government. It was the fishermen, after all, who manned the ships of war when the need arose, which in England's case was not infrequently. 'Fish days' would be declared nationally to boost their trade and keep up the number of vessels of the fishing fleet – and the national reserve of seafarers. Edward III intervened between 1357 and 1360 to keep fish cheap and maintain an open (or free) market. Only fast London boats were allowed to buy at Kirkley Roads – the rest of the catch had to be sold freely in Yarmouth.

The Statute of Herrings of 1357 fixed prices, clarified the definition of a 'last' as 10,000 herrings, and gave protection to the local curing industry: there was to be no curing within seven miles of Yarmouth except that of the fishermen curing their own catches. Alas, the outcome was not what the monarch might have hoped: with a remarkable predictability the fishermen boycotted the port and the king had to lift his clamp on prices and settle instead for free selling at the end of the tide on which the fish was landed. His insistence on daylight dealing irritated the fishermen by losing them time at sea. Compounding the king's problems were the London merchants – never slow off the mark – who had moved in on the trade with their own fish-houses at Little Yarmouth. The men of Great Yarmouth, upset by the encroachment, took a violent revenge from time to time and the Londoners, complaining that their trade was being disrupted, would find the local bailiffs turning a deaf ear. In the circumstances the king's good intentions were no doubt frustrated by his own dependence on the capital's financiers. By the close of the fifteenth century, however, the biggest threat to East Anglia's ports was coming from the Dutch. A report of 1614, when Yarmouth itself had about 1,000 fishermen and at least 200 boats, observes: 'to Yarmouth do daily come into the haven up to the key the most part of the great fleet of Hollanders and all the herring they do bring in, they sell them all for ready money to the Yarmouth men'. From the later fifteenth century the Netherlanders had been fishing the East Coast grounds under treaty, going from strength to strength, and arousing a growing bitterness. Their herring fleet fished everywhere – even in the Scottish lochs. Years of depleted stocks fanned the resentment, until in 1636 Charles I, in a move that was to cast a long and sinister shadow, banned the Dutch from English waters, and fearful of their navy, imposed his 'ship money' tax.

The herring trade suffered a setback with the Dutch Wars. Yet the fair revived somewhat with William III's accession to the throne, and a decade or so after William's death Yarmouth and Lowestoft between them were still curing 40,000 barrels of red herrings a season in the shoreline colony of curing sheds, for export by merchants to Italy, Spain and Portugal – and Holland. With the barrels went 'very great quantities' of Norwich's worsted products. Further quantities of herrings were snapped up by dealers for sale round the adjoining countryside.

The town was filled with great breeches, and the country flocked in to see the sight

The Napoleonic Wars, closing Europe's ports to commerce, virtually put an end to the trading significance of the herring fair, though it continued to be marked by the old festivity and carnival atmosphere of Dutch Sunday – to which the 'Hollanders', scorning earlier enmity, still flocked in droves. The Sunday was that closest to Michaelmas, when the Dutch traditionally had descended with an armada. One observer, a Dr Aikin, writing about 1785, reported: 'We have a great deal of amusement here from the annual visit of the Dutch fishermen. About fifty of their schuyts [flat-bottomed craft] come up our river and lay for three or four days at the Quay in an uniform regular line. The town was filled with great breeches, and on Sunday all the country flocked in to see the sight, so that the whole length of the Quay was crowded. The gradual

A queen looks down. Victoria turns her marble back on the commotion around Bostock and Wombwell's renowned menagerie at Nottingham's Goose Fair in its earlier location. She may not have been amused. Star of the show Captain Fred Wombwell, always spruce and bemedalled, was a fearless animal trainer

approach of the schuyts with their yellow sails glittering in the sun, and their progress up the river in a line, one after the other, were very striking 'spectacles'.'

Another commentator remembered that the foreigners would have their boats decorated with flags and *en fête*. All the length of the Quay would be one huge, jostling crowd, with everyone in his or her Sunday best. By the evening of Dutch Sunday, the start of the herring bonanza, the tourists would be in high spirits. C.J. Palmer in *The Perlustration of Great Yarmouth* reports that 'the Dutch went about the streets bawling tunes, but there were no quarrels. On the Monday they laid in their provisions and put to sea. During their stay in Yarmouth they carried on a considerable traffic in pipes, dried flounders, "Dutch toys", gingerbread and "domino clumps"; the latter being balls of crystallized white sugar, with a piece of lemon peel in the centre.' Palmer, after a period that had closed the Dutch ports but fortuitously revived Yarmouth's fortunes, recalled the poignant if brief interval of reunion: 'On the 25th of September, 1814, being "Dutch Sunday" . . .

a number of schuyts arrived, after an interval of twenty years. The old custom was revived, and the scene attracted a large assemblage of visitors from the neighbourhood. In 1832 thirty sail of Dutch fishing boats came up to the Ballast Quay, since which time very few have entered the harbour.'

Yarmouth's herring fair, without question, was one the country's big fairs, but not so great as Stourbridge, the fair that seems to have had every covetable commodity under the sun. The Cambridgeshire occasion in the 1730s with its horse fair, hop fair, wool fair, coal, iron and timber fairs, its basket fair, pot fair, leather fairs and oyster fair, had many other 'streets' and 'rows' that comprehensively delineated its astonishing range of supplies: Booksellers' Row, Brush Row, Cheese Row, Fish Hill, Joyners' Row, Soap Hill, Tallow Hill, Trunk Row, Turners' Row. Only a few of the old fairs could match its air of electric excitement though many, for good or ill, might acquire the kind of reputation that spread their fame. And most, as night drew on and the shadows lengthened between their booths, were still the scene of that oldest and most feverish of all transactions, sometimes hurriedly and drunkenly undertaken.

CHAPTER TEN

CAPITAL ENTERTAINMENT

London's Bartholomew's was a cloth fair. It claimed at one time to be the biggest in the land and maybe it was; certainly it was the most scandalous. Ben Johnson's disreputable play *Bartholmew Fair* with its cut-purses and prostitutes and pimps and its uninhibited bawdiness may have done no more than mirror the event itself. Or so it would seem. Round London's suburban rim today – on Wanstead Flats, on Hampstead Heath, at Pinner and Mitcham, Blackheath Common and Barnet – the fair, like the travelling circus, makes its pitch and unremarkedly moves on. It is a tame spectacle set against the high malarkey and misbehaviour that once marked out Bartholomew's yearly August fair as capital entertainment – and, for most of its long reign, a capital problem.

By the dawn of the seventeenth century the fair – held to the lowing accompaniment of the City's Smithfield cattle sale – was well on its way to consolidating its raffish reputation: nearby was Cock Lane, the haunt of bawds and crowded with brothels. It suffered a relapse into some sort of decency under Cromwell – the Puritans frowned on its frivolity and woeful morals. But it was a joker's fair, founded by a royal jester who got religion, and was again soon reflecting it as the Restoration and the rogue-ish behaviour of the Merry Monarch himself brought the recovery of its ill-repute. Bartholomew's, like the capital's other fairs, was at its wicked worst as Londoners shed the restraints of Commonwealth rule. Thus the lure of Old Bartlemy's excitement and the shameless hyperbole of the handbills of the later seventeenth century proclaiming its attractions: 'These are to give Notice to all Gentlemen and Others, That there is joyned together Two of the Best Companies in England, *viz* Mr Jacob Hall (Sworn Servant to his Majestie), and Mr Richard Lancaster, with several Others of the Companies; by whom will be performed Excellent Dancing and Vaulting on the Ropes; with Variety of Rare Feats of Activity and Agility of Body upon the Stage; as doing Somersalts and Flip-flaps, Flying over Thirty Rapiers, and over several Men's heads; and also flying through several Hoops; Together with severall other Rare Feats of Activity, that will be there presented: with witty Conceits of Merry Will: in the performing of all which They Challenge all Others whatsoever, whether Englishmen or Strangers, to do the like with them for Twenty Pounds or what more They please.' For Bartholomew's, after all, was circus and fair rolled into one.

The rope-dancer was, of course, today's high-wire artiste and Hall, one of the accomplished performers, a man with whom the Lady Castlemaine liked to spend some time when she was not with the king, Charles II, or perhaps when he

THE FORM OF THE PROCLAMATION

FOR PROCLAIMING

The Fair of Saint Bartholomew:

AT 12 o'CLOCK OF THE NIGHT,

PREVIOUS TO THE DAY ON WHICH IT IS PROCLAIMED

BY THE LORD MAYOR OF LONDON.

O yez! O yez! O yez! All manner of persons may take notice, that in the Close of Saint Bartholomew the Great and West Smithfield, London, and the streets, lanes and places adjoining, is now to be held a Fair for this day and the two days following, to which all people may freely resort and buy and sell according to the Liberties and Privileges of the said Fair, and may depart without disturbance, paying their duties. And all persons are strictly charged and commanded in His Majesty's name, to keep the peace, and to do nothing in the disturbance of the said Fair, as they will answer the contrary at their peril, and that there be no manner of arrest or arrests, but by such officers as are appointed: And if any person be aggrieved, let them repair to the Court of Pie-Powder, where they will have speedy relief, according to Justice and Equity.

GOD SAVE THE KING.

. Communicated by the Steward of Lord Kensington (Lord of the Manor) 1830.

A cry in the streets. Beginning the bacchanalia: the proclamation that gave sanction to the licence of the capital's infamous Bartholomew Fair

was with another of his countless mistresses. The fair, then, plumbed a grossness at times that thoroughly shocked the diarist John Evelyn. Not so Hogarth; born so to speak on its doorstep; he came to sketch frantically, a man in his element, immortalising among others the great Cadman, an artiste whose daring on the rope outshone even Hall's. Pepys's visits were confessedly to see the sideshows, the rope-dancers and the tumblers but were covertly no doubt enjoyably enhanced by his other abiding interest, the spectacle of young London womanhood in all its gauzy finery. By then the fair had spread itself into four

High malarky. Front-of-house paraders on their platforms try to entice the fair throng at Bartholomew's. The ubiquitous Richardson was there, as were Saunders and Wombwell, with a gin palace conveniently at hand

parishes and, given even the king's liking for such things, lengthened its duration from the normal three to fourteen days.

For a time, appalled by its own excesses, the capital's great fair strove to mend its ways, redeeming itself by the *gravitas* of its theatrical presentations. It drew back the quality to witness performances by some of the best actors of the age and in turn, in the eighteenth century, encouraged the revival of the old mystery plays – the masques of the 'Creation' and 'Noah's Flood' – something Bartholomew's had been noted for in its earlier days. These made use of animals, of course, and possibly heightened the feeling of circus, and certainly of spectacle. About 1770 the fair remained a phenomenal draw for all (or perhaps because of) its licentiousness and was still attracting the nobility, mainly male and young and intent on amorous dalliance, and even royalty, to mingle in the pleasures of the *hoi polloi*. That Fifties historian of English fairs William Addison may have put his finger on the occasion's perennial appeal in *English Fairs and Markets* when he said: 'Every component of a fair was there from the beginning, every manifestation and expression of piety, its feasting, its greed, its folly – and all it seems, in melodramatic proportions. We have the rabble of sick and diseased gabbling their prayers at the altar, the chapmen haggling in the porch, pedlars crying their wares and chaffering in the churchyard, minstrels, mummers and acrobats – or tumblers – with clerks and friars going among them to beg alms, and the way being cleared every few seconds for a mounted knight or dignitary of the Church to ride through, all to the accompaniment of the lowing of oxen, the neighing of horses, and the bleating of sheep. Slaves were bought and sold here as well as the cloth on which the wealth of the priory was ultimately to depend. Nearby, at Skinners' Well, the Company of Parish Clerks performed their miracle plays, sometimes before the king and his court and usually with nobility present. And it is more than likely that the first plays at St Bartholomew's Fair, for which long afterwards the London theatres were to close, were representations of the miracles that Rahere the jester alleged had been performed in his church. These would be succeeded by "mysteries", which in turn were followed by "moralities", while just outside the priory gates, on the site of the fair – or part of the site – were the martyr fires, the most lurid and terrible spectacle of all.'

The last indeed were 'spectacles' that sent their fever like an virulent virus through the crowd, but never more so than on the opening day of the fair in 1305. Fair-goers fought and jostled to see a man butchered like a Smithfield beast: that morning the Scottish patriot Sir William Wallace, who had long earned the reigning Edward I's obsessional hatred, perished on the green under the notorious Elms of Smithfield. It was the chosen place of execution when an example had to be made to the nation. They watched as the hero of Scotland's fight for independence – brought to the capital but the previous day, hastily tried, condemned and dragged into Smithfield that fair morning behind horses – was half-hanged, cut down to be disembowelled while still alive, and then burned. The act, and the ferocious barbarity of it, can only be understood by the monarch's fear of the man who had so resolutely defied and eluded him. There is a plaque in Smithfield today that records the savage justice of the warrior's punishment but not that of the many others who were martyred by Smithfield's dreaded fires, which would not be dowsed until the seventeenth century. By then Smithfield was long inured to the stench of the burning flesh of heretics, a saga of martyrdom which had started with the fifteenth century. It was here that Henry VIII, in 1538, had the Greenwich prior John Forest dangled over a slow fire in an iron cage till he roasted to death; here in Queen Mary's thankfully short reign that most of the 277 people condemned to the flames for their firmly held beliefs were burned. The usual place of incineration was opposite the entrance to St Bartholomew the Great, with the victim facing to the east and the vast gate of the church. The prior of St Bartholomew's presence would be requested, and things being as they were, the invitation could not be refused.

The usual place of incineration was opposite the entrance to St Bartholomew the Great

It was at Smithfield that the end would come suddenly for the rebel of another cause, just when he thought he held all the best cards. In that historic arena on a Saturday morning in June 1381, as the Peasants' Revolt over the imposition of a poll tax and a simmering general discontent finally erupted into town, Wat Tyler and his mob faced the young King Richard II. The king had drawn up his small troop outside the church of St Bartholomew and the parley was carefully orchestrated and apparently amicable between king and subject when one of the royal retinue recognised Tyler as a Kentish highwayman. The rebel, lunging for his accuser, found his action barred by London's Lord Mayor and drove his dagger at him instead. The Lord Mayor that morning had had the foresight to don armour

In the name of the saint. The colour and convulsion of Bartholomew Fair in its hedonistic heyday, and as it faltered as a serious trading event, from the brush of Egbert van Heemskerck the Younger (1634–1717)

under his coat and was unscathed as another of the king's men, John Standwick, ran the rebels' leader through with his sword – twice. There is uncertainty about the fine detail of the encounter but it is generally agreed that stunned by the swiftness of events, the peasant band quickly dispersed, leaving Tyler slumped, badly wounded, on the ground. Barely alive, he was carried into Rahere's hospice, where his wounds were treated before he was again hauled out to what shortly before had seemed the scene of his triumph – and beheaded. It was a fate not without its crude justice; it was one that his men during their rampage had inflicted on many of their own hapless victims. In the custom of that barbarous time, Tyler's head was displayed on London Bridge, a dire warning to all who would tangle with authority.

It is hardly possible, as Addison hints, adequately to catalogue the sum of Bartholomew's 'entertainments', but there was, as we have seen, an early element of circus; and when the death-defying deeds and more vulgar attractions palled, there was a weird and apparently talented bestiary: the five-legged bull, for example; or the dogs that did Morris-dancing. (In 1668 Pepys was amazed by 'the mare that tells money'.) Assuredly, the London fair was never for the genteel or for those with a delicacy of feeling. Yet under the gaudy skin of its good-humoured hedonism Bartholomew's hid the activity of serious business. Besides its cloth market, held by the north wall of St Bartholomew's Church, and cattle dealing there were cheeses and horses and, as the playwright Ben Johnson, writing at the height of the occasion's notoriety, makes clear, all the usual trinkets and geegaws of the thorough-going fair. There are reminders still, in Smithfield's street names – Cloth Fair and Hosier Lane, for instance – along with its aura of

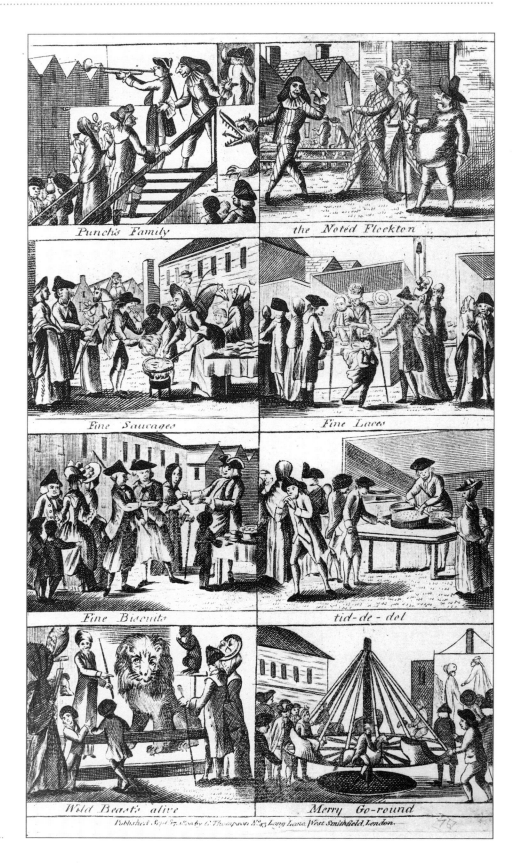

Eat, drink and take a whirl on the merry-go-round. An advisory panel on what to see and enjoy among the less dissolute attractions of the disreputable Smithfield carnival

history, of the importance of its cloth market and of that time when cloth-making was England's wealth. Its charter was granted by Henry I, who also gave the royal joker Rahere the land on which to build his priory and hospice of St Bartholomew's, which he did about 1133. The jester had decided that life was serious after all, and resolved to mend his ways after being visited by a vision of the saint while critically ill. He was the lord of the fair, given to fund the priory and held initially for three days from the eve of St Bartholomew's Feast (24 August), which brought the cold dew and, in the medieval calendar, was the first day of autumn. Rahere was still a jester at heart, however, and occasionally reverted to his old profession, doing juggling tricks to amuse the fair-goers.

The fair at first – like so many – was held in the churchyard but soon overspilled on to land adjoining the priory. Disputes over the tolls between the priory and the City's cattle market led to the two becoming joint lords of the fair. It survived the Dissolution better than most, however, soon finding its way into the hands of Sir Richard Rich, the astute sprig of a family of London mercers, who acquired all the fair's rights and promptly moved himself into the priory house. To establish title beyond doubt, he further rechristened the occasion the Cloth Fair. It was a futile ploy, however. Soon further dissension led to the fair's transfer, in 1604, into the hands of the Corporation of London. Controversy would seldom thereafter be missing from its chequered existence, and Rich's cloth fair was perhaps less successful than he would have hoped. By 1750 it had lost much of its grandiose clout in the miasma that was forever Bartholomew's. The memory of its cloth-trading high point, though, would be kept alive by the City's tailors, who met yearly on the eve of Bartholomew's at the Hand and Shears pub (still a welcome landmark in Cloth Fair) to march as a body to the priory gate, where, scissors in hand, they performed their ceremony of 'snapping the shears'. If it was an elaborate excuse for a night out, it did also commemorate that time when every self-respecting London tailor would have his booth in the fair. Respectability was never the great fair's forte and there is precious little evidence to suggest that it strove manfully to make it so. By the early nineteenth century its coarseness was again a byword and an embarrassment to the respectable citizenry – and increasingly a threat to its own continued existence. Soon it would disappear from the capital's fair calendar leaving few regrets behind it.

For almost as long as Bartholomew's reigned there were periodic 'St Bartholomew's fairs' on ice – sans charter or saint – as the capital's river froze over. These were spontaneous affairs, as they had to be. In 1150, it is said, 'after a very wet summer there was in December so great a frost that horses and carriages crossed upon the ice as safely as upon the dry ground'. That year the iron-clad weather lasted through to March. In the winter of 1564/5 we hear of archery and football and dancing on the Thames and it was reported that Queen Elizabeth – a lady much experienced in treading thin ice – took a turn round the fair's booths and stalls with her plebs and watched the ox-roasting. But it would be over a century later, in 1683/4, when a prodigious frost gripped the capital from the start of December until February, that the Frost Fair was truly born. A

The Queen took a turn round the booths with her plebs and watched the ox-roasting

Fighting beak and claw. When even Bartholomew's palled, there was the spectacle of cock-fighting at nearby Clerkenwell, but this (depicted by Rowlandson and Pugin) was Boswell's preferred venue, the Royal Cockpit in St James's Park, where a bout between ferocious cocks could last for hours. Afterwards Boswell liked to take a stroll in the Park, where he was certain to be approached 'by several ladies of the town'

coach and six was driven on to test the ice – for a wager. It held – and the fair began. An entire street of booths called Broad Street (but also at times Temple Street and other names) spanned the Thames from the Temple to Southwark's Bear Garden selling cloth, plate, earthenware and so on, as well as meat, drink and tobacco. The Thames became a thoroughfare. Galloping sleighs charged hither and thither sending fair-goers scampering in fear of their lives. The Frost Fair had everything any land fair, even Bartholomew's, could muster: menageries, bull-baiting, bear-baiting, cock-fighting. Winding through the throng according to one observer were 'Bawds, Whores, Pickpockets, Jilts and Cheats'. In addition to the many gambling dens there were lewder places 'dedicated to the provision of more dubious, more fleshly diversions'.

Besides the cross-river traffic, the coaches plying at fifteen-minute intervals from Temple Stairs to Southwark, there were others which ran with timetable regularity up to Lambeth, Westminster, Whitehall and Vauxhall. At its full roaring height the Frost Fair could stretch from London Bridge up to Vauxhall. As a ballad of the time perceptively stated:

> I'll tell you a story as true as 'tis rare,
> Of a river turned into a Bartlemy Fair.

Noting the event in his diary for 24 January 1684, that Deptford diarist and man-about-the-capital John Evelyn – having himself crossed the river on foot to dine at Lambeth with the Archbishop of Canterbury – is more explicit: 'The frost continuing, more and more severe, the Thames, before London, was still planted with booths in formal streets, all sorts of trades and shops, furnished and full of commodities even to a printing press, where the people and ladies took a fancy to have their names printed, and the day and year set down when produced on the Thames: this humour took so universally, that it is estimated the printer gained five pounds a day, for printing a line only, at sixpence a name, besides what he got by ballads, etc. Coaches plied from Westminster to the Temple and from other stairs, to and fro, as in the streets; sleds, sliding with skates, or bull-baiting, horse and coach races, puppet-shows and interludes, cooks, tippling and other lewd places; so that it seemed to be a carnival on water. . . .'

The Merry Monarch – it goes without saying – was partial to the frozen revels and took a royal party on to the petrified river amid the milling crowd to have their names printed in the booth of the enterprising printer, whose name was George Croom. There was in fact no end to the entrepreneurial surge that sought to turn a buck on ice:

> Here also is a lottery, music too,
> Yes, a cheating, drunken, lewd and debauch'd crew;
> Hot codlins, pancakes, ducks and goose, and sack,
> Rabbit, capon, hen, turkey, and wooden jack.

Booths sudden hide the Thames, long streets appear,
*   And numerous games proclaim the crowded fair*

Thus said John Gay (1685–1732), the poet who wrote 'The Beggar's Opera', in his verse to the capital's occasional Frost Fairs, depicted here in a quite delightful painting by the Dutch artist Thomas Wyck (1616–1677)

There on a sign you may most plainly see't,
Here's the first tavern built in Friezeland Street.
There is bull-baiting and bear-baiting too.
There roasted was a great and well-fed ox
And there with dogs hunted the common fox.

The king, it is reported, further reinforced his fun-loving image and cemented loyalty with his subjects by taking part in the foxhunt. Roger Morrice, recording the phenomenon, noted: 'And so it continued to the second of February, on which day, not far from Whitehall, a whole ox was roasted upon the Thames. The king came to eate some of it and give them a ginney and many Lords of Counsell, etc, the Dutches of York, and many ladyes and very many others, an exceeding great concourse of people.'

For all its notoriety and questionable pleasures, all of them enhanced no doubt by the novelty of the setting, the Frost Fair – sometimes called the blanket fair because of the thicker material needed for the booths in the severe wintry weather – was still a market, a trading occasion, but with a penalty: the prices would be higher than for a fair held on terra firma.

There were further great frosts in 1715/16 and 1739/40 and again Smithfield supplied an ox of suitable girth for the turnspit. In 1788/89 the fair was strung out from Putney Bridge down to Rotherhithe. And during the 'frost of the century' in 1813/14, during the greatest Frost Fair of all, there was even a grand mall starting from Blackfriars Bridge and called City Road, where the Thames watermen, deprived of their living, imposed tolls of 2d and 3d on fair-goers and made sure of collecting them by cutting channels along the river bank so that assistance was needed to cross them. Like Old Bartlemy, London's ice fair was clearly a fun occasion. But unlike the annual Smithfield orgy, it ended not in a slough of self-disgust but much more mundanely when Sir John Rennie's new London Bridge of 1831 allowed the Thames to flow faster, with little future possibility of significant freeze-up and an excuse for such capital jollity.

Bartholomew's was by no means the first of London's fairs to give offence; others had been equally scandalous – guilty of a long litany of questionable conduct that had begun when Westminster's St Edward's fifteen-day fair (its 1257 charter given by Henry III to the abbot and canons of St Peter's), with its worldly ways, was evicted from St Margaret's Churchyard. Southwark's Our Lady Fair, in September, was one of the great fairs of Old England, thought by some to rival Stourbridge and certainly ranked next to Bartholomew's. Its charter, given to the Corporation of London in 1462, was confirmed to the village of Southwark by Edward VI in 1550 and its three days in its heyday would stretch to a fortnight or longer. Sometimes it was called St Margaret's Fair from the former name of its venue, St Margaret's Hill. It was an uninhibited carnival that took place in the shadow of St George's Church beside the Tabard Inn, on the roads from Dover and Canterbury, giving entrance to the capital for Continental travellers. It was a street lined with inns, a thronging thoroughfare, until 1750, leading to the only bridge across the river. It was from its famous Tabard Inn, built in 1307 as a town

For all its novelty, the Frost Fair was still a market, a trading occasion

Riotous assembly. Southwark Fair, 1733, in all its fascinating Hogarthian detail and with its full cast of actors, acrobats, conjurers, musicians, magicians and highwire specialists. William Hogarth (1697–1764) pictured the capital's top performers and its louche characters in his portrayal of the notorious fair held near the old Tabard Inn and St George's Church in what is now Borough High Street

house for the Abbot of Hyde (near Winchester) that Chaucer's pilgrims set out for Canterbury and the shrine of St Thomas à Becket in the cathedral – something pilgrims would do for centuries – having gathered at the inn the night before. Opposite the church of St George's stood the cage, the pillory, stocks and whipping post for the punishment of the fair's piepowder court offenders. The 'cage' was a small prison or cell but in case that were not enough, five real prisons stood cheek by jowl with the inns, willing to receive serious disturbers of the peace.

Space was always a problem and stalls and booths nudged themselves off what is now Borough High Street into the nearby alleys and took over the inn courtyards. The draw of its excitement was tremendous:

> From various parts, from various ends repair
> A vast Mix'd multitude to Southwark Fair.

It offered spectacles almost beyond belief: monkeys dancing on the ropes, turning somersaults while carrying baskets of eggs and jars filled with water without

One man and his dog. Every performing dog got his day at the fair and this one is obviously part (and perhaps the novel mainstay) of his strolling master's act. His next bone, like the entertainer's next meal, will depend on the whim of the crowd. This 1874 painting is by the London artist William Weekes

spilling a drop. The daring acrobat Robert Cadman in his time enlivened the fair (and gave a taste of things to come) by swinging across the street from the tower of St George's to the Mint, the former home of the Duke of Suffolk taken over by Henry VIII to mint the currency the ruler most desperately needed. Understandably it was another of Hogarth's favourite haunts and it was here in 1733 that he did his familiar work which includes some of the famous figures of London's old fairs: Cadman, the breath-taking slack-rope performer; James Figg, the 'fighter' who attracted the crowds with his repertoire of unusual skills such as 'foil-play, back-sword, cudgelling and boxing'; Violante, the renowned tumbler; and Fawkes, the illusionist who did tricks with Italian birds. Amid the fair's freaks, its abundance of prostitutes and the usual pickpockets, the artist found a rich mélange. Evelyn here saw asses dancing and his eye (in 1660) was taken by a weight-lifter and even more beguiled by an 'Italian wench' rope-dancer ('All the Court went to see her'); Pepys was there, his fancy equally captivated: 'To Southwark Fair, very dirty, and there saw a puppetshow of Whittington which was pretty to see; and how the idle thing do work upon people that see it, and even myself too! And thence to Jacob Hall's dancing on the ropes, where I saw such action as I never saw before and mightily worth seeing.'

The capital's May Fair was a late starter, a puking babe to Bartholomew's cackling crone, but like Bartholomew's and Southwark Fair, it could continue for

Amazing character. Impeccably dressed and the perfect little gentleman, this studio study of 1870 shows one of the many dwarfs who travelled the fairs circuit intriguing the crowds. He was known as 'Major Tom' and was a regular in the 1890s at Islington's World's Fair, a Christmas-tide occasion intended to compensate the capital for the loss of its orgy, Bartholomew's

six weeks. The Smithfield fair had passed itself off under the innocent flag of a cloth fair; the May Fair, staged on ground margined by Tyburn Lane (now Park Lane), Curzon Street and Half Moon Street at the east corner of Hyde Park, was, in the words of its charter, for 'the buying and selling of all manner of goods and merchandise'. The fair started promisingly enough. It ran from 1 May for fifteen days, the first three of them – as befitted its then village status – for live cattle and leather. Its entertainments, however, imitated those of Bartholomew's. It seems that it may have inherited the wild bohemian spirit of St James's Fair, dedicated to St James the Less but alas, as early as 1664 banned for 'looseness and irregularity'. The May Fair was a resuscitation by the Earl of St Albans. In 1689 James II licensed a fifteen-day event whose booths spread to Piccadilly and Park Lane and threatened even to eclipse both Southwark and Bartholomew's in its licentious character. It soon faced suppression yet somehow survived. In its 'revival' about 1735 Edward Shepherd built his market in the village centre and in consideration no doubt of the cattle sales gave over its lower storey to butchers' booths and its upstairs to a theatre. (At the time Mayfair had over fifty butchers, still droving their animals to their shops for slaughter.)

In its heyday the yearly fair that took place around it had all the ingredients of the boisterous occasion, with booths for jugglers and bare-knuckle boxers; besides rope-dancers it had fire-eaters, ass-racers, eel-divers and hasty-pudding eaters as well as the almost obligatory bull-baiting. One of its attractions at least was particularly repellent. It gathered a sporting crowd around its ducking pond, where the quarry for several small dogs was a solitary duck. The dogs' owners and spectators wagered heavily (yes, in the nearby Dog and Duck) on the outcome: how long could the duck elude its attackers by diving under the water? Yet there were more seemly distractions: among the characters who strutted their stuff there was Tiddy Dol (commemorated nowadays in the name of a restaurant), a fairground dandy in a white satin suit trimmed with lace, a lacy ruffed shirt, white silk stockings, the lot topped off with a lace hat sporting a feather. Tending his gingerbread stall, he took the precaution of donning a spotless white apron.

CHAPTER ELEVEN

FAIRS OF THE FRINGE

So the great central fairs of old London peaked and passed away, eclipsed by the growing gentility of the time, their rowdy bacchanalian behaviour banished to the capital's fringe – to such 'country fairs' as those of Enfield, Edmonton, Camberwell, Bow and Stepney and Mitcham, Pinner and Greenwich, whose three-day Easter and Whitsun fairs had them flocking down the Old Kent Road in every imaginable conveyance – stage, gig, omnibus, donkey cart and even coal waggon. In high holiday mood they crammed on to steamers that would take them down the Thames. Greenwich's Easter fair it was said was 'the first London festival of the year', and all roads led there:

> Over St George's Fields they flock,
> From Kent Street, Rotherhithe, Greenland dock
> Jolly tars in coaches come,
> With flashy girls from Gravel-lane.

Even Walter Scott, it seems, was a witness to the great exodus from town:

> For Greenwich now they sweep along –
> Oh! What a sight was there.
> Old Thames smiled to view the throng
> That jockied to the fair.

Most of the fair-goers in 1834 still came on foot 'from all parts of the metropolis'. For others seeking more effortless ways to get there, every inventive dodge was encompassed. According to one newspaper report of the day: 'The regular and irregular stages were, of course, full inside and outside. Intermingled with these, town carts, usually employed in carrying goods, were filled up with boards for seats; hereon were seated men, women and children till "the complement" was complete, which was seldom deemed to be the case till the half-killed horses and spare and patient donkeys were overloaded. Now and then passed, like "some huge admiral" a full-sized coal waggon, laden with coal-heavers and their wives . . . these solaced themselves with draughts of beer from a barrel on board. . . .' The report, rather tellingly, concludes: 'The fair itself was nothing, although the congregated throngs were everything, and filled every place.' Just as surely, the Easter holiday brought a fleet of strange craft on to the Thames to convey the crowds to the fair of their choice.

A day for horse-trading. Barnet's fair in its better times, as the copers come from town to view the animals on offer. The village by the Great North Road was an ideal location for a horse fair: it had inns galore! The painter is John Frederick Herring, Sen. (1795–1865)

At Whitsun in 1842 steamboats were leaving Nicholson's Wharf every fifteen minutes (fare: 4*d*). At similar intervals they were departing from Hungerford Market Pier. By 1845 200 steamboats would be plying the river. Vessels ran services not only to Greenwich and Stepney Fairs – the latter having that year spread itself over two fields and acquired two performing elephants – but downriver to Woolwich and Gravesend; and upriver to Putney and Kew, Richmond and Twickenham. In particular the Watermen's Steam Packet Company plied between Adelphi Pier and Greenwich from 8 a.m. until midnight. The Greenwich Railway that year brought thousands. It was, one observer noted 'one continuous fair from the Elephant and Castle to the entrance at Greenwich.'

The river traffic especially caused alarm, the reckless air of the fair itself extending to the Thames. Despite chilly weather, the fair of May 1836, reported the *Morning Herald*, was more crowded than ever, most coming by steamers which decanted their human cargoes every five or ten minutes. Only fifty steamers were plying the river, 'many of them crammed in a most shameful manner', the bodies being 'wedged together as close as bales of merchandise in the hold of a ship'. As the crowds swarmed off them, the vessels dipped alarmingly, bringing the portholes close to the waterline. Many of the craft were tugboats, joining in the fun, some of them 'rotten and worn-out vessels'. Between nine and seven o'clock, it was estimated, they brought 150,000 to the fair. The *Herald*'s reporter warned: 'It is high time that the Government should enforce some regulations with respect to the steamers on the Thames both as regards their speed and the numbers they are in the habit of carrying, unless the evil is to

Call of the wild. The travelling menagerie, with its beasts from the jungles and forests of the world, was a colossal attraction as Frederick Piercy painted this work in the mid-nineteenth century. Soon its central appeal would be diminished as the fair found a new dimension with steam-powered rides

work its own cure in an accident too appalling to dwell upon.' But nothing seems to have been done: at Easter a decade later, the *Illustrated London News* was echoing the *Herald*'s fears, complaining that the steamers for both Greenwich and Stepney were still 'fearfully overcrowded. Indeed such was the pressure to get passage to Greenwich at all costs that passengers were prepared to queue for two or three hours.'

They came to revel, the *hoi polloi*, in a king's playground, a place well used to celebration and banquets and balls and high jinks; a headquarters for great jousting spectacles and splendid hunting parties. Greenwich Palace had been the preferred residence of the Tudors, Henry VIII particularly, and Greenwich Hill provided a sweeping view over the capital. (The fair-loving Pepys, as Secretary for the Affairs of the Navy, would have found himself on familiar ground there.)

What they encountered when they got to, say, Whit Monday's fair, five miles out of town, is recalled by another observer: 'They found the principal street filled from end to end with shows, theatrical booths, and stalls for the sale of an infinite variety of merchandise.' But for the fond swain and his lass, the lure – in their brief and precious moment of freedom – was the Park, 'a beautiful piece of

High hilarity. All the skittish, uninhibited fun and heedless excess of the fair, marvellously captured here at Greenwich's carnival, which Dickens called a 'three days' fever'. Richardson presented 'a melo-drama (with three murders and a ghost), a pantomime, a comic song, an overture and some incidental music, all done in five-and-twenty minutes'

ground made venerable by the old oaks of Henry and Elizabeth, and . . . by the towering observatory the youth and maidenhood of London carried on a series of sports . . . The favourite amusement above all was to run your partner down the well-known slope between the high and low levels of the park. Generally a row was drawn up at the top and at a signal off they all set; some bold and successful in getting to the bottom on their feet, others timid and awkward, tumbling headlong before they were halfway down. The strange disorders of this scene furnished of course food for no small merriment; the rule was to take every discomposure and spoiling of dress good-humouredly.' The writer puts it delicately; the sport was to watch the lasses rolling hopelessly *déshabillé*. In fact the results of rolling one's sweetheart down Observatory Hill 'to the derangement of their mobs and bonnet caps' could be considerably more serious: there were always a large number of mishaps, including heads cracked open by colliding with trees. Sometimes, tragically, these injuries would prove fatal.

In 1761 Greenwich was attracting crowds of 15,000 or so, modest by the standards of later times and perhaps reflecting the strong competition from such established East London fêtes as Stepney. By 1838, however, the Easter fair – its main focus now the space near the Creek Bridge – had a strong circus element, including lion- and tiger-taming acts. It had also become a bacchanalia for some

200,000. Besides the beasts, the fair now had the famous Richardson and his booth installed in Bridge Street and presenting ten-minute plays (such was the attention span of the average fair crowd), with the programme also featuring panto, comic turns and comic songs and so on – a variety bill of staggering scope. The Naval Hospital's pensioners, glad of the chance, made themselves a penny or two (or a ha'penny at least) by lending their telescopes to fair-goers so that they could view the panorama spread before them – as far as Epping Forest it was said. Gruesome but infinitely more fascinating in earlier times, were the bodies of 'pirates' strung up in chains along the riverside. The sight of their skeletal remains shaking in the wind can but have deliciously sharpened the appetite for all the day's pleasures, legal or illicit.

The sight of skeletons shaking in the wind sharpened the appetite for pleasures

Charles Dickens was a fond devotee of the fair; he was also a seasoned reporter. In *Sketches by Boz* he called the occasion 'a three days' fever which cools the blood for six months afterwards'. He requests: 'Imagine yourself in an extremely dense crowd, which swings you to and fro, and in and out, and every way but the right one; add to this the screams of women, the shouts of boys, the clanging of gongs, the firing of pistols, the ringing of bells, the bellowings of speaking trumpets, the squeaking of penny dittos, the noise of a dozen bands, with three drums each, all playing different tunes at the same time, the hallooing of showmen, and an occasional roar from the wild beast shows; and you are in the very centre and heart of the fair.'

He describes another of the fair's attractions: 'The grandest and most numerously frequented booth in the whole fair . . . is "The Crown and Anchor" – a temporary ball-room – we forget how many feet long, the price of admission to which is one shilling. Immediately on your right hand as you enter . . . is a refreshment place, at which cold beef, roasted and boiled, French rolls, stout, wine, tongue, ham, even fowls, if we recollect right, are displayed in a tempting way. There is a raised orchestra, and the place is boarded all the way down, in patches, just wide enough for a country dance . . . In this artificial Eden – all is primitive, unreserved, and unstudied. . . .' Thus wrote the great novelist, drawing a modest veil over the temporary ballroom's frantic hedonism. Although its measurements varied from year to year, the Crown and Anchor booth in 1837 was 380 ft long by 46 ft wide. A year earlier, the *Morning Herald*'s reporter, too, had declared the vast dancing booth 'well worth seeing, from its extraordinary extent, and its internal decorations. One part, about 100 feet in length devoted to parties taking refreshments, and the other, consisting of four compartments, 300 feet in length by about 60 in width, is appropriated for dancing.'

By about 1840 the 'dense crowd' at the Easter fair and the fair's stalls and sideshows would sprawl all through the town. Unsurprisingly, by nightfall – as was usual with fair crowds – drink would have worsened their behaviour and considerably coarsened their perception of what was seemly in a public place and Greenwich, too, would come to the ignominious end of all big fairs. Its easy bonhomie blew apart, finally, when it was at its mid-century peak, in rioting and a vicious orgy of destruction. After that its fate was sealed.

Prelude to madness, 1745. Proclaiming Chelsea's disreputable Horn Fair with solemn ceremony, soon to give way to wild abandonment. Defoe memorably said of the London fringe fair's mob that they took 'all kinds of liberties, and the women are especially impudent . . . as if it was a day that justified them giving themselves a loose to all manner of indecency and immodesty'

The capital's fun-seekers would have to move farther afield to find their uninhibited pleasures. The choice was wide; nineteeth-century London was ringed by a 'necklace' of fairs, some of them chartered events that had been saved by the coming of the railway and an easier communication with what were not yet the suburbs, almost all of them regarded by local magistrates as an unacceptable nuisance. Those without charter rights could often be easily dealt with, though not always. As one legal expert observed, hedging his bet in the superb manner of his kind: 'It is at all times difficult by law to put down the ancient customs and practices of the multitude.' Perhaps he was thinking of Greenwich's Observatory Hill.

In 1839, it is reported, nearby Deptford's fair was particularly well attended, 'the Cockneys having availed themselves of the railway to an unprecedented extent'. The fair was held on Trinity Monday. Waxing full by 1825, it was still relatively new but had everything a good fair needed: theatre shows, waxworks, wild beasts, dancing, balloon ascents, weight-lifting, freak shows, boxing booths, fortune-tellers – and gallons and gallons of beer. Fair-goers one year were implored not to miss the Surprising Irish Giant and the Learned Pig, the stars apparently of 'entertainments' held all round the capital.

Neighbouring Charlton's fair was something else. Defoe for once was unkind, calling the place 'a village famous or rather infamous for that yearly-collected rabble of mad people at the Horn Fair'. It was, none the less, an occasion that the people of both Greenwich and Deptford sallied forth to in their droves.

Charlton, it should be said, had once had a perfectly respectable three-day fair granted in 1268 to the Prior of Bermondsey by Henry III. It was no match for the later aberrations of the Horn Fair. When the folk of the neighbouring parishes set off to see the fun, most would already have horns on their heads. In the fair itself, each booth would be similarly adorned – and rams' horns were abundantly for sale to those who felt naked without a pair. Even the gingerbread was horn-shaped. The *raison d'être*, ostensibly, for this peculiar trait was that the fair honoured St Luke's Day (18 October), the saint's symbol being a horned ox (as represented in the windows of the local church). But there was another reason, hinted at by the fact that fair-goers would gather to form into a procession – with a king (and sometimes a queen) – from Bishopsgate by way of Cuckold's Point, Greenwich and Blackheath. The circumnavigation of St Luke's Church three times would be followed by a sermon before the fun really started. The Charlton Fair was staged at Fairfields, in the eastern part of the parish; even if it were more carousal than carnival, it had goods for sale – all made from horn.

Adjoining Camberwell and Peckham Fairs were scarcely more respectable; both were considered 'subversive to peace and good order'. Camberwell's three-day affair at the height of its fame (or infamy) would go on for three weeks: it had 'a theatre, a zoo, fairground rides, sideshows, drinking booths, dance-grounds and other attractions'. Reported *Bells Weekly Messenger* breathlessly in 1806, there were 'players, conjurers, the Irish Giant, the Polish Dwarf, along with lions, tigers, panthers, hyenas, serpents, kangeroos, ourang-outangs, beavers, wolverines, ostriches, cassowaries, pelicans and storks' all adding to the wonder (and one wonders about the reporter!). Half a dozen roundabouts were in 'rapid rotation'. There was music, poetry, ballads from singers accompanied by blind fiddlers, harpers and hurdy-gurdies (yes, one definitely suspects the reporter). And as night came on 'all was a blaze of illumination, and din and clamour, laughter and merriment; the theatres were all crowded, the ladies all delighted, the swains all happy; a few trivial ebullitions of vivacity, vulgarly called boxing-matches, here and there adorned the field, and enlivened the roads to town.'

Among the freaks of 1831 were the Two Miss Westons, Canadian Giantesses, the presumably home-grown Norfolk Dwarfs (a Mrs Walpole and her son) and an Italian girl, her hair snow-white at the age of twelve. One year a 'fat boy' from Scotland named (unbelievably) William Wallace weighed in at 400 lb – at the age of thirteen. More intriguingly, however, if a print of about 1800 can be believed, the fair may long have been denied its place in history as a pioneer of the merry-go-round. A writer for *Hoods Magazine* early in the century describes 'a horizontal wheel, supporting a circle of horses, saddled and bridled, with red nostrils, and flowing manes, and a few double-bodied phaetons at intervals for the accommodation of timid riders. Men, women and children mounted it with equal eagerness, and I observed that the various colours of the horses, black, white, piebald mottled, striped, gave rise to much fastidious picking and choosing, even among the adults.' The writer thought the attraction well named 'merry' for 'it not only exhilarated its riders but seemed to sprinkle centrifugal fun among the crowd'.

The circumnavigation of St Luke's Church three times would be followed by a sermon

Girl at the sharp end. There were folk of the fair, as in the circus, who lived dangerously. This shapely but vulnerable half of the knife-throwing act in Richard Shufflebottom's celebrated Wild West Show was at work at Hull Fair. The Shufflebottom family long travelled the country's fairs with a show that focused on the culture of the American frontier

In later years one of the theatres was the famous Richardson's, 'the greatest theatre in the universe'. The old showmen really were no strangers to hype! All the same, the former strolling player's turnout does seem (as we have already seen) to have been a bit of an extravaganza, showing a wonderful variety of animals and housing an audience of a thousand at a time, each at a sixpence. Hype really was the order of the day, earlier in 1795, when the old fair may have been flagging a bit. A balladeer, perhaps out of pure self-interest but more probably for remunerative gain, distilled the message:

> This is an invitation song,
> For London lads and lasses,
> Camberwell Fair, I now declare,
> All others now surpasses.

The singer, promising 'rural scenes upon the green', went on to name other inducements, including Browsy Nan's sausages.

Camberwell's fair, held for 600 years, was associated with the feast of St Giles – a highly popular saint with many fairs gathered to his name. In its prime the fair stalls stretched from the Cock Tavern to Camberwell Gate. The occasion was officially a three-day event; it dated from about 1297, Edward I's reign, but no charter has ever been found for it, something that would tell heavily against it in its mid-nineteenth-century fight for survival. It was first staged, like most fairs of the time, under the patronage of the Church and was held in the churchyard. Traders stored their wares inside the church until Edward I's Statute of Winton caught up with the fair, when it moved to the High Street (its eighteenth-century focal point was opposite the Cock Inn). Later it claimed Camberwell's famous Green, which, says a contemporary report, 'seethed like a great anthill'.

On its site of Camberwell's famous green the fair 'seethed like a great anthill'

Camberwell came first but Peckham, chartered by King John, closely followed, being held in North Field in its neighbour's parish, hence the close linking of the two. Peckham, still a rural village in the days of the cattle droves, was a convenient stopping point on the way into the London markets. Like Barnet, its High Street was lined with inns where the drovers girded their thirsts for the rest of the drive (the Red Cow remains, the Red Bull, alas, is no more, rebuilt in 1960). The village's three-day fair unsurprisingly centred on their favourite, the 'once-merry hostelry', the Kentish Drovers.

As the capital's transport system expanded through the outer fringes, South Londoners had yet another fair to descend on: Mitcham's, in August, was less than pure of pedigree, passing itself off as a charter fair when it was nothing of the sort. Indeed it had started humbly on wasteland as a three-day rendezvous for the sale of horses and cattle. There are rumours, less than persistent, that Queen Elizabeth I on a late-life visit to the village's bucolic celebrations on the Green decreed a yearly fair. Again, alas, there is not a tittle of evidence that its charter was ever granted. The earliest news we have of Mitcham Fair is the recorded fact of 'Christopher Helstead, a fiddler, that came to the Fair and died at Mr Merrett's'. The year was 1732.

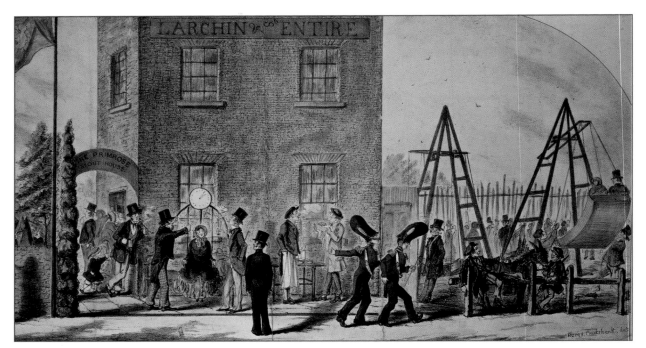

Swings . . .
The inn was at the heart of the fair, usually the hub of its activity, with sideshows and ox-roasts in its yard. The carnival atmosphere here, in Percy Cruikshank's painting of the Primrose Tavern at Chalk Farm, is being suitably augmented with swingboats

Even the fair's great golden-key opening ceremony, it seems, has a lot more to do with sheer showmanship than hallowed tradition. There was no great fanfare for the event in Victorian times. In the 1880s, one old resident would later recall, 'at 12 noon the organ of the roundabout let go, the whistle blew, and that was that'. The golden-key ceremony in fact dated from just before the First World War, and would continue with embellishments. The fair had weathered censure in the late eighteenth century. But having cleaned up its act it was allowed to carry on with attractions that included a travelling circus, the usual troupe of performers and freaks, dancing booths, boxing booths (with stooges planted in the crowd) and women wrestlers. Its sideshow prizes, however, tended to the exotic, and offered items such as gilt Prince Albert watch-chains and wedding rings as well as dolls and cigarettes. It had grown into an occasion that the ubiquitous Richardson could not afford to miss. To the danger, as usual, of all other road users, it drew the gypsies – to Mitcham Common – to trade horses and ponies, mainly among themselves. Some at least would linger on as the fair ended, to help with the local lavender harvest.

Beyond Greenwich, Blackheath's fairs were among the most popular – and not a little scandalous. History and highwaymen lurked there where Watling Street crossed its dark soil. Blackheath's first fair had been a cattle sale in 1689, by Evelyn's account to give trade to a local tavern. But the heath, too, had seen pageantry and meetings of men. Tyler's rebels had gathered there before Smithfield's showdown; a different kind of man, John Wesley, in the 1730s had staged revivalist meetings in its airy spaces, preaching to thousands. Eltham had a plethora of fairs, its first, Holy Trinity Fair, chartered to the lord of the manor,

. . . and roundabouts
A bucolic (and some might say drunken) frolic on the merry-go-round before the power of steam set the gallopers off on their reign of fairground supremacy. Somewhere at its centre a couple of well-muscled men or boys are cranking frantically

John de Vesci in 1299 and sympathetically renewed by Henry VI in 1436 'in consideration of the increase of his lordship, and the slender means of his tenants'. Later fairs were held on Palm Sunday, Easter Monday, Whit Monday and on 10 October, a market for horses, cattle and toys, mindful no doubt that Christmas was drawing nigh.

Undoubtedly these fringe occasions excited their own loyalties, flourishing in importance as the capital usurped the available spaces where a fair could be held. Each had its own eccentricities: Croydon, for instance, with its sheep, horse and cattle fair in October and its cherry fair in July, both from fourteenth-century charters, had a penchant for starting them at midnight, somewhat rare but not unknown. The dealing done, however, the circus performers and the menagerie took the limelight – along with the lithe lady dancers in their muslin skirts.

To the north of the river lay the equally popular heath of Hampstead, with its Roman road bound for St Albans. Once the washerwomen of London laboured there and the farm men made hay till nearly 1800. Almost certainly, when they let their hair down on holiday, their steps would turn, Whittington-style, to the sound of Bow bells and the uninhibited revelry of Cockney London. The capital's Bow Fair was just as bawdy, and its pleasures just as dubious as those of Bartholomew's:

The watermen with Wapping whores
Over the fields do come by scores.

Bow, then indeed surrounded by green fields, was a village that had grown, as it became the great unloading point for the corn cargoes brought by barge down the River Lea, into a place of mills beside the river but would mushroom only in the mid-nineteenth century. Today its medieval settlement is recalled only by the church in Bow Road, which once stood at its centre. Its fête was held on land alongside what is now (appropriately) Fairfield Road, long swallowed by London's eastward development. Its scandalous fair, many felt, took on the mantle of the suppressed May Fair. Held on the Thursday, Friday and Saturday of Whitsun week, it was billed as a toy fair, but there is, frankly, some confusion over its credentials. According to Hughson (*Circuit of London, Vol. VI*) there was an annual Michaelmas Day fair granted in 1664 to the Earl of Cleveland to be held on Mile End Green, or at any other convenient venue within his manor. A notice of 1733 to 'all Gentlemen, Farmers, Graziers, and whom else it may concern' advertised a yearly Michaelmas event called Mile End Fair to be staged beside the Artichoak in Mile End old town in the parish of Stepney. The site was a 5 acre field and the notice proclaims primarily a livestock sale. Two years later the fair-goers at what was often known as the Stepney Feast included those of such quality as the Duke of Bedford and the Earl of Lichfield. (Fairs of East London changed venue and identity with alarming nonchalance, sometimes disappearing without trace.)

In time, however, the fair seems to have been translated to Stratford Bow (still in the parish of Stepney) just along the road and rescheduled for Whitsun, attracting 'vast throngs from London', and becoming 'generally the scene of

Country fair in Croydon. In 1833 the rural community's occasion was a mixed affair, still mainly for livestock but with a menagerie, circus acts and dancing girls (in see-through dresses). The fun started at midnight. Fifty years later, with metropolitan spread, the small market town would be a London borough

inebriation and dissoluteness'. The fair also had another name, Greengoose Fair, perhaps the legacy of an even earlier existence, and in the reign of Charles I had to be suppressed as its venue was 'where the plague doth more increase than in any other parish within or without' London. A year or two earlier, before disaster struck, the so-called water poet John Taylor (1580–1653) had celebrated the fair's orgiastic attraction:

> At Bow, the Thursday after Pentecost,
> There is a fair of greene goose ready roast,
> Where as a goose is ever dog cheap there
> The sauce is over somewhat sharp and deare.
> There (e'er they scarce have feather on the backe)
> By hundreds and by heaps they go to wracke;
> There's such a baking, rosting, broyling, boyling;
> Such swearing, drubbing, dancing, dicing, toiling;
> Such shifting, shanking, cheating, smoaking, stinking;
> Such gormandising, cramming, guzzling, drinking.

Two hundred thousand people beat their way to Greenwich Fair's biggest rival

The possible explanation is that the Earl of Cleveland took over a good-going goose fair and the conundrum is further cracked by the knowledge that Stepney Green, as late as 1703 at least, was known as Mile End Green. It was where Richard II had ridden for his first encounter with Tyler and his rebels.

Stepney by 1844 was considered a part of the capital; a news report in March of that year refers to a 'renewal' of its fair – probably the banned Bow Fair, suppressed twenty or so years earlier. The fair, the report claims, had been 'revived' two years earlier and eulogises the attractions of an Easter Monday affair, which included plays 'equal to representations in minor theatres' and a vast dancing booth. Two hundred thousand people beat their way to what was clearly Greenwich's biggest rival, and that figure may well have been exceeded in later years as they rolled up on the increasingly popular rail excursions.

Farther out on the capital's fringe the gentlefolk of Edmonton on the east bank of the busy Lea had hired their servants at the statute fairs at Northall and Waltham Abbey until finally an appeal to the hundred's high constable secured the village a fair of its own (admittedly sans charter). It, too, became something of a nomadic event, being held in its first two or three years, about 1680, in mid-September at the George and Vulture (near the corner of what would later be Marsh Lane). It then moved across the road to the Cross Keys, settling there for a time before taking itself in turn to the Five Bells and then the Three Blackbirds. And it didn't stop there: thereafter it was taken to the King's Head at Winchmore Hill, next the Cock at Bowes Farm until, about 1730, it returned to its old haunts and the Bell Inn (now the Angel) at Edmonton, where it was continuing as W. Robinson published his *History of Edmonton* in 1819. By then, he says (and who could be surprised), the fair had already lost sight of its origins and become a 'holiday' – and, he adds, a noisy nuisance.

Edmonton Fair, somebody once said – and it may have been Defoe – was famous for nothing. But that is hardly so: surely no other fair so eloquently demonstrates the essential central role of the inn in the staging of the Old English fair? Edmonton's 'statty' was still functioning – but only just – as the First World War began. Once, it appears, the area had three fairs, a further two (once held on top of Clay Hill) on Ascension Day and on St Giles Day. Both, designated Beggars Bush Fairs, were staged on the edge of the Chase, near Southgate, on ground around the old Crown Inn, given by King James I. The king loved hunting and was hardly installed in the capital in 1603 when he swapped the manor of Hatfield for that of game-rich Theobalds (which became a royal palace). A short time later when he added Cheshunt land to his estate, including the site of the intriguingly named Beggars Bush Fair, he granted it (in letters patent) a new location in fields on Chase Side. The name remains something of a mystery. The answer perhaps is that the 'bush fair' was the forerunner of the mop – and like the hiring fair an occasion of suspect jollity and pleasure drawing crowds whose aim was not always to find work. Southgate's own fair, always the curtain-raiser to the maelstrom of Barnet, faded before the First World War.

Enfield was just as lucky when it came to courting royal favour. It was an earlier king, the warrior Edward I, whose charter in 1303 to Humphrey de Bohun, Earl of Hereford and Essex and lord of the manor of Enfield (who had the foresight to marry the king's daughter Elizabeth) gave it a weekly Monday market and a licence for two annual fairs, each of three days. These were 'on the eve and day and on the morrow of St Andrew the Apostle', the other similarly on the Assumption of the Blessed Virgin 'unless such fairs be a nuisance of the neighbouring markets and neighbouring fairs'. Whatever he did to Wallace, Edward could be scrupulously fair to his own!

The August fair slipped into September without apparent reason, having long ceased to be a significant trading occasion and become simply Enfield Fair and, according to G.H. Hodson and E. Ford in their 1873 *History of Enfield* 'a source of immorality and disorder and a growing nuisance to the inhabitants'. The fair 'was crowded with stalls which sold oysters, mussels, cookies and sandwiches'. There were toy and gingerbread stalls, stalls for skittles, nut shooting and wheels of fortune. And beyond that: exhibitions, legerdemain and feats of strength, a steam roundabout and swings. Not a puny event! Lord George Sanger's circus was the highlight of 1892, an extravaganza with 300 horses, two herds of elephants, a troupe of camels and performing lions.

The St Andrew's Day cattle fair brought a different crowd to town – the drovers – perhaps appropriately since many of them must have been Scottish dealers, desperate men who had missed out at St Faith's. The fair was hugely attended. Sweating cattle-hands jostled round Hubbard's gingerbread stall to gulp down pastry pigs filled with mincemeat at a penny apiece. The town's Church Street as well as Market Place would be thronging with men and animals. Yet it was as much for its cheeses, brought in from the hinterlands of Essex, that people initially flocked to St Andrew's. The shops and the inns would be stacked high with them! But by 1870, reported one source, St Andrew's was a

Shops and inns would be stacked high with cheeses brought in from the hinterlands

(*Opposite*) the toy-seller. Long before some fairs designated themselves 'toy fairs' the itinerant trader whose trifles were for the young was a familiar figure among the booths. He confidently cried his wares, knowing that the man who had found a good price for his livestock would buy something to take home to his children. The painting is by John Burr (1831–1893)

fair 'now chiefly resorted to by horse-dealers and cattle jobbers'. Latterly that function also faded and the fair became more for 'the amusement of the idle, than for the bustle of business' while clinging sadly to the King's Head Inn, whose licensee leased it and gave it a 2 acre site.

Local historian Edwin M. Ware claimed Pinner's Whitsun fair to be 'world famous'. Though his loyalty is commendable, his judgement may be just a trifle extreme. Certainly thousands flocked to it – and it is still bringing chaos to Pinner's narrow winding streets as a day for family fun on the roundabouts, the helter-skelter, the waltzers and of course the gallopers. Posters announcing the fair in more recent times have proclaimed it as 'founded upon a charter granted to the Lord of the Manor and Inhabitants by King Edward 3rd in the 10th year of his reign, 1337'. In fact, the charter granted two fairs (besides the usual weekly market) after some special pleading and an approach made to the Archbishop of Canterbury when the locals suffered a loss of pannage and their swine had to go hungry in an acorn shortage caused by the felling of the local oaks.

The three-day fairs honoured that saint of the wool merchants St John the Baptist (24 June) and his Decollation (his beheading) on 29 August. The charter was granted to the people; they were people's fairs and local residents still have the right to set up a stall. Now only one fair remains – always on a Whit Wednesday – the other having been abandoned in the mid-nineteenth century. Boys at Harrow sneaked out to sample the fair's grown-up pleasures, returning late through windows on which the screws of the iron bars had earlier been loosened. For one at least, the memory of that day and the evening dancing in the pub was indelible: 'The dancing was in a small room, and the atmosphere, impregnated with the smell of beer and tobacco, and the noise of dancing in chaw-boots, etc, to a merry fiddle, was something indescribable.' Thus were the excitements of adulthood glimpsed before a fugitive return to the dorm. The writer: the Revd Henry Torre.

There were other, earlier diversions, more adversarial, such as cudgel-play or quarter-staff fighting. Illusionists presented breath-taking 'beheadings'; bears danced and performing dogs delighted the genteel fair-goers. The high amusement in 1831 was 'gingling': the pursuit of one blindfolded man by another blindfolded man with bells attached to him. But the fair still had its traditional dimension. That year cattle were still the dominant business. Sheep were driven in to the fair (and penned at the top of the High Street) until the mid-nineteenth century, and, anecdotal evidence suggests, it was also a hiring fair. Almost alone of the notable fairs of Old England Pinner's seems to have managed to remain an occasion of innocent amusements, free of the viciousness that could seriously mar the more boisterous of Cockney knees-ups.

There can have been no single event that so united the whole of the capital's East End as Hainault Forest's Fairlop Fair. It was unique, a carnival that stretched from Wapping to Barking, one of reckless high spirits when a boat 'sailed' through the streets. It had all started innocently enough, about 1745. At weekends Daniel Day, a jovial ships' blockmaker in Wapping, liked to escape,

'The noise of dancing in chaw-boots to a merry fiddle was something indescribable'

Van dwellers. Life for this travelling showman's family may have been one of constantly moving on from one fair to the next but in 1900 their living wagon was the last word in luxury

with his faithful housekeeper Hannah, from town to the country delights of his small estate at Fairlop. Beside his house there grew a large, majestic oak and Daniel's joy was to sit under it, after a week of business stress, in the last of the mellow evening sunlight. Daniel was not a selfish man and he was a considerate employer. Indeed his workfolk called him 'Good-Day'. How nice, he thought, if they, too, could forsake the mean streets, at least once a year. So he invited them to his Hainault haunt for a dinner of beans and bacon, doubtless accompanied by suitable refreshment, on the anniversary of his own first visit to his Fairlop retreat, the first Friday of July. There was just one proviso (for Daniel was also a mischievous man): they were to arrive at the very door from Wapping by boat, using no other transport. That one, Day's workers solved quickly; they built the Fairlop Boat on wheels, a *coup de théâtre* that would electrify the streets of east London and establish Fairlop Friday, and eventually Fairlop Fair, leaving its story lingering in the air right up to our own time.

The blockmakers' boat was called the Maggot, a trifle unromantic even if the 'maggot' was a part of the ships' tackle that Daniel's firm manufactured. The land vessel was drawn by a team of horses, adorned for her 'voyage' by enormous bouquets of flowers and manned by a jovial crew who had put aboard suitable provisions: i.e., an ample barrel of beer. Soon other skilled watermen and tradesmen were building boats of their own to join the throng. Fairlop's magnificent oak, spreading its branches over a 300 ft diameter, became their mecca and by 1840 the procession was clearly an imposing one. 'Vehicles of every description were in requisition, and numberless vans, each drawn by two horses, covered with awnings and gaily decorated, followed each other in rapid succession along Lea Bridge and Mile End roads. Great confusion sometimes prevailed at the turnpike gates from the number of vans, gigs, omnibuses, carts, etc, waiting to pass . . . The impositions of some of the turnpike men were loudly complained of, and they would have been greater but for the attendance of the police. The great attraction of the day were the amphibious vehicles, the watermen's and blockmakers' boats, mounted on carriages, and each drawn by six post horses, with postillions superbly dressed. At half-past seven the Unity [the watermen's boat] got under way from Green Bank, Wapping . . . and being unable to pass under the arches of the Blackwall railway . . . passed over Old Gravel Lane, Ratcliff Highway, Upper East Smithfield, the Minories and Whitechapel Road. The wives of the watermen followed in an open landau, and the rear was brought up by a large van, covered with an awning, containing fifty persons and a band of musicians . . . In the Mile End Road the procession was joined by the Maggot [which had started from the Builders' Arms in Grundy Street] followed by open barouches . . . containing the blockmakers' wives.' Truly it was an occasion of Coronation dimensions!

The fair that year – restricted to one day so as not to spread over and desecrate the Sabbath, as it had earlier done, drew a crowd of 200,000 – some Essex countryfolk but mainly East Enders – to swings, roundabouts, Houdini acts, fortune booths and, yes, Richardson's theatre. Thankfully 'the thimble and pea-rig cheats were not so plentiful as they were at Egham and Ascot'. There were fire-eaters, a man who would eat broken bottles, and archery contests.

But dusk, as always at any fair, brought a change of character, a highly charged atmosphere: 'the fun waxed fast and furious. The blare of unmusical instruments, the shouts of hilarious youths, and the shrieks of timid maids caused a perfect pandemonium of sound. Lads with squirts discharged streams of not so clean water into each other's faces; some, armed with "ticklers", strolled up and down in search of mischief, and horseplay increased as it grew dark. Strolling singers bawled broadside ballads in questionable taste, dancing was indulged in without restraint, and a gay rollicking, riotous scene brought the day to a close.' The *East London Advertiser*'s correspondent was writing some years after the end of the fair and distance had lent its usual enchantment. The reality was somewhat more vicious. The day ended in scenes that shocked the countryfolk, and the return of the boats to Wapping at night brought chaos to the streets of East London – Stratford, Bow, the Mile End Road – as crowds gathered along the route. Pubs were packed. Predictably the high spirits of Fairlop's fair day degenerated into a disorderly rout of robbery, drunkenness and violence.

Day, at least, was spared the worst excesses of the event he had founded. When his great tree (rumoured girth: 36 ft) lost one of its seventeen branches (each as thick as a tree trunk), sombered by the omen, he had the timber made into his coffin and, it is said, frequently laid himself into it to test the fit. He was

'Strolling singers bawled broadside ballads in bad taste, dancing was without restraint'

Fair in the forest. The frantic gaiety of Fairlop, round its large-girthed oak at Hainault, began well and ended badly, its name a byword for excesses that scandalised Essex country folk. The capital's entire East End, it seemed, flocked there, creating a July carnival that stretched from Wapping to Barking

laid into it for the last time in 1767, aged eighty-four, a remarkable man whose first interest had been to honour the skill of his workmen. He left behind him another of his odd stipulations: that he be conveyed for burial at Barking by boat. He had a fear of horses. His favourite tree, damaged by fire in 1805, was blown down in 1820 and, in that curious paradox that is history, its wood went to make the pulpits of St Pancras Church. The carnival would continue, though, where Good-Day's oak had stood. And the Fairlop Boat sailed on, sometimes renewed or refitted and the last built in 1891, until the present century, when it sailed into oblivion . . . a voyage of mystery that would be rekindled only in 1952 when its ruined wreckage was found lying in a Romford cottage garden.

Just as perennially favoured were the Flats of Wanstead and the Forest of Epping, the Cockneys' paradise, a place where they could escape from the drab streets of the capital's East End and the world of unrewarding work. In the 1920s 102,000 people arrived through Chingford station on their way into the forest in a single day; huge forest 'retreats', refreshment rooms, could serve 2,000 at a single sitting. Each summer weekend – and especially on Easter Monday and Whitsun and August bank holidays – saw them decanting with their numerous offspring at Chingford. William Addison, lifelong guardian of the forest as well as its historian, describes the scene: 'No matter what the weather might bring, thousands of Cockneys on pleasure bent bundled themselves out of trains or wagonettes from early morning till noon. Some of the mums were already smelling of gin and my-dearing everybody as they waddled out of the station yard, followed by their bairns like proudly clucking hens with their chickens fluttering behind them. The men of those tended to be as stunted as the lopped hornbeams in the Forest itself. Few of the girls were beauties by modern standards. Life in East London was too hard for that. But friendliness and good humour were universal – at least until drink got the better of the more hard-bitten.'

At times there would be as many as 13,000 people milling across Chingford Plain, riding the showmen's switchbacks, shrieking, laughing, patronising the donkey rides, the coconut shies or astride the gaudily painted gallopers (or the cockerels) of the merry-go-round. Here, too, Easter's fair was the highlight, the curtain-raiser to summer's gaiety. It was boisterous, uninhibited jollity as only the East Enders knew how to enjoy it. Addison again, in *Portrait of Epping Forest*, described that piece of equipment that became a favourite at the Easter fair and unfailingly tempted the exhibitionists: 'The flying trapeze consisted of a series of ropes with handles, or loops, to be grasped by the flyer as he or she swung round daringly from a ring attached to an upper rope. The flyers enjoyed the security of knowing that if they lost their hold they would fall into the rope net suspended below them; but the buxom girls thought chiefly of the moment when they would be caught in the arms of the strong youth waiting for them at the end of the flight, where the custom was to seize them and carry them screaming to a safe distance for a rough and tumble on the grass.'

Amid it all, the hucksters cried their wares; a bear or two danced. Boats were for hire on Connaught Water (tuppence a time). Fortune-tellers did a roaring trade, as they always did among people who had nothing to lose and plenty to hope for. Donkey men, in the flush of trade, sometimes so far forgot their responsibilities as to get thoroughly tight and have their animals impounded. But the day wore on. The children got fractious, exhausted, and wailed. Lovers strayed deeper into the undergrowth where they would not be disturbed – and the forest's alehouses filled with thirsty men and their gin-swigging partners. Mainly they are still there today, the inns where they congregated: the Royal Forest, the Royal Oak, the Robin Hood, the Wake Arms and The Owl at Sewardstone, places where the singalong continued into the lilac dusk to the accompaniment of jangly pianos, or a barrel organ in the yard. Understandably the quality avoided the forest and found another way home. Through the months of summer – it seemed then that the sun always shone – the Chingford Plain was an almost permanent fair. There were Cockney families who even brought their tents and their utensils with them, determined not to miss a minute of it, doubtless hoping that they might never have to go home.

CHAPTER TWELVE

SCANDALOUS BEHAVIOUR

The fair has no racial barriers; its appeal is international, its brash assertiveness is the same in any language. Nobody is needed to translate its magic – and the people of Britain are as susceptible as those of any other nation. It is rather like life itself: swings and roundabouts. Life is a carousel, old chum . . . We are grateful for its moments of dizzying excitement. Yet there are those who find it all a little louche, who are unpersuaded by its mood of festal jollity and as dubious as the writer J.B. Priestley. He visited Nottingham's great carnival, the Goose Fair, in the autumn of 1933 for his *English Journey*, a book about his pilgrimage round the country – at a time when the old-fashioned travelling fair was still in its heyday. The blunt Yorkshireman was distinctly uncertain about it all and said so – bluntly. 'Its narrow avenues were so thickly packed with people that you could only slowly shuffle along, pressed close on every side . . . The brazen voices of the showmen, now made more hideous and gargantuan than ever by the amplifiers and loudspeakers, battered our hearing, which could not pluck words out of those terrifying noises. The mechanical organs blared in batteries, so closely ranged that the ear could never detect a single tune: all it heard was the endless grinding symphony. The real patrons of the fairs of this kind are youngsters in their teens; and there were thousands of them pushing and cat-calling and screaming in the crowd: the boys, their faces grinning and vacant in the whirl of coloured light, sometimes looking like members of some sub-human race surging up from the interior of the earth; the girls whose thickly powdered faces were little white masks without lines but daubed with red and black, looked like dolls out of some infernal toyshop; and the appearance of them all was fascinating and frightening.'

In his memories of the fair, G.C.A. Austin, the city's Clerk of the Markets for thirty-seven years (1907–44) could cast his mind back to the last years of the nineteenth century. He recalled that frightening surge of humanity, mindlessly intent on pleasure: 'It was impossible to change one's direction once one was in the stream . . . All but the most vigorous . . . would most likely be lifted off their feet and carried along bodily by the throng.' The mood could pass from one of revelry to abandon heightened almost to anarchy as the rougher element ran amok with 'ticklers' (small, long-handled brushes) whose precise purpose Mr Austin forgets to tells us (though we may hazard an educated guess) and little rubber balls that squirted water. The sight and size of such crowds thoroughly alarmed one French commander, taken prisoner at the battle of Blenheim (1704) and detained at the king's pleasure in Nottingham. After visiting the goose fair he

wrote urgently to the French king, advising him to give up the struggle. He had just seen enough men in one English market-place to overrun the entire French kingdom!

Priestley hints at the mood of menace that lurked under the arc-lights; that existed under the surface even where the pleasure seemed simple and unalloyed. In that earthy gaiety was the potential for explosive and unpredictable excess. Riots that erupted periodically helped to seal the fate of London's great fairs. Southwark's fair was a byword for drunkenness and debauchery, like St Bartholomew's and Greenwich. Later, on the capital's eastern rim, when the fair came to Wanstead Flats, the middle-classes by then ensconced in its suburbia feared for their property if not for their lives as rival gangs from Whitechapel and Hoxton took advantage of the occasion to settle old scores. In the West Country, Lansdown Fair, near Bath, had always been an unruly event, but by the mid-nineteenth century it was sinking from bad to inexcusable. Lord George Sanger, the veteran showman, who cannot have been easily shocked by the behaviour of fair-goers, thought it one of England's roughest fairs. It erupted in 1848. The impresario himself, in *Seventy Years a Showman*, described the mayhem that suddenly broke loose: '. . . at length [we] found ourselves at Lansdown . . . for the big cattle, sheep and pleasure fair that then used to be held annually on August 10th at the hill village which is some two miles from the old city . . . Bath at this period had in its slums what was considered to be the most brutish and criminal mob in England, and for these people Lansdown fair was, as they put it, "their night out".

'Though it lasted but one day, the fair was always a big one occupying a great space on a broad hillside. On this booths, shows and refreshment tents of all descriptions were erected to form an enormous ring, in the centre of which were the droves of sheep, cattle and horses that formed the staple of the fair to which the country folk flocked from all the district round . . . As dusk came on the regular business people – the farmers, graziers and others who had been dealing in the horses, cattle, farm produce, and such-like – left the fair to the pleasure-seekers. The drinking booths, gingerbread stalls and shows began to twinkle with lights . . . As night advanced the character of the fair crowd gradually changed. It grew rougher and rougher. Fights were frequent. Oaths and screams were mingled with coarse songs from the drinking booths, which were filled with a motley throng.'

With the arrival of a crowd from the city, 'the scenes that followed are almost indescribable. Not content with drinking all they could, the ruffians turned on the taps, stoved the barrels, smashed up bottles, and let the liquor run to waste. Then they started to wreck the booths. Canvas was torn to shreds, platforms were smashed up and made bonfires of, wagons were battered and overturned, show-fronts that had cost some of their poor owners small fortunes were battered to fragments. Everywhere was riot, ruin and destruction.'

The fair in riot was an alarming spectacle and Lord George Sanger's is a terrifying account, though by no means an isolated one. Priestley was right to be uneasy. The fair's seemingly relaxed gaiety could erupt for all manner of

As the night advanced the character of the fair crowd changed and it grew rougher

(*Opposite*) a penny to see the peepshow. Naughty or mischievously innocuous, who can say what revelations are about to be revealed to the dubious young punter in John Burr's painting

Wickedly observed. The artist has buried a message at the core of this gallery of grotesques at Bartholomew Fair, where the dips quietly work the crowd. Pickpockets were an ever-present danger at the fair – and the reason why Pepys left his wallet with an innkeeper before venturing into the throng

reasons, and Nottingham's great fair was not immune. Some time about 1766 the fair was reduced to chaos by a cheese riot, an incident duly recorded by one of the town's chroniclers: 'There was a tumultuous riot, on account of the high price of cheese, which was selling at from 28s to 30s per cwt. The violence of the people burst forth like a torrent, in open fair, cheeses were rolled down Wheelergate and Peck-lane in abundance, and the Mayor, in his attempt to restore peace, was knocked down with one in the Market Place. The Riot Act was read: a detachment of the 15th Dragoons was called in, many of the rioters were taken prisoners, and one innocent man was shot by the military.' When a press-gang swooped on Bow Fair in the early eighteenth century the fair erupted into a riot in which the constable of the then country village, trying to keep order, died from the injuries he received. London was always a city at the mercy of the mob. Greenwich Fair, prone to bad behaviour, at Easter 1850 exploded into an orgy of destruction when sixteen artillery men from Woolwich and six marines clashed with civilian fair-goers and also attacked Richardson's theatre, tearing away the steps, rushing on to the platform, pulling down lamps and breaking up painted partitions, urns and so on. It took police and mounted militia to restore calm. And always, general assault was a commonplace at the fair.

That the fair in the past also had an alternative social purpose was shrewdly understood by yet another of the Goose Fair's commentators, writing around 1910. 'Our Autumn carnival,' he confided, 'undoubtedly acts as a safety-valve through which the super-exuberancy of a large section of the community may lightsomely escape instead of finding vent in other and far more reprehensible forms of madcap prankishness.' A local reporter in about 1860, with the weary cynicism of his profession, saw the fair in similar orgasmic terms as 'the great attraction of our hard-working, but somewhat thriftless, Nottingham, which annually, for several days, and we may say nights, also, occupies all thoughts, and absorbs all attention.'

Describing the occasion as a 'chartered saturnalia', he adds: 'Hundreds, we may say thousands, of the youthful portion of the surrounding populations, may be seen pouring into town from every direction, but all hastening to one point, the Market-place.' For some the milling, mindless mob posed a problem: 'It is not altogether clear . . . whether some of the monstrosities provided for exhibition at the fair may not be excelled in point of extravagance by the outrageous proportions of some of the young lasses, whose crinolines, swollen to the amplitude of rick coverings when leaving home, are doomed to frightful collapse in the effort to squeeze them through the compact masses of unpitying, or envious, rivals in the race after fashion and pleasure.'

Dickens, too, understood all too well that the day of the fair was a day of catharsis. In *Sketches by Boz* he calls Greenwich Fair 'a periodical breaking out . . . a sort of spring-rash'. He confesses to being, in his young days, a 'constant frequenter' of the fair, once making his foray 'in a spring-van, accompanied by thirteen gentlemen, fourteen ladies, an unlimited number of children, and a

On with the show. The great Richardson's extravaganza at Greenwich. Despite its attractions the showman's booth was torn apart in one of the many disturbances that finally kept the middle-classes at home and sent the fair into a spiral of dissolute behaviour and decline

Smithfield in gaudy fair
mode. John Nixon's superb
watercolour of the capital
frolic of Bartholomew Fair
about 1810, before its fall,
is a visual feast to the eye.
Pepys adored the fair, and
Ben Johnson based his play
on its louche characters

barrel of beer'. Sometimes, he hints, he was himself a little under the weather on
the homeward run. There was a tension in the air as the fair convoy of 'cabs,
hackney-coaches, 'shay' carts, coal-waggons, stages, omnibuses, sociables, gigs
and donkey chaises' rolled along, the dust flying in clouds, the ginger-beer corks
popping off in volleys: 'the balcony of every public-house is crowded with
people, smoking and drinking, half the private houses are turned into tea-shops,
fiddles are in great request, every little fruit shop displays its stall of gilt
gingerbread and penny toys; turnpike men are in despair; horses won't go on,
and wheels will come off; ladies in 'caravans' scream with fright at every fresh
concussion, and their admirers find it necessary to sit remarkably close to them
by way of encouragement; servants-of-all-work, who are not allowed to have
followers, and have got a holiday for the day, make the most of their time with
the faithful admirer who waits for a stolen interview at the corner of the street
every night, when they go to fetch the beer – apprentices grow sentimental, and
straw-bonnet makers kind.' It is a masterly evocation from a masterly pen: the
picture of a powder-keg of emotions ready to ignite.

Truly all human life was there at the fair, something the novelist and satirist
Thackeray also well knew: his *Vanity Fair* opens with a delightful curtain-raiser
that sees the fair as a metaphor for our imperfect society. As manager of the
performance he is about to unfold, the author himself looks out on the scene:

'There is a great quantity of eating and drinking, making love and jilting, laughing and the contrary, smoking, cheating, fighting, dancing, and fiddling: there are bullies pushing about, bucks ogling the women, knaves picking pockets, policemen on the look-out, quacks bawling in front of their booths, and yokels looking up at the tinselled dancers and poor old rouged tumblers, while the light-fingered folk are operating upon their pockets behind.' Yes, he tells us, not a moral place! He admits: 'Some people consider Fairs immoral altogether and eschew such, with their servants and families; very likely they are right. But persons who think otherwise . . . may perhaps like to step in for half an hour.'

Few would resist the invitation. The sights and sounds of Stourbridge Fair – to his eyes the distressing sights – were said to have been Bunyan's inspiration for the fair of his *Pilgrim's Progress*. Beyond question the Bedfordshire man's work shows an intimate understanding of the fair's then central role and function in society. For Bunyan it was not only heedless distraction that was encompassed there – the fair was indeed a mirror of life itself with all its thoughtlessness, beckoning pleasures and deep troughs of temptation. The name of his fair town is Vanity; the fair was kept 'all the year long'. It had 'jugglings, cheats, games, plays, fools, apes, knaves, and rogues of every kind. Here too are to be seen – and that for nothing – thefts, murders, adulteresses, false swearers . . .'. The way to the Celestial City is through the lusty fair. All humanity passes between the booths. Dwelling as he did in the country, Bunyan knew the fair's temptation for rural youth and the impact on the health and morals of those drawn to its excess. It pleasures were deleterious, like the 'prizes' of life, in themselves practically worthless and quickly snatched away from us. Satan is the prince of the fair.

Obliquely Sanger, the veteran showman, in his account reminds us of the old pattern of the traditional fair, with its mornings mainly for commerce, its afternoons for gossip and extended dealing, and the evening for the kind of bacchanalian excess that made circumspect men who had brought their daughters take them home again by nightfall. Increasingly, the genteel would stay away from the fair, offended by its squalor and made apprehensive by its unpredictability. For all that, it was by such occasions that the countrymen of Old England would continue to chart their days; they gave significance to their lives, so that meeting over a tankard in the Fleece and Whistle or the Plough and Harrow they would reflectively wrinkle their brows and recount their stories with the recollection that 'T'were just past Priddy' or 'It b'aint long a'fore St Giles'.

For writers especially – Priestley excepted – the fair was a focus of delight: its temptations were boundless, sometimes irresistible. It was a stage ready-made for declarations of love, the discovery of treachery; the fulcrum of their plots find their location in the lightly disguised setting of some well-known event. Thackeray did not think too highly of fairs it seems: in *Sketches and Travels in London* he betrays an antipathy in introducing a character who is 'a frequenter of races at Greenwich Fair and such amusements in questionable company'. In *Far from the Madding Crowd* Thomas Hardy, novelist and ruralist, immortalised (as Greenhill) Woodbury Hill Fair, held over several days within its ancient

The fair was a mirror of life: all beckoning pleasures and deep troughs of temptation

earthworks near Bere Regis, which drew traders from all over the south and west of England. His scene of wife-auctioning in *The Mayor of Casterbridge* is set at Weydon Fair, which is Weyhill. His hay-trusser Henchard enters the Fair-field (of the 1840s) late in the day to find that the big fair's 'standing places and pens where many hundreds of horses and sheep had been exhibited and sold in the forenoon . . . were now in great part taken away . . . but little business remained on hand, the chief being the sale by auction of a few inferior animals, that could not otherwise be disposed of, and had been absolutely refused by the better class

What HARM is there in going to the FAIR!

1. ASK AT THE WORKHOUSE! *Fairs promote Idleness*—Idleness causes Poverty—Poverty brings Pauperism! Many are driven at last to a Workhouse, who began to waste their *time* and *money* at Fairs!

Recollect that *Time is Money* to the industrious artisan. Think what you *might* have earned to-day to increase your domestic comfort. If you can, by industry, procure more wages than you at present want, save some against another day, and do not spend what you labour to earn, upon rogues and vagrants.

"Go to the ant, thou sluggard; consider her ways, and be wise. She provideth her meat in summer, and gathereth her food in harvest." Proverbs vi. 6. "Time is short." "Redeem the time, because the days are evil."—St. Paul.

2. ASK AT THE HOSPITAL! *Fairs are the haunts of Vice!* There, abandoned women wait for their prey. *Vice produces Disease!* Who can describe the sufferings of the miserable wretch who is thus defiled? He exchanges a Brothel for a Hospital, and noisy mirth for agonizing groans! Observe his pale face, his sunken eye, his wasted frame, his exhausted strength, his early death!

Flee then the resorts of a whorish woman.

"Remove thy way far from her, and come not nigh the door of her house, lest thou give thine honour to others, and thy years to the cruel, and thou mourn at last when thy flesh and body is consumed. For her house inclineth to death, and her paths unto the dead—her end is bitter as wormwood. Her feet go down to death, her steps take hold on hell!" Proverbs v. 4—20; ii. 16—19.

"Whoremongers and adulterers God will judge." Hebrews xiii. 4.

3. ASK AT THE MAGDALEN, the Penitentiary, or any other Asylum where poor girls, with ruined characters, find a shelter from reproach and shame! They will tell you, *that Fairs corrupt the morals of females, and lead on to seduction.* There, at the dancing-room, the drinking-booth, and the lewd shows, are to be found wretches of both sexes, who, by promises which they never intend to fulfil, seek to destroy female virtue, and dare to *ruin two souls at once!*

"Evil communications corrupt good manners." St. Paul.

"A companion of fools shall be destroyed."—Solomon.

4. ASK AT THE MADHOUSE! *Drunkenness is a common Vice at the Fair*, or why are all the ale-houses and liquor-shops crowded, and the drinking-booths thronged? *Drunkenness leads on to Madness!* Ask at Bethlem Hospital, or St. Luke's, and they will promptly tell you *that it is one of the common causes of madness!* See it in that poor drivelling Idiot; and in that raving Lunatic, whom chains can hardly bind.

"Wine is a mocker, and strong drink is *raging*, and whosoever is deceived thereby is not wise!" Proverbs xx. 1.

"Woe unto the drunkards, whose glorious beauty is a fading flower." Isaiah xxviii. 1.

"NOR DRUNKARDS shall inherit the kingdom of God." 1 Corinthians vi. 10.

5. ASK AT THE PRISON! *For Fairs lead to Felony!* Many servants are tempted to rob their employers every year, that they may have money to spend at the show-booth, the dancing-room, the gaming-table, or the brothel! Thus they begin a career of vice, which leads them on to the *Jail! the Hulks!! the Gallows!!!*

"Thou shalt not steal." "Let him that stole, steal no more; but rather let him labour, working with his own hands the thing which is good, that he may have to give to him that needeth." Ephesians iv. 28.

"Exhort servants to be obedient unto their masters: not purloining, but showing all good fidelity." Titus ii. 9, 10.

READER, you may not intend to practise any of these Evils. Then why expose yourself to the temptation? Why come near to those who commit them?

"Avoid it, pass not by it, turn from it, and pass away." Proverbs iv. 15.

No. 3. Published by the London Christian Instruction Society, 5, Paternoster Row.

Fair warning. This contemporary handbill leaves no sin unturned in its desire to denounce the dire consequences, physical and moral, of succumbing to the enticements of the fair

Sweet teasers. The fair called them 'paraders', but by whatever name these provocatively dressed Naughty-Ninety girls were the kind of delicious distraction that a farmboy could find irresistible at the end of a hiring fair day. You paid your money for what followed, inside the booth

of traders'. Yet the crowd is denser, more disorientated, more disaffected, the 'frivolous contingent' including 'journeymen out for a holiday, a stray soldier or two come on furlough, village shopkeepers and the like, having latterly flocked in; persons whose activities find a congenial field among the peep-shows, toy-stands, waxworks, inspired monsters, disinterested medical men who travelled for the public good, thimble-riggers, nick-nack vendors, and readers of fate'. Hardy loved a fair and left us a lingering record of their flavour. He was about the last to do so; the old fairs, even then, had dwindled in their importance and were fading from the landscape.

Cobbett was a man out of a similar mould. Having settled comfortably in Kensington, and himself forsaken the farming life, he set out on the journeys of his *Rural Rides* and began to call his hard-pressed countrymen to account. He declares his intent at the start: 'my object was, not to see inns and turnpike-roads, but to see the country; to see the farmers at home, and to see the labourers in the fields; and to do this you must go either on foot or on horse-back. With a gig you cannot get about amongst bye-lanes and across fields, through bridle-ways and hunting-gates; and to tramp it is too slow.' He was an early Studs Terkel, folklorist as well as polemicist. Between 7 October and 1 December 1822 he covered 327 miles, taking him through Hampshire,

Berkshire, Surrey and Sussex. His method was simply defined: 'I went to the Swan Inn to dine with the Farmers. This is the manner that I like best of doing the thing . . . But I do not like Dinner-Meetings on my account. I like much better to go and fall in with the lads of the land . . . at their resort; and I am going to place myself . . . in the midst of all the great fairs of the West . . . I shall be at Weyhill Fair on the 10th of October, and, perhaps on some of the succeeding days; and, on one of those days, I intend to dine at the White Hart at Andover . . . I wish to see many people, and talk to them . . . What better reason can be given for a man's going about the country and dining at Fairs and Markets?' What better reason indeed!

There are times when this history of fairs leans heavily and without shame on Cobbett's journeys of discovery, as it does on Defoe's *A Tour Through the Whole Island of Great Britain*, one hundred years earlier, counterpointing their observations. During Defoe's peregrinations, the fairs of Old England were still at their height; in Cobbett's time they were – along with the nation's agriculture – in decline. If there are reasons for accepting Defoe's accounts with some caution, his nevertheless is a reporter's eye, registering eclectic but often significant detail. Cobbett's is a closer social scrutiny, occasionally a rant, as the railway age is about to dawn and change the entire fabric of country society, making the old-style fair redundant.

The artist, too, would provide an invaluable record, drawn by the fair's colour and its characters; it was a feast to the palette. Hogarth, born in St Bartholomew Close nearby and baptised in St Bartholomew's, grew up in the sleazy shadow of Smithfield and cannot have been unaffected by the life of the heaving humanity he saw in its surrounding streets and alleys; Sir Edwin Landseer, far too romantically, mirrored the Highland drover and his beasts on the eve of his departure for the trysts; Rowlandson haunted Barnet and Harlow Bush; Sir Alfred Munnings, who captured with his brush for all time the bucolic essence of the horse fair at Lavenham, was as we have seen captivated by the solid strength and decoration of the carthorses as they stood in rows awaiting the coper's gaze.

Yet those inspiring occasions they depicted, which so often opened with such high intent and impressive ceremonial, could, as we know, quickly deteriorate into unsavoury scenes of drunken revelry and dubious pleasures that sat ill with the celebration of a saint's day. There had always been that contradiction at the heart of the fair: the holiday was also a 'holy day'. The Middle Ages had found it difficult to reconcile itself with the scenes of sometimes lewd behaviour that followed, and possibly accompanied, the service of solemn dedication to its particular saint, and it was this, more than anything, that accelerated the fair's expulsion from the sacred precincts of church or cathedral. Kings offended by such conduct could take against fair gatherings. William's celebrated arrival on the English scene had placed an early control on things with the proviso that fairs must be held in the cities and towns. Sharp dealing was not the problem; it was the riot and unrest inherent in these markets, both large and small.

There had always been that contradiction: the holiday was also a 'holy day'

Rope trick. Tightrope walkers were in the top echelon of entertainers and could command a crowd, especially if one was a girl. The eighteenth-century artist Joseph van Aken has captured that moment of awe as thousands of eyes watch in hushed silence

The Vatican in the twelfth century forbade fairs in the cathedral precincts because of their immoral behaviour and general rowdiness. The Catholic clergy were banned from attending them – wherever they were staged – doubtless because of the temptations they held. Edward I, too, bore down heavily on fairs. When a parliament at Winchester, the old Anglo-Saxon capital, produced the Statute of Winton (or Wynton) banning these unruly events from all churchyards, many thought it was not before time. Its decree was unequivocal: 'the King commandeth and forbiddeth that from henceforth neither fairs nor markets be kept in churchyards for the honour of the church'. It may indeed have been a matter of religious concern to him, though it cannot have done him any harm to keep on the right side of the bishops (who balanced the power of the knights). Edward, anxious about the excessive tolls that were sometimes levied, and the latitude for corruption, also came up with the idea of the King's Seal, a guarantee of fair trading.

Outwith the shadow of the Church the fair would only slide the faster in the way it inclined. At Yarmouth's Herring Fair in the late fourteenth century there was an attempt to keep the peace and curb the worst excesses by making the carrying of arms unlawful at the fair, along with a local curfew that kept the boat crews on board their vessels between nightfall and dawn. Much later, another monarch, King James I, that wisest fool in Christendom, would rail against the mischief and noisy behaviour of the fair and strive to limit the damage the fun of it did to students' studies by banning such occasions within a 5 mile radius of Cambridge. Alas, he failed miserably. Such is the lure of the fair, it would prove impervious to the royal wish. The students of the time, it must be remembered, at Oxford as well as Cambridge, were loutish and ill-behaved, rich men's sons who roistered their nights away, swaggering through slothful indolence in the latest foppish fashions (along with sword or rapier), neglecting their books for cards and dice in the beer parlours of the time, fencing, and watching the brutish spectacles of bull-baiting and cock-fighting. Their tutors stood terrified of them – and even more so of their wealthy, indulgent fathers. University life quite possibly encompassed other wayward diversions: seeking the early closure of St Radigund's nunnery in 1496 the then Bishop of Ely had done so on the grounds of the 'dissolute disposition and incontinence of the religious women . . . by reason of the vicinity of Cambridge University'.

Refreshment was always a concern at the fair; the 'furmity' dispensed by Hardy's old wife in *The Mayor of Casterbridge* may have been innocent enough unlaced (which was seldom the case) but usually the liquor that flowed so freely had disastrous results; the behaviour of the hiring fairs claimed a yearly toll of lost innocence, with all the regrettable consequences. Even Cardinal Wolsey, they say, as the young rector at Limington in about 1500, once got himself into a disgraceful state at Somerset's Lopen Fair and had to be lodged in the stocks to cool off. There was constant regulation governing the consumption of ale – without much success, for a fair crowd, above all, was in the mood to eat, drink and be merry. Even in the reign of Charles I, when tighter legislation brought down the shutters on unlicensed ale-houses, and heavy fines and heavy whipping in default (since few of their keepers could afford the fine) there was still an unbridled freedom allowed for fairs and similar occasions. Anybody could sell malt liquor from a fair booth.

The behaviour of the hiring fairs claimed a yearly toll of lost innocence

The fair indeed could drastically alter the character of a town. Horncastle, given its primary trade, had a plethora of public houses, though never enough, it would seem, to quench the collective thirst that went with horse-dealing. By the close of the eighteenth century it had about fourteen inns; by 1826 there were twenty-one; by 1860 there were forty-eight inns and beerhouses with licences. Normal 6–11 p.m. opening hours stretched at fair time from 5 p.m. to midnight. The horse-dealers had their favourites, the Irish as their presence grew from about 1860 finding congenial havens in the Fighting Cocks, the Rodney and the New. They were, reported the *Horncastle News*, 'a jolly lot of men and go in for rollicking fun'. The inns of the town had extensive stabling; the larger establishments would each have room for one hundred horses and more, yet there was always a shortfall and accommodation usually had to be found for man and beast in the surrounding villages. By the end of the nineteenth century, the town alone had stabling for over a thousand animals.

The village taverns of Church Brough and Market Brough, at the foot of the worst coaching road in Britain, the Stainmore Pass – where the settlement had grown up around the Roman fort – had long been havens for weary travellers. Down Church Hill the multitude of inns had increased year by year – among them the evocative Pack Horse Inn and the Green Tree Inn. Beside the old fording place in the square was the Bridge Inn. In Market Brough were the Grapes Inn and the Fleece Inn, the Hole-in-the-Wall Inn and the George and Dragon (transcended now into the One-stop Shop emporium), the White Swan Inn, the Shoulder of Mutton Inn and the Malt Shovel Inn and the George Inn. In all, Brough had at least seventeen inns, including the Castle Hotel and the Black Bull Inn.

The mood was merry and as frequently acrimonious as deals began to be considered

On fair nights, when Brough was at its peak of importance during the eighteenth and nineteenth centuries, they were crammed to the doors, mostly with gypsy horse-traders. The mood was merry and as frequently acrimonious as the deals of the day began to be considered under the influence of drink. The village left its autumn hearths to come and see the fun; ten extra policemen were drafted in to cope as the fist fights developed over imagined slights or a horse that now seemed less the bargain it had been cracked up to be. 'They fought like devils,' one old-timer recalled. 'By six o'clock they would be dancing in the inns – and this would go on right through the night. The language was terrible.' His grandfather had been one of the policemen. One thing the small village would find shocking during the inter-war years was the number of women and girls in the inns during fair time: 'They came from Leeds and disappeared back there.' Scots people, too, would come to Brough Hill Fair, adding to the general mêlée: 'People would sleep anywhere – under hedges, wherever. They were all half-tight anyway.'

At the time of St Faith's cattle fair every cottager around would put out his green branch above the door to help the Norfolk village's eight inns assuage the appetites and thirsts of men at the end of the long drove south. The inns would open all day and all night and every fiddler living within a 10 mile radius of Norwich would gravitate there, sure of steady work.

For all its inns, Horncastle, too, was unable to cope with the demand and private houses would buy a barrel of ale and a five-shilling bough licence and as 'bush houses' put out a branch of greenery to turn a penny and slake the fair's raging thirst – and no doubt add to its misbehaviour. In the inns men gambled their money on cards and other games of chance; the thimble-riggers – which thimble was the pea under, an early variant of the three-card trick – prospered quietly. Some of the beerhouses were pulsating brothels, some more discreetly so, the most notorious being Daft's Tap in St Lawrence Street, which no doubt accommodated the 'ladies or nymphs of the pave' who came 'to ply their avocation'. It is likely that business boomed after the town got gas lighting in 1834. The place in those early Victorian days was a rough town of drunken

Rogue fair. Lansdown, held on a hillside just outside Bath, had a disgraceful record and drew the riff-raff from the city's slums who made sure the fair ended in deplorable scenes of violence. Thomas Barker (1769–1847) shows in oil on canvas a corner of the fair and a game in progress – with money almost certainly staked on the outcome

shenanigans where the farmboy, or more likely the horse-coper, could take the pick of a bed companion for the night and where the prostitutes hawking their wares were a constant threat to the morals of the young men of the town.

The horse fair, in its closing stages particularly, when the serious dealing was ended, drew in the unsavoury dregs, wringing protest from citizens who were 'coming in daily contact with the profane swearing, blasphemy, and filthy lewdness given utterance to by the very dross of creation who now infest the place'. Condemnation does not come stronger than that. With the girls came the pickpockets – 'from the South, from Scotland, Ireland, anywhere,' said one ninety-year-old, now living in what was one of Brough's many inns – going from fair to fair, mingling with the throng; the horse fair, with its wads of raw, ready money passing from hand to hand was a rewarding affair. It was awash with cash. They watched where the money went, perhaps following buyer and seller to the inn where they were drinking to their bargain, marking out their victims, waiting for the chance to move in. Horncastle, in its heyday, was no different, and men who had drunk unwisely were regularly waylaid as night fell on some lonely stretch of road.

The shrieking, hair-pulling fights between gypsy girls at Brough Hill were always suspect: such distractions were staged to draw a crowd and provide rich pickings. The technique might be sophisticated, the work of an accomplished dipper, or considerably cruder, like that used commonly by the pickpockets who stalked the unwary at Greenwich Fair about the 1830s: 'A young man . . . was standing with a friend looking at the performances which were going forward, when he suddenly received a violent blow from behind, which forced his hat over his eyes. On raising his hands to his hat both his arms were held forcibly above his head, and his pockets were turned inside out; and on his obtaining the use of his eyes and hands, he found himself minus one sovereign and a half in gold, 15s 6d in silver, besides an excellent silver watch, which, with its appendages, he had purchased the same morning in the Strand for £7.' Pepys, visiting Southwark Fair, and knowing the talents of the so-called 'swell mob', took the precaution of leaving his wallet with an innkeeper before mingling with the revellers.

At Nottingham's Goose Fair, however, the dips might well have an unpleasant surprise: 'Beggars, pickpockets and imposters of every kind are swarming about, little aware that argus-eyed detectives are in the midst of them.' Darker deeds, too, were done at the fair and left their mystery to be uncovered many years later: when Horncastle's Queen's Head Inn (now the Farmers' Club) came to be modified after the Second World War, two skeletons were found under the kitchen floor. The horse fair, it should be said, also had its honest-to-goodness diversions; London's glove-fighters came up for the event – as they did to Lincoln Fair – to take on all-comers and it was here that the legendary Jem Mace, aged only eighteen, made a name for himself by fighting the local unloved champion to a standstill.

Undoubtedly the liquor that lubricated the gaiety also inflamed the passions. Another horse fair, Stow Green in Lincolnshire, was a June affair that persistently lingered into July, John Byng reported, with many publicans erecting 'booths on the green for the sale of beers and spirits; and the fair has usually been visited by so many gypsies, pedlars and other disorderly persons, that the magistrates have found it necessary to send a number of constables to keep the peace'. The gypsy horse-dealers at Sherborne's romantically named Pack Monday Fair frequently fell to arguing with whips; sailors from Plymouth who went to Tavistock Goose Fair for a drunken awayday tangled regularly with the locals in the White Hart, which often ended fair day knee-deep in the debris of their disagreement. To facilitate matters – that is, their rapid ejection – the publican removed the inn's doors during fair days, and as much else that was moveable.

But the fair was also an occasion for feasting, and in that time before the hot-dog and the hamburger satisfied an instant need, the food of the old-time fair was arguably more wholesome. It could not be Poole oysters for all but there was hardly a fair where one could not have a slice off the roasting ox or, in the autumn time, perhaps a sliver of roast goose. At Tavistock's fair between the wars the local auctioneers regularly went one better, yearly treating up to two hundred farmers to a traditional goose dinner in one of the town's hotels. It is true that the fair's catering standards in the past would have horrified today's hygienists. An old shepherd would recall his first time at Findon's big sheep fair, in 1853 'when I was only ten years old. I had to mind the flock up at the end of the field while shepherd went to find the pens he was to use. Near to me was a thing like a round table with hooks all round it. It was set near to a big fire. A pig was cut up and the joints were hung on the hooks. The big turnspit took the joints round and round, and when they were cooked folks bought roast pork for

At Sherborne's Pack Monday Fair gypsy horse-dealers fell to arguing with whips

their dinner.' The memory was confided to the folklorist Barclay Wills and is recorded in that delightful selection from his writings, *The Downland Shepherds*.

Each fair and each region would have its traditional fair-day menu. The Scots drovers finding themselves finally at St Faith's and having slept rough and subsisted for six weeks on oatmeal (which they carried with them in a bag), onions and a lump of cheese – bleeding a beast now and then to make black puddings – fell ravenously on the fair's favourite, roast pork and apple sauce. With Norfolk dumplings, of course. (Long after the fair had faded many local families would not let its anniversary of 17 October pass without such a meal of remembrance.) The quality, however, were more likely to opt for cakes and oysters. Oysters were the recognised treat for the tastebuds at Mitcham Fair; the Green would be littered with oyster stalls and 'cartloads were consumed'. Pickled salmon was also a favourite; slices of 1 lb cost a shilling. At Croydon's fair the fancied dish of the day was oysters and sausages.

Corby Glen's traditional sheep fair fare was stuffed chine, and one could eat well – nay, extravagantly – at Greenwich in 1845: 'ham sandwiches, pigs' trotters, fried sausages, roast turkey, cold and boiled mutton, mock turtle and pea soup'. Refreshment at the fair was taken in salons such as the Crown and Anchor, where the respectable citizenry danced the day out. The gamier fair-goers, however, may have preferred its more exciting rival, the romantic Gipsies' Booth, where the dusky Romany waitresses wore long, dangly ear pendants and were undeniably sexier to look at, their eyes flashing a promise of wicked delights (probably never to be fulfilled) for those who took their fancy. In *Bartholmew Fair*, Johnson's play, much of the action takes place round Ursula's booth, which is selling roast pig. Camberwell Fair, in 1806, having narrowly escaped closure, celebrated, reported *Bells Weekly Messenger* with a grandiose turn of phrase, 'in its wonted splendour. Three rows of booths, stored with customary refreshments, courted the prurient appetites of the multitude. Gingerbread nuts, bearing the favourite names of British victors and victories, everywhere claimed consumption from loyal and patriotic purchasers: the names of St Vincent, Nelson, Abercrombie, Sir Richard Strachan, Trafalgar and the Nile emblazoned every cannister which contained those sweetmeats.'

For Brigg's fair day a special kind of Lincolnshire plum bread was baked, and that, too, is a tradition that lingers on. Hardy's furmity-wife, distilling her brew from wheat husks boiled in milk, is at work on her stove in the big marquee of the fair during the moments of his novel's high drama. Such vast tents, with tables ranging their entire length, were typical of the big fair's concern for the stomachs of the crowd. But refreshment tents would be dotted all over the fairground, some of them with the kind of ale-wife who could say with the furmity seller: 'I've stood in this fair-ground, maid, wife, and widow, these nine and thirty year, and in that time have known what it was to do business with the richest stomachs in the land.' Hardy's old dame's once-grand pavilion is no more, but she can reflect with pride: 'I knew the clergy's taste, the dandy gent's taste; I knew the town's taste, the country's taste. I even knowed the taste of the coarse shameless females.' So perhaps it was at Weyhill. At Brough Hill the big-tent

In the Gypsies' Booth the dusky Romany waitresses were undeniably sexier

menu would run to roast beef and boiled ham with boiled potatoes; in the Methodist tent the fare might be only sandwiches but it came free to the poor at the fair and, as we have seen, without strings or offers to save the soul.

At the big autumn hiring fairs almost without exception the great ox turned and sizzled – whole and publicly, as it did in front of the Garrick Inn at Stratford's well-known mop. In many pub yards, too, other innkeepers would be roasting a pig or two for the revelry that ended the day. As the succulent juices ran on chin and cheek few would have cared to be told that the ox-roast was perhaps a sinister link with that long-past time when the ancient hilltop gatherings were the scene of human sacrifices. Most would want to believe that the hill-sitings were fortuitous, simply places where the old ridgeways met. They may be right. Yet the human fancy has always been excited by the morbid and the bizarre, and in the fair – the old travelling fair especially, with its strange and exotic attractions, its sub-human creatures – such things found their truest expression. In the booths one entered an arena of the macabre, one with more than a whiff of seediness, an underworld of licence.

Defoe hints darkly at Charlton Fair's notoriety but then draws a veil over the general drunkenness as if shocked by what his eyes have seen. Edward Warde, in his *Frolicke to Horn Fair* in 1700 is less fearful of giving offence. Of the fair, he said comprehensively: "Tis a sanctuary for ill manners, a protection for all rudeness, an encouragement of wickedness, a revelling of young libertines, a looking glass of confusions, hurtful to all good manners, and hateful to all good men.' It seems to have been, among other things, a fiesta for transvestites, for the men often wore women's clothes – as well as those horns as headgear. There is an intriguing scandal rumoured to the fair and the reason for its charter in the first place, about the king and the miller's amorous wife, caught in flagrante in their intimate delight by the miller. The culprit, it is said, was King John, who had been hunting in the neighbourhood when he beheld the lady involved. In reparation he gave the miller both the fair and land to go with it. The fair became known as the Horn Fair (horns being the symbol of the cuckold) but was also called St Luke's (after the local church) and held on St Luke's Day, that saint being particularly associated with cattle. The London fair was at its peak and flourishing mightily through the eighteenth and nineteenth centuries, when thousands came by boat – and later by river steamer – dressed as queens and kings and millers. And all of them wearing horns! Those who converged on the South London festival of gender confusion and cross-dressing across Blackheath additionally indulged in a little pre-fair fetishism: crossing the heath the men would lash the women fair-goers with branches of prickly furze. All, they said, was fair at Horn Fair. Nevertheless it greatly perturbed and long infuriated the local clergy and their more sober-minded church-goers.

In Johnson's play, Justice Overdo steps down from his magisterial bench to observe with bewilderment the inanities of his fellow humans in another bacchanalia, Bartholomew Fair. It is an astonishing encounter, but hardly less so than the real event itself. The smell of roasting ox and of the live animals must have been obnoxious, mingling with the other odours of 'this wicked and foul

There is a scandal rumoured of the king and the miller's amorous wife

Bear bites back. The popular 'sport' of bear-baiting was a common spectacle of the old-time fairs and in the capital's Bankside area, and was even enjoyed by the monarchy. Henry Alken (1785–1851) has recorded a moment when one of the bear's tormentors appears doomed. Bear-baiting was outlawed in 1835

fair', not least the sweat of its thronging humanity – it was all too much for that fastidious man John Evelyn. Pepys, though, had a passion for the fair, and given its nature it is easy to guess the reasons for his fascination, one being the voluptuous Countess of Castlemaine. In his dreams the celebrated diarist toyed with the king's mistress – only to wake up in a cold sweat, overwhelmed by his audacity and fervently thankful it was only a dream. At St Bartholomew's he may well have found consolation before the night was out.

It is difficult now to shake off the belief that Smithfield and Bartholomew Fair deserved each other. Outwith the City walls, Smithfield, so long the site of London's livestock market, was a fine, dry, airy space well suited to its purpose and well used to crowds. Before the famous fair had laid claim to it, it was the venue not only for horse markets but for knightly tournaments: in 1357 'great and royal' jousts were held there before the kings of England, Scotland and France; in 1362 the king was present along with English and foreign nobility. Combat was either by single opponents or by knightly teams and the arena would be set conveniently close to the fair. It was one of the early spectator sports with pavilions for the knights and stands for those who came to watch the combatants compete for the end-of-tournament prizes – and perhaps for possession of some gentle lady's garter. The fair, besides, staged archery contests and wrestling and even football. That early chronicler Fitz-Stephen who attended its horse shows, understandably thought London 'the most noble of cities' and 'a pleasant merry place'.

Folk who did not come to Smithfield for either the market or the fair would come for the floggings and the torturing of wrongdoers – and of course, the gruesome executions and the horrendous spectacle of the 'Fires'. Two years after Wallace, the Scottish patriot, had died under the Elms, his brother also perished, along with two brothers of Robert the Bruce. The 'smooth field' was where, in essence and so abruptly, the historic Peasants' Revolt ended. And it is impossible in its precincts to forget those 200-plus unfortunate Protestants who perished for their beliefs in Bloody Mary's sixteenth-century crusade to revive Catholicism – burnt alive while the crowd watched their pitiful agonies. It is, after all, hard to die bravely. But history lurks in every corner and stone of the London market for it has been in its time an arena for almost every activity fit to mention – as well as a few best forgotten.

Smithfield had been an arena for almost every activity fit to mention

It had always attracted the underclass of the capital. Whores, banished from the City, congregated there, particularly in Cock Lane, with its brothels and its personal tragedies for many of the prostitutes once were immigrant Flemish girls who had been unable to find work and instead plied their bodies on market days – and every other day. As dusk fell they sallied forth from Cock Lane, retiring to 'low taverns . . . to receive their gallants'. By 1500 the whole area had become built up and both Smithfield market and its roaring fair were notorious. Among the other fair attractions at this place of 'frays and common fighting' in Pepys's day were bare-fist fighting, badger-baiting, fights between women, between a man and a dog, and cock-fighting was to be had for those who headed over to Clerkenwell. And mingling as always with its milling humanity were the pickpockets.

Wherever a great fair gathered the gullible together, there had always gathered the tricksters and cut-purses and whores. St Ives in its heyday had harlots in droves, apparently under the auspices of the barbers, who brought their booths to the fair. Bury Fair was probably little better, with its ladies of the fringe whose role was in the lower levels of entertainment. Observers of the time leave a certain ambiguity in their reports. We know, however, that widowed Letitia Rookes, whose coffee-house was enjoying a wide reputation in 1748, exploited her two daughters – comely wenches, no doubt – to lure in passing trade. Defoe, visiting the Suffolk fair, is circumspect, unwilling to impute the worst, though it is clear that by then the fair had become an occasion for outrageous flirting between the sexes or even worse, a venue for discreet assignations. Defoe uses the journalist's well-known denial technique so that he can mention the shocking matter without being accused of giving it outright currency: 'It is true Bury Fair, like Bartholomew's Fair, is a fair for diversions more than for trade: and it may be a fair for toys and for trinkets, which the ladies may think fit to lay out some of their money in as they see occasion. But to judge from thence, that the daughters of Norfolk, Cambridgeshire and Suffolk, that is to say, for it cannot be understood any otherwise, the daughters of all the gentry of the three counties come hither to be pick'd up, is a way of speaking I never heard before.'

The worst condemnation was reserved for the capital's fairs, and those on its fringe. London was a city bent on hedonism. In the eighteenth century people were visiting its new pleasure gardens to do more than simply stroll. Privacy was harder to come by then; one garden proprietor went to prison for keeping a disorderly house! In the Georgian capital the bull- and bear-baiting drew the crowds to Bankside; cock-fighting (not illegal until 1849) tournaments were being held throughout the country in inn yards. Boswell visited London's Cockpit and found 'a circular room in the middle of which the cocks fight. It is seated round with rows gradually rising. The cocks, nicely cut and dressed and armed with silver heels, are set down to fight with amazing bitterness and resolution . . . The uproar and noise of betting is prodigious.'

Southwark, in particular, where the roads from Kent, Surrey and Sussex converged, and with its profusion of inns and ale-houses – and just beyond the City limits – had long had a reputation for seedy pleasures. Its countless brothels stood perversely on the estate of the Bishop of Winchester, their unfortunate whores enjoying the designation of 'Winchester geese'. Even in Victorian London the oldest profession plied as enthusiastically as ever – there were an estimated 80,000 practitioners in 1859, advertising the city's dreadful poverty. They collected like taxi-cabs in ranks in such areas as the Strand, the Haymarket, near the Bank of England, in Ratcliff Highway and Shadwell High Street. In such a licentious climate the 'escape valve' of the fair could not but be an excuse for the wildest excess. When fire struck the inhabitants of Southwark during the fair of 1689 some considered the extensive damage an overdue judgement brought on them by allowing the 'Disorderly Booths which were created in this Fair, and by the just Vengeance of God for permitting such pregnant cause of Licentiousness.'

By the nineteenth-century height of its infamy Greenwich Fair's drinking booths had become 'places of disrepute, shunned by the middle classes'. Protesting its desire to defend the right of the working man to his moment of leisure at the fair, the *British Mercury* was deploring the fact that far from it being the resort of the working classes – the labourer, the mechanic, the ploughboy – the fair-goers were the 'profligate scum of an overgrown metropolis, thrown together for the purposes of unrestrained vice and debauchery. The lower classes for whom such scenes provide amusement are the pickpocket, the prostitute, the needy stroller, the gin-dealer, the gaming sharper and such worshipful tribes of mankind; and the sports carried on are drunkenness, obscenity, roguery, gaming and swindling.' Another observer, in 1819, also put the case for what must have been a temporary fall in attendance, citing 'the corrupt taste of the lower classes, and their increasing fondness towards habits of profligacy'. All the 'low tippling houses' were filled with men and women drinking 'bad porter and worse gin' and dancing to 'vile fiddle-scrapers, while mobs of sailors, soldiers, common women, and pickpockets, were collected round the show booths, and annoyed all who had occasion to pass along'. Even in the Frost Fair of 1683/4 Roger Morrice laments, 'The concourse and all manner of debauchery upon the Thames continued upon the Lord's Day.' Among the so-called Frost Fair ballads of that time was one which could not have been more explicit: 'Oh London! Th'adst better have built new Bordellos'.

What was true of the great central fairs was echoed in those of the fringe. Viewing Camberwell's wanton descent into pleasure the rhymester George Alexander Stevens (in an alliterative cascade) saw a scenario in the still rural village of orchards and

Drinking booths had become places of disrepute shunned by the middle classes

smallholdings of 'shrill fiddling, sharp fighting and shouting and shrieking'. The motley of the fair included 'Pimps, pawnbrokers, strollers, fat landladies, sailors, Bawds, bailiffs, jilts, jokers, thieves, tumblers and taylors'. Edmonton's statute fair, in fine weather drawing crowds of 30,000, in time was a 'fair perverted to the use of holiday people, chiefly of the lower ranks . . . and is a source of great moral injury'. Next-door Enfield was obviously little better. The Market Place, from the parish pump to church rails, complained one correspondent with indignation, 'was filled with a monster booth of which the least said the better; we will merely remark that persons least expected in such places were sitting at the entrance, and young children, late at night, sleeping through scenes of revelry that morality shudders to witness'.

Young children slept through scenes of revelry that morality shudders to witness

Even famous Fairlop, started with such open-handed kindness, degenerated badly. In 1839, just before it cleaned up its image and strictly (for a time) confined itself to one day, missionaries on duty on Fairlop Sunday, a continuation of the Friday fair with a crowd of up to 60,000, were shocked by what they saw. 'Among the booths one counted 108 places where drink was sold; and many vans were supplied with beer from the booths by men who went with jars into the wood to sell it. There were numerous shows; and gambling was practised in the most open and impudent manner. The missionaries counted 72 gaming tables . . . They also observed that temporary places were erected in the wood for the filthiest crimes.'

Alas, by 1876 the fair had slipped back into its old ways and the East End's temperance movement was attempting reform. It was on the home trek especially that temptation lay in wait. A movement that saw drink only in the most distempered terms could be relied on to oppose strongly the idea of fair merry-making, and it did: 'Fairlop Friday is the great drinking bout of the year for East Londoners . . . upon the night of Fairlop Friday the Mile End road presents a scene which taxes the ablest pens to describe. Here some two hundred and fifty thousand people are gathered to witness the return of the Boats, of which there are never less than two and sometimes six . . . It is now about half-past ten, and presently the unceasing hubbub deepens into a roar, echoed and re-echoed – subsiding and swelling – as the first Fairlop boat approaches. Look down the road now, at the mass of moving heads; at the thousands of firelit faces; at the tremulous heaving of the vast crowd! Hark! to the sounds of brazen trumpets, of harsh voices, of screams, of yells, of cheers; all is tumult and discord. Gaze about you – first at these devils incarnate, inflamed with liquid fire, and then at these poor little mortals who were never children but were born cunning old men and women, rich in their knowledge of the world. Groups of swaggering youths, arm-in-arm, cigar in mouth, and singing so-called "popular" songs, pass you; girls, ragged, dirty, with a sensual look in their faces, follow. And what have we here? Respectable coats on backs belonging to gentlemen – at any rate they would have us consider them so. Yes, gentlemen! City gentlemen who have come down to the East to see the "fun" and behaving as wantonly, as loosely, as the lowest of the low! For them there is no excuse. . . .'

The pen itself is an able one, one which Dickens or Priestley might well have acknowledged, shackled perhaps to an unyielding cause but no doubt truthful in its portrait of the detritus of fair day, whether it was Greenwich, Camberwell,

Stepney or Bow. It throws into context the contemporary concern of society and explains the growing nineteenth-century revulsion with the old-time fair. Away from the capital the spirit of the fair may have been less threatening and provoked a little less censure. Nevertheless, its high emotions and uninhibited excitements were always a potent mixture.

Each September those much-mentioned (and maybe maligned) women of pleasure made themselves available, as the saying goes, by visiting Yarmouth's Herring Fair, and certainly even the great Stourbridge had its scandalous side. There was more than a degree of high spirits in the initiation ceremonies that took place at many of the old fairs and Stourbridge was no exception. Horse fair day, ending the great fair, began at the Robin Hood Inn with a 'christening' ceremony that climaxed with its main attraction, the large bowl of punch, paid for almost certainly by that year's novitiates.

The Cambridgeshire fair had another name, in the circumstances not inappropriate given its reputation as a rendezvous for transient liaisons. Though reporters like Defoe hinted at its fringe curriculum, they were careful of a frankness that might alienate their readers. E. Ward avoided all such sophistry in his account of 1700, *A Step to Stir-Bitch Fair*, and makes clear his low opinion not only of the fair's crowds but of the dealers who attended it. He is alarmingly candid about the merchants' motives for being there. Men off the marital leash may have been easy prey, though most, in Ward's view, were by no means fighting temptation. 'Their pretence is coming down to meet their customers; tho' it's plain by their Loitering, they have little else to do but to Drink, Smoke, and Whore, and to help support the fair in its Ancient Custom of Debauchery.'

One thing in particular that would have struck the casual visitor to the Cambridgeshire fair was the extraordinary number of London hackney carriages that had come to ply for hire there. Any regular fair-goer would have explained their purpose: usually the 'fare' behind each carriage's discreetly drawn blinds would be a lady of pleasure entertaining a client to the gently rocking motion of the cab as it wheeled through the country lanes. The fare rate for such a novel boudoir was 1s 6d, the service, as always, a matter for negotiation.

Vigilantes patrolled hourly to combat the fair's nightly capitulation to pleasure

At Stourbridge, the university – sharing authority over the fair – took a high moral stance on such goings-on. It was the proctors' job to 'seek out and punish lewd women' of whom there were obviously such a goodly number. If caught they were held in the Spinning House – the house of correction – to await chastisement from the town-crier, whose conditions of employment included the onerous duty to 'discipline the Ladies of Pleasure with his whip'. The university, as a matter of concern, appointed a corps of eight vigilantes in its effort to combat the fair's nightly capitulation to pleasure: they did hourly patrols in their bright red coats while warning all and sundry of their approach with shouts of 'Look about you there!', presumably giving strumpet and client time to reach a satisfactory if hurried conclusion of their business before safely eluding discovery.

CHAPTER THIRTEEN

FINALE FOR THE OLD-TIME FAIRS

The notoriety of the fair, the sleazy side that brought prostitutes to town in platoons to sell their favours among the seedier booths or in the scrub of the common with drink-sodden punters, had by the nineteenth century made it a thing of censure bringing widespread protest and a demand for its suppression from a Victorian society generations distant from the old earthy, rural communities that had seen nothing very strange in such human behaviour. An astonishing number of fairs would disappear during the century in what were, perhaps, the final, jaded days of Merrie England and the bawdy pleasures it had enjoyed – or at least long countenanced. The 1871 Fairs Act helped the movement and that decade accelerated the closures. That astute clergyman, the Revd N.F. Hulbert, who made a detailed survey of Somerset's fairs, summed up the situation with some regret: 'as with all decaying institutions, that which was least wholesome remained to the end, and enabled the last factor to operate against its [the fair's] survival. The growing sophistication and increased refinement of manners of English life found it impossible to gain adequate enjoyment from the time-honoured fun of the fair, or to tolerate the accompanying licence and disorder which was natural to an earlier time.'

Yet the fair had always had its scenes of saturnalia and there were many, even more relevant, reasons why the century would witness such a dramatic decline in its fortunes. The effects would be deep and far-reaching, inflicting vast change on society and on rural communities especially. History had always borne heavily on the fairs of Old England: the Black Death at its height in the fourteenth century had put a curb on such events; the Hundred Years War with France, fought essentially to preserve our wool trade with Flanders, severely interrupted trading connections with Europe's landmass, dealing an injurious blow to the great fairs, one from which few of them ever fully recovered; the Dissolution from 1536 – when Henry VIII sold off something like one-fifth of the land, from the monasteries into the hands of his favourites – devastated many more as they found themselves unable to rise from the ashes; all were affected, like today's trade fairs, by the fluctuating economic health of the nation.

Growing industrialisation and with it the drift to the cities would modify and sometimes end the vital role of many of the old country fairs; better roads would let buyers deal directly with manufacturers; commerce, liberated first by the cutting of canals that would take commodities such as cheese, butter and malt more easily to new and distant markets, and then by the coming of the railways, would redraw the old trading map of England. And this time it would be for ever.

The railways would fracture the tight texture of that rural society for which the fair had been the hub of the year; they broke families and dispersed them far from the place that had nourished their generations; soon they would bring in the cheap imported food products that would drive many small farmers to the wall. As for many more, the rapid distribution they offered was the final blow for Yarmouth's once-famous Herring Fair. But they gave life as well as took it away, diverting trade overnight from long-established markets and re-routing it to other fairs closer to the tracks, which, for a time at least, prospered greatly; they betrayed the local craft industries, offering them a wider market while bringing them fierce competition; they brought town crowds from the 'satanic mills' to enliven and change the whole character of the bucolic occasion, seldom for the better; and they took the country-dweller, whose option had been only the ponderous carrier's cart, ever more swiftly into the city.

Towns had always been jealous of the fair's impact on their trade: during Horncastle's horse fair the town's normal trading came to a virtual halt. Now the situation had gone into reverse: no longer did goods come seeking a buyer, the buyer went to seek *them* as the spreading ribbons of metal – the unstoppable conquest of rail – linked each town with its neighbour and the industrial hinterland beyond.

The steamship, followed so quickly by the railroad, spelt the end for the hardy drovers as fresh meat was whisked overnight from local slaughter-houses to the capital and turnip-fed fatstock sales took a stronger stance in the regional farming economies. The Galloway Gate, that ancient ridgeway route for cattle beast and packhorse train and pedlar man – with its 'stations' where inns served the ever-passing trade and blacksmiths stood ready by their anvils – that stretched down from the south-west of Scotland through Cumbria into Lancashire, would fall eerily silent. Farming, meanwhile, after the euphoric boom of the Napoleonic years, had slumped badly and abysmal prices made a mockery of the old fair's bonhomie. The auction mart, pioneered in Scotland's Border country but hindered by tax impositions until 1845, was fast and efficient, and a man went home with the price of his beasts in his pocket, even if it was not the price he had wanted – and maybe not what he might have secured at Brough Hill or Stagshawbank. It grievously cut the banter and thrust of the guileful negotiation that had always been part and parcel of the fair, the thing that was for most of the old farmers and dealers the very essence of the occasion. Against the old noise and clamour the auction sale was a cold, colourless thing, but it would rapidly move south, dealing a cruel *coup de grâce*.

Crewe, with its famous rail junction, would come suddenly to prominence and have no fewer than ten cattle fairs up and running by 1860. Rugeley, with

Against the old noise and clamour, the auction sale was a cold, colourless thing

The bitter end. The final and farcical act for Stourbridge Fair as the Clerk of the Peace and the Mayor of Cambridge defiantly proclaim the fair in 1933, nearly eighty years after it had effectively ceased, ludicrously reflecting the antagonism that had always existed between town and gown

two annual fairs dealing desultorily in horses (among other livestock), suddenly flared into significance with an important horse fair, entirely due to its position by the rail trunk route through to Holyhead; the trains brought in fine Irish stock and in turn the military purchasers for them, not only from the British Army but from those on the Continent. Other fairs managed to survive by reasons of need or their geography, Barnet, Appleby and ancient Brough Hill among them, though the latter's trade had turned to horses and had been curtailed officially to just one day. And Barnet would have to withstand a bid by the local lord of the manor to have it closed, following a setback in 1871 when High Barnet station was built where the raffish races were held and the further decided inconvenience of having the railway routed right across its fair field, thus altering the character of the event. But there were compensations: those singing Welshmen could now load their animals at the railhead and ship them direct to the fair – and some more of them could stay at home. Barnet may not have been ungrateful. In time it would become largely a pleasure affair. Horncastle was still bringing in copers from far and wide. Northallerton, on the other hand, slid swiftly from its eminence to be almost a local market: the town must have felt a deep sense of betrayal as its neighbour Bedale edged it into

'A Border Fair.' This vivid canvas by John Ritchie is a remarkable record of the old country fair and the folk who flocked to it. His subject is Stagshawbank, primarily for sheep but with every other kind of livestock and commodity needed in the early years of this century by a remote community in the lee of Hadrian's Wall

oblivion. Generally, by the mid-nineteenth century the fair's drift into decline was deepening. Even that 'great mart' and important port King's Lynn had fallen on hard times. Once its six-day event had brought traders from all corners of the kingdom.

The 'great fair' as an institution, as a pillar of the country's economy, had probably passed its high plateau with the end of the Middle Ages; now it was unravelling the social fabric. If we can take Hardy's Weydon to more or less accurately reflect Weyhill, Susan Henchard's return in *The Mayor of Casterbridge*, after nearly two decades, is to a fair in which 'the pens for sheep, the tie-ropes for horses, were about half as long as they had been. The stalls for tailors, hosiers, coopers, linen-drapers, and other such trades had almost disappeared'. Cobbett, among others, would chart the reason for that and for the demise of a once-important occasion and, in 1826, point a bitter finger at the forces responsible. Having eulogised the rise of the turnip through Hampshire, he turns in his travels to lamenting the changes now afflicting the countryside:

After quitting Soberton Down, we came up a hill leading to Hambledon, and turned off to our left, to bring us down to Mr Goldsmith's at West End . . . at about a mile from the village of Hambledon. A village it now is; but it was formerly a considerable market-town, and it had three fairs in the year. There is now not even the name of the market left, I believe; and the fairs amount to little more than a couple or three gingerbread-stalls, with dolls and whistles for children. If you go through the place, you see that it has been a considerable town. The church tells the same story; it is now a tumble-down rubbishy place; it is partaking in the fate of all those places which were formerly a sort of rendezvous for persons who had things to buy and things to sell. Wens have devoured market-towns and villages; and shops have devoured markets and fairs; and this too, to the infinite injury of the most numerous classes of the people. Shop-keeping, merely as shop-keeping, is injurious to any community. What are the shop and the shop-keeper for? To receive and distribute the produce of the land. There are other articles, certainly; but the main part is the produce of the land. The shop must be paid for; the shop-keeper must be kept; and the one must be paid for and the other must be kept by the consumer of the produce; or, perhaps, partly by the consumer and partly by the producer. When fairs were very frequent, shops were not needed. A manufacturer of shoes, of stockings, of hats; of almost anything that man wants, could manufacture at home in an obscure hamlet, with cheap house-rent, good air, and plenty of room. He need pay no heavy rent for shop; and no disadvantages from confined situation; and, then, by attending three or four or five or six fairs a year, he sold the work of his hands, unloaded with a heavy expense attending the keeping of a shop. He would get more for ten shillings in booth at a fair or market, than he would get in a shop for ten or twenty pounds. Of course he could afford to sell the work of his hands for less; and thus a greater portion of their earnings remained with those who raised the food and clothing from the land. I had an instance of this in what occurred to myself at Weyhill fair. When I was at Salisbury, in September, I wanted to buy a whip. It was a common hunting-whip, with a hook to it to pull open gates with, and I could not get it for less than seven shillings and sixpence. This was more than I had made up my mind to give, and I went on with my switch. When we got to Weyhill fair, George had made shift to lose his whip some time before, and I had made him go without one by way of punishment. But now, having come to the fair, and seeing plenty of whips I bought him one, just such a one as had been offered me in Salisbury for seven and sixpence, for four and sixpence; and, seeing the man with his whips afterwards, I thought I would have one myself; and he let me have it for three shillings.

Cobbett's impatience is evident: 'Does not every one see, in a minute, how this exchanging of fairs and markets for shops creates idlers and traffickers; creates those locusts, called middle-men, who create nothing, who add to the value of nothing, who improve nothing, but who live in idleness and who live well, too, out of the labour of the producer and the consumer . . . The fair and the market lay every thing open: going to either, you see the state of things at once.' It was a cry against the wind, and the crusty old warrior would have known it. All the same, his claim holds true, for such was indeed the case at England's old country fairs. For centuries they had been central to the functioning of rural life. It was here, in the dealing round the fair's sheep and

Bargaining round the cattle and sheep pens set farming's price parameters

cattle pens or in the horse market, that the day's bargaining would effectively set the price parameters for livestock and commodities, often for the whole year ahead. They apprised the countryman of his financial worth. Now, however, the stock prices Cobbett encountered merely reflected the depressed state of the nation's farming: in an earlier foray, in 1822, he had visited Chertsey's September fair 'for horses, cattle and pigs. I did not see any sheep. Every thing was exceedingly dull. Cart colts, two or three years old, were selling for less than a third of what they had sold for in 1813. The cattle were of an inferior description to be sure; but the price was low almost beyond belief. Cows, which would have sold for £15 in 1813, did not get buyers at £3. I had no time to inquire much about pigs, but a man told me that they were dirt-cheap.' Such was the abyss into which English farming had been plunged. The rural fair was scarcely in better shape.

The shops as ready, year-round centres of supply would deal the final blow, but already there was widespread defection from the fair, doubtless by men who could not bear the stark message its prices conveyed to them, but also by others who had lost faith in its role as the beating heart of the community. Though it might still set commodity values, and though such knowledge was as vital then as it is to the farmer now, these men in future would more and more seek their commodity prices – whether for hops or hired help – from the columns of their local newspaper. Some of those fairs once so important to the health of the countryside would slough off their past to assume new identities; more than a few would be so sadly diminished as to become purely pleasure occasions. Some indeed were already so. Discreetly and somewhere along the way, a few would manage to salvage a little of their character and transform themselves into agricultural shows.

Some would simply fade, unmourned, from the social calendar. Many were already a memory in the rural year. County by county they would disappear: Somerset, for example, once so flush with fairs – it had 180 in 1729, and later, it was rumoured, up to 300 – would be down to 34 by the 1930s. (Somerset, oddly, in spite of its impressive spectrum, would never have a 'great' occasion.) Most of the West Country fairs in fact functioned, sometimes faded shadows of their old importance, into the nineteenth century. Most of the strictly county fairs would shrink in time to the status of markets. And one by one even the burnished names would fall away into the void of history, stars extinguished from the firmament.

One by one the burnished names of the past fell away into the void of history

The extinction of the capital's fairs had a sad inevitability. Southwark's fair of Our Lady had been an early casualty, causing outrage by its excesses and debauchery. There had been complaints of 'irregularities' and disorders by 1678; it had ceased to be a trading fair even by 1733 and given itself over entirely to pleasures which a decade later were still continuing for fourteen days, when it was ordered to be 'cried down' by the bellman, apparently with little success. Hogarth in his famous depiction has fun with the fair, perhaps, like the novelist, seeing it as a metaphor (or parable) for life itself. The fair where the booth-keepers had collected money for the prisoners in the nearby Marshalsea, where

Playing to the galleries. Southwark's Tabard Inn took the overspill of Our Lady's Fair in its courtyard; in the eighteenth century plays were performed there. Chaucer's pilgrims rested there on the night before leaving for Canterbury and later it became a carrier's depot sending out waggons to destinations all over the south of England. Its proud story ended in 1873 with the dawn of the railway age

the conditions were beyond the primitive and where a debtor could be incarcerated for his lifetime, was finally abolished by order of the Court of Common Council in 1762; by 1874 the renowned Tabard Inn, where galleried bedrooms ringed the inn yard, and which was so much a part of the fair's wild revelry, would also have gone, demolished before the ever-onward march of the railway. Like many other such inns throughout the country it no longer had a role to play.

There was confrontation in close-by Camberwell by 1806, when Surrey magistrates declared themselves 'disposed to use all lawful means for suppressing the fair' but found, unexpectedly, resistance from the lord of the manor, who made clear an intention to hold the fair, even should force be necessary to do so. The magistrates, miffed by their failure we may be sure, were forced to confine their powers to the prevention of such behaviour as they were allowed to rule on. In this fashion, they claimed, they had suppressed gaming, forced the inns for once to close at a reasonable hour and 'prohibited Dancing at the Public House, a practice which in former Fairs at this place has led numberless females to ruin'. They had, they further asserted, 'protected the inhabitants against a lawless rabble which without such Interposition much Mischief was to be apprehended. They have in short prevented the Fair from being what it has hitherto been of late years, a scene of terror and unbounded licentiousness during the whole of the nights. Their Interposition has moreover had the effect of reducing the duration of evil to three days to which the Claim of its Continuance is Confined.' (Catch the anger in those capitals!) The magistrates, sniffily, made the further point that fairs were supposed to be marts of trade not 'sources of Dissipation and riot'. And Camberwell had no need of the former. Their adversary, the lord of the manor, one Dr Letsom, apparently felt that the banning of the fair was likely to lead to a riot greater than any inconvenience the fair would produce and threatened that if the magistrates persisted in their opposition he would chop down every tree on Camberwell Green and, what's more, cover the Green with cottages for the labouring poor.

The fair was saved. But only for a time. In 1823 the local newspaper was reporting: 'A numerous gang of London pickpockets assembled at Camberwell Fair . . . all committed the most audacious attacks on the persons and property of the company.' The following year complaints to the petty sessions court by local residents sought an end to it and questioned the legality of the fair, along with that of Peckham's. But when the end came it was truly machiavellian. The local gentry, to whom the fair had become a 'nuisance', in 1856 raised £3,000 by subscription (a not inconsiderable amount then), formed an abolition committee which bought the rights to the event (for considerably less) from the lord of the manor, obtained a hundred years' lease of the Green for a peppercorn rent – and promptly surrendered to the Crown its right to hold the fair. And just to be sure, the abolition committee declared the fair to be illegal. They were in the nick of time: notice of the ban was posted only a month before the August date of the fair. The committee throughout had struck a high moral tone, alleging that the community had too long 'enjoyed a most unenviable celebrity – namely that of attracting to itself, for several days every year, during the Fair, much of the vice and pollution of the worst haunts of the Metropolis'. With suitable disdain, and reflecting society's generally changing attitude to the fair, it added that the event was 'a stigma upon the very civilisation of the age'.

So ended, officially, Camberwell Fair's highly chequered history (first attempts at its revival came five years later). Its suppression was part of a capitalwide move against the unbridled hedonism of the fair. Greenwich's turn would come a year later. It, too, had outlived middle-class tolerance; magistrates there, too, believed 'that the enjoyments of the festival involved much disorder and impropriety'. But nobody, claimed the local *Mercury*, was keener to suppress this 'scene of tumult and profligacy' than the good people of Greenwich themselves. There were moves towards suppression as early as 1825. Magistrates and parochial officials made their best endeavours, invoking the lack of a charter for the fair, a common tactic, and concluding that the fair was therefore illegal. Stallholders were warned not to return the following year, a threat that was comprehensively ignored: workmen went ahead in the run-up to the Whit fair, erecting the booth for the famous Crown and Anchor tavern even as bills were being posted in the streets proclaiming the magistrates' intention to 'put down' the fair and prohibit the setting up of such booths. Richardson continued with the erection of his usual theatrical booth, along with the proprietors of drinking

Camberwell's suppression was part of a capital-wide move against London's fairs

Show on the road. Like the earlier strolling players who walked the ridgeways, the itinerant entertainers of the nineteenth century took their acts round the summer fairs and villages, hoping their talents would elicit appreciative coin. The observer is the painter Francis Barraud (1879–1924)

and dancing booths and of the gingerbread stalls. On the Saturday specially sworn constables demanded that they all be dismantled. Richardson stood firm; others followed his lead. The impresario's resolve buckled, however, when the officers threatened to tear down his 'establishment' and he left, with many of the other showmen, for the less contentious reaches of Wandsworth Fair in a few days' time. The Crown and Anchor owners took a tougher stance and were finally left in peace – along with the roundabout, some swings and no fewer than twelve other drinking booths. It was a mellow fair, and not to give offence the Crown and Anchor closed on the knell of midnight and turned its 4,000 dancers out to the night. And for once the fair seems to have been devoid of trouble. But the showmen had a powerful card to play. They had been in the habit of subscribing to the parish funds. Such donations in the past had been misapplied, they now claimed, prompting an inquiry which seems to have silenced for some time all further threats of closure.

By 1839, however, the fair had become somewhat ragged, more down-at-heel – 'straggling', as one observer noted sadly, 'the booths reaching almost to Deptford Creek'. All the same, in 1848 it was thronged as never before. Forty steamers were engaged, each making seven or eight trips during the day, each carrying at least 400 people at a time and in some cases up to 1,000 or even 1,500. Yet these human cargoes, hell-bent on pleasure at all costs, along with those swarming there by rail, were adding to the fair's problems. There were those already prophesying its doom. There was increasingly a sense of déjà vu. As a contemporary report confessed: 'Some may imagine that the entertainments have changed their character, to keep pace with the improving spirit of the age. Not in the least: there are the same booths, the same giants, the same nut-targets. Not a single additional character has made his appearance among the unwholesome *dramatis personae* of the gingerbread stalls. The Learned Pig has not acquired a solitary trick within the last forty years. There is no alteration in Richardson's play-bill; not a single new feature in the way of pasteboard noses.' The confession, ironically intended to convey the fair's perennial appeal, falls sadly short of its aim. The fair in fact was moribund, as were so many others. In 1856 it was reported to be 'little more than a confusion of unwashed and shabbily dressed people, presenting a mobbish appearance'. Greenwich's fair, a pioneer of the circus and wild-beast shows, was suppressed a year later – but not before being generally (and possibly unfairly) credited with establishing a new dimension, at Easter 1835: that great showman's innovation, the merry-go-round, the Voyage Volante – four 'boats' hung from timber beams connected to a central mast – cranked from underneath by two muscled, sweating men.

Charlton's disgraceful Horn Fair, whose start had been so unpropitious, would go out in 1872 not with a bang but in a slow whimper, reduced apparently to a 'poor goose fair where none but the meaner people repair'. By 1820 this 'Frolicke', described as 'an encouragement of wickedness, a revelling of young libertines', had moved from Charlton's Green to the east of the parish and the site called Fairfields. Its charter was finally rescinded 'for the public good' by an Order in Council.

The capital's May Fair, an earlier casualty, was in trouble from its inception with a chorus of disapproving voices demanding its closure. An attempt to do so by the constables of St Martin's met drawn swords and left one of their number dead behind them. A few years later it was thought to be finally suppressed but again sprang to life, as many of the old fairs did in fitful revivals. Its outrageous saturnalia was finally quelled in 1764, leaving only its rowdy name to become fashionable, after the Earl of Coventry took exception to its disturbance at the rear of his Piccadilly town house and local residents complained equally bitterly of its lewd and drunken scenes. In 1820 St Edward's Fair, that scourge of Westminster, was banished to Tothill Fields, and finally to Rochester Row, before dying out entirely, having offended for too long.

The age of the colourful Frost Fairs came to a close in 1825 when they demolished Old London Bridge with its many piers; it had long led the raffish clientele of the capital to the city's main brothel area. Peckham's occasion beside the Kentish Drovers' Inn was 'put down' in 1827, quite possibly with good reason (the famous pub itself closed only in 1954). For the confusion of fairs that brought the East Enders out in their clamouring hundreds of thousands from drab factories and drab lives to the Easter and Whitsun holiday sunshine the end came gradually and – true to form – confusedly. Bow Fair, after its eventful career, fell foul of an Act of Parliament in 1823; the Act gave the justices power to suppress any fair within 10 miles of London if it were not held by 'charter, prescription, or other lawful authority'. When the

The notorious Horn Fair would die out with a slow whimper not with a bang

Last orders. A sad ending for The Kentish Drovers, Peckham's famous drovers' inn and their last stop on the way to the capital's markets. It despondently sold its last ale and shut its doors in 1954 – to become a shop

petty sessions court summonsed one John Giles of Bow, the occupier of the fairground, to show by what authority the event was held, Giles could cite only the law of ancient custom (his lease had in any case expired) and it was declared illegal, with warning notices pinned to all the church doors in the parish. The manor itself was in the hands of the receiver. In all this there may well have been a grave injustice done to the Cockney fair that sought to ape its May Fair better, for its pedigree, though tortured certainly, may have been unimpeachable – if it was in fact the nomadic fair granted to the Earl of Cleveland back in 1664, and, according to Hughson's *Circuit of London*, that 'denominated Bow Fair'. A news report of 1823 succinctly records the fair's demise:

SUPPRESSION OF BOW FAIR–Yesterday, pursuant to adjournment, a Petty Sessions was held at Lambeth Street Office, calling on the proprietors of certain land in the parish of Bow, to show by what authority they held Bow fair annually. It being admitted that neither charter nor prescription could be produced, sanctioning the holding of the fair, the Magistrates declared it to be illegal, and expressed their determination of suppressing it for the future.

They may have been less than successful. A news item of 1825 states blandly and without further explanation: 'Bow Fair held annually in Whitsun week was attended by vast throngs from London, and was generally the scene of inebriation and dissoluteness.' A later writer in the letter columns of the *East London Advertiser* in 1900 was determinedly claiming that Bow Fair was 'put down within the last twenty years': he was recalling a fair held on the Thursday of Whitsun week that 'was long a favourite resort of the holiday makers of London'. Official or not, it seems unlikely that the Cockneys would have surrendered their annual knees-up.

Stepney fell foul of similar laws and the Police Act when the owner of land near Bancroft's Hospital in Mile End Road was summonsed to show right and title to the fair in 1855. The event was declared unlawful. Old residents would remember its last flickering years 'around 1860'. Here, too, Victorian rectitude, long outraged, had finally triumphed.

Fairlop's celebration fared better, though it was a close-run thing. In 1836 there was an attempt before Ilford petty sessions to quell the July 'outrage' which now made its weekends disorderly. It had changed deplorably from the quiet feasting of Daniel Day's time. Drunken orgies and scenes of hideous dissipation were alleged – though the event was defended as being no worse than the other merry-makings of bucolic England. Its boisterousness was curbed in 1840 when the London City Missions, appalled, succeeded in having it legally abolished – except that it continued as an annual Friday rendezvous for the East End watermen and blockmakers, better, it is said, than it had ever been. But at least the Sunday was no longer being defiled. Fairlop's feast petered out only at the end of the nineteenth century; the famous Boat was taken to the forest for the last time about the end of the 1880s, bringing an end to those riotous shenanigans along the Mile End Road. In its final throes the fair inhabited different sites: first, near the Old Maypole (accustomed to housing 2,000 in earlier days); a field at Fencepiece Farm and finally, a patch of ground near Chigwell's Bald Hind Inn.

Yet they did not go unlamented into the void of history, those old fairs of East London. Far from it. An *Elegy on the Death of Bow Fair* in 1823 would be a requiem for all those colourful if dissipated occasions condemned and extinguished by the Victorian age:

> The Bow Bell tolls the knell of Bow Fair fun,
> And Richardson winds slowly out of town;
> Poor old 'young Saunders' sees his setting son,
> And Gyngell pulls his red tom-tawdery down.

Fairlop's fair-day brought riotous shenanigans the length of the Mile End Road

No more shall cockeys don their Sunday coats,
Stepney, Brook Green or brighter Bow to fill.
No folk shall row to Greenwich Hill in boats,
And roll in couples down One Tree Hill!

No lucky bags, no drums, no three-hand reels,
No cocks in breeches, no tobacco sots!
No more shall Wapping learn to dance quadrilles,
Or shake a hornpipe 'mid the pewter pots.

Outwards, doubtless, went the old showmen, to the fairs round the fringe, to Epping Forest with its woodland, grassland, heathland, bog, lakes and ponds, dedicated in 1882 by Queen Victoria 'to the use and enjoyment of my people for all time'. It would continue to provide an escape from those mean and dreary streets. So, too, would Wanstead's Flats, still with three fairs a year – as has Hampstead Heath at Easter, spring and summer bank holidays, which can bring anything up to 100,000 people on to the heath. Blackheath again has two, held on the old common, after its original May and October fairs had to be suppressed for familiar reasons in 1872.

Each September Barnet's pony fair still makes a nostalgic nod to the past

Barnet's fair has suffered by slow cuts. The races stopped in 1871 when High Barnet's station took occupation of the field where they were held – much to the chagrin of Father Bampfield, a local priest who, like not a few of his cloth, had a soft spot for the horses. But the horse fair continued – despite attempts to abolish it – with most of its old panache in fields on either side of the intruder, giving a toll on every beast to the manor. Barnet was a thorough-going fair right up to 1868, when it was stricken by cattle murrain, a disaster from which it never quite recovered. In 1888 it found itself again facing extinction when the lord of the manor petitioned parliament for the fair's abolition – only to find himself vigorously opposed by the local townspeople, who protested to the Home Secretary that the loss of the 50,000 head of cattle being traded yearly (and they may have crunched the numbers in their own favour) would seriously imperil local prosperity. The townspeople prevailed, though building development would bring a change of site. Today a huddle of horse-lovers still gather for what is left of the old horse fair, now held in the suburb's Mays Lane, where it coincides with the borough's longer pleasure fair in Barnet Lane. In a nostalgic nod to the past each September a few animals are still trotted up and down the lane in the old, time-honoured way.

As the cattle sickness struck Barnet, nearby Enfield Fair was in trouble of a different kind, its immorality such a source of concern that the local tradesmen and residents joined the magistrates and clergy in their petition. Their plaint was familiar. The fair, according to one report, 'was inundated with a crowd of the lowest classes of the population of London . . . for three days business was brought to a standstill, there were such disgraceful scenes of debauchery and drunkenness that the residents and tradesmen of the town were almost unanimous in urging suppression'. The fair had 'for many years ceased to answer

Way out West. The Shufflebottoms took their cowboy cavalcade round the country's fairs, including King's Lynn Mart (seen here in 1926, with the family members of the troupe in costume), perpetuating the then not-so-distant skills and folk myths of the wild prairie

any legitimate purpose of trade'. They presented their petition to the Duchy of Lancaster, the Secretary of State and the Commissioner of the Metropolitan Police – and the September fair was duly declared unlawful. Or, as a later historian, David Pam, put it: 'Thus was Enfield Fair killed off, while it was still at the height of its popularity, by a holy alliance of nonconformist and evangelical zeal.' An act of bravado the following year in attempting to perpetuate the fair proved ill-judged, one of the defiant booth-holders being thrown into prison for a day for contempt – and maybe to emphasise that in Enfield, the wild days of the fair were over. Edmonton's occasion similarly offended around the same time and just as abruptly faded for ever from the fairs calendar.

But there were survivors, notably Pinner and Mitcham. Neither escaped the puritans' scrutiny. As early as 1829 some of the principal tenants of Pinner, and older and highly respectable residents, were writing to Lord Northwick protesting themselves 'much hurt by an imperious and arbitrary order from the Magistrates of Edgware to put down Pinner Fair'. They made clear an intention 'to defend their public right in every legal way'. The fair continued. In 1873, under the Fairs Act of 1871, the then Lady Northwick, claiming ownership of the fair, consented to its abolition. But again the fair – a mop into the present century – continued. In 1894 some of the residents again approached the magistrates with a petition but so inflamed the feeling of other locals they quickly recanted. The folk of Pinner had defended their fair bravely: it still clogs the main streets yearly and spills into the side-roads.

Mitcham of the flawed pedigree and the golden key has triumphed over comparable vicissitudes. There was a bid to suppress the by then mainly toy fair in 1905 as the Common's conservators blanched before the imminent extension of the capital's tram system to the village – and the trouble this would bring. Here again the Home Secretary's consent was sought but the showmen, undaunted, claimed the Upper Green as usual and gained the villagers' support – provided the fair in future was held on the Common. With that proviso, the Home Secretary, too, acquiesced. But the fair never moved. The First World War intervened and Upper Green became the Fair Green until 1923, when the event moved to Three Kings' Piece. There it stayed until sixteen years later and another outbreak of hostilities, when the fair site went under the plough in the wartime food drive. It would be 1948 before the fair reclaimed its site. It reached its highpoint through the Fifties, fell out of fashion and finally failed completely before staging a revival in 1983, once again on the quaintly named Three Kings' Piece.

Like Pinner it would be one of the few that would weather the nineteenth-century purge that rode on the back of legislation like the Fairs Act, which condemned all fairs as 'unnecessary' (true in the trade sense) and 'the cause of grievous immorality'. The fever to put down the old fairs was nationwide, a sweeping away of a past that then could be seen only as shameful in the history of Old England. Some, long in decline, would take the chance to fade discreetly from the social calendar; others (as we have seen) would exit with ignominy. Even East Anglia's hallowed Bury Fair – unquestionably one of the greatest – in its later years would suffer a severe fall from grace, perhaps for the reasons Defoe hinted at, and was finally banished from the genteel space of Angel Hill and penned into St Mary's and St James's Squares and the churchyard of the cathedral, its ancient site. It was closed down by order of the Home Secretary in 1857 for its impropriety and regular scenes of drunkenness.

The behaviour of Stourbridge's bawds can have done little to help its survival. Their scandalous conduct had been enough to make the preacher from nearby Barnwell village take his portable pulpit and Bible into the heart of the fair's worst decadence to exhort its sinners to mend their ways. (There were those who believed he might more profitably have stayed at home, since Barnwell itself, so close to Cambridge's students, was said at other times to supply a similar comfort and need.) The famous fair, in such vigorous health when the indefatigable Defoe toured that way, was ailing badly by the close of the eighteenth century but came in reality to an end when the Vice-chancellor called the fair on the Cambridgeshire stubble on 18 September 1855 – though in that contrary way that had existed throughout its life between town and gown, the mayor defiantly continued to proclaim it until 1933. It would prove a ludicrous artifice and in 1931 the attendance was only five: two of them

The fever to put down the old fairs would sweep away a shameful history

policemen. Two years later there was an ice-cream barrow and two women with babies. 'Thus,' laments Addison, who seems to have been there, 'ended the great fair which at one time was both the busiest mart in the realm and the merriest rout.' St Ives in the end would outlast its old adversary, but only as a feeble squib, the palest of lacklustre one-day Whit Monday affairs. It must have seemed a hollow victory.

It was as though Bartholomew's could not go on alone without its great country counterpart. In 1855, after 700 years, it too eventually bowed to the pressure of Victorian gentility, not a moment too soon. It had become a capital embarrassment. In 1708 the Court of Common Council had sought to curb its earlier excesses by cutting back its yearly reign to three days. Now the authorities had simply had enough of its rowdiness; its jugglers and freaks, its dwarfs and rope-dancers, its gingerbread men and hot-pie and orange sellers moved on, scattered who knows where. The rapscallion fair had survived better than most, certainly better than it deserved to. As the nineteenth century dawned the crowds were as big as ever. Astutely, it had modified its fare to the times. Horror had become the theme in the theatre booths, though there were still the ever-familiar attractions of the Learned Pig and the Fireproof Lady. But its capacity for the licentious was undimmed. Neither the nobility nor the genteel could any longer afford to be seen there. The young blades, however, continued to attend; so, unsurprisingly, did the ladies from Cock Lane. That 'airy space' of London, the scene of so much of the capital's history, that had pulsed with life, became suddenly quiet. For that year, too, Smithfield, one of the most famous livestock markets in the world, fell silent. The last market bell would ring down the curtain at 3.15 precisely on Monday 11 June 1855.

Amid the increasing sprawl of building that enclosed it the market had become a beleaguered arena; beasts being driven through the streets at night left a sea of cow-sharn in their wake to the fury of fastidious residents. The slaughter, too, was distasteful, taking place nearby and so close to their doors. The colourful language of the shouting drovers disturbed their sleep and doubtless offended the ears of the quality whose carriages must needs pass that way. And besides, there was the custom the market activity engendered in its adjacent brothels. After seven centuries, its smells and clamour, its noxious fluids and trails of excrement were outlawed to the outskirts of the city and the less congested Copenhagen Fields in Islington, where the market was 'opened' by Prince Albert on 13 June 1855. Its new home, six times bigger than its old space just beyond the City walls, cost £350,000 and maybe as a sop to the country that had been its most faithful supplier, it was named the Caledonian Cattle Market. It would continue to trade until 1939.

No longer could the nobility and the genteel afford to be seen there

Thirteen years after its closure, on its old site there would rise the 'new' Smithfield, the florid palace of the dead-meat trade, an imposing edifice with towers and domes and thirty entrance gates – and a bit like some super-sports arena. Designed by Sir Horace Jones, it opened with a grand lunch for 12,000 guests on 24 November 1868. It was owned and run by the City Corporation of

London, though not always amicably, as events in recent years have shown. It signalled the way things would go. It had an imposing new name: London Central Markets. The romance has gone; the cattle no longer come clattering in on the slithering hoof through the streets of the City. Now the capital's meat begins to arrive as dusk falls, in large refrigerated vans. But read their legends, the towns and counties blazoned on their sides, and the realisation dawns: London's beef comes still from those distant regions where the old drovers gathered up their beasts for the long drove south to their goal of Norfolk's St Faith's.

Once a mêlée of lowing Scottish 'runts', it is now a quiet community beside the airport on the fringe of the county's capital. But the barley still ripples in the breeze on the broad acres of Bullock Hill. Close your eyes in the swirling mist of an October morning and maybe you can imagine the barking of the dogs and the curses of the men who once brought their cattle droves there. The famous fair would weather the change, but only for a time. The mid-century had brought the peak years for the droving business. At Falkirk's trysts of August, September and October in 1850 some 150,000 beasts were sold. But that was the highwater mark and the end would come with astonishing speed. By 1870 the Scottish tryst was but a pallid shadow of the occasion it had so lately been; by the end of the century it would be an almost unbelievable memory.

Forty years earlier its St Faith's equivalent had been officially 'closed' by a Royal Proclamation Against Vice but the fair continued as a gathering for cattle-selling, in 1844 still taking three weeks to clear its livestock. It would succumb to the pressures of change – and the increasing dominance of Norwich's weekly cattle market – with a last sale in 1872, its closure order being obtained by Viscount Ranelagh, the owner of the fairground, under the Fairs Act of 1871. The drover men drinking in the village's Highland Laddie Inn (alas, no more) would not have been surprised. From the early half of the nineteenth century the long-drove trade had been under threat, negligibly at first but then with increasing impact as the steamship established its reliability, frequently opening up new markets. The railways when they came merely hastened the end, as the new turnip husbandry coalesced with both modes of transport to deliver livestock direct to market, ready-fattened, circumventing the old need to 'finish' the beef on rich English pasture. Indeed, by 1849 half of the two million animals sold yearly at Smithfield were already coming by rail.

Harlow Bush Fair, held on the common, became a casualty in 1879, at the close of the decade that had seen the end of so many such occasions. Not unreasonably it was thought time that the common was kept clear – for the commoners. A decade later Carlisle's autumn fair (Carel Fair), which had once launched the big droves south, was facing the poignant truth with a heart-rending muster of only fifty beasts. So, round the landscape of Old England, the great names lost their ancient glister. Somerset's venerable Whitedown Hill went bereft of its traditional hides trade as the new roads took the tanners

In the morning mist you can hear the barking of dogs and the cursing of drovers

elsewhere. By 1845 its Whit Monday and Tuesday affair was heading the way of all fairs but still viable, confidently billing itself: 'The first day will be for the sale of horses etc, and the second for sheep, bullocks and all other kind of cattle.' It had a horse race (for non-thoroughbreds) over hurdles as well as a foot hurdle race. Trowbridge's St James, with its charter from 1200, was in decline by 1814. By 1830, though still a considerable fair, it was incurring calumny as a disorderly affair, decidedly bawdy with 'improprieties of conduct'. In 1871 its 'din, dust and buffoonery' were outrageous and as the genteel stayed away it began its drift towards its nemesis of 1892 by Home Office Order.

A little earlier Birmingham's Onion Fair had finally been banished from the famous Bull Ring to the fringe of the city because of its uncontrolled scenes of drunkenness, rowdiness and general debauchery. Cornwall's Summercourt would shed its prideful purpose, the sale of sheep and oxen and prime steers, and give itself over to pleasure. Its switch was typical. King's Lynn would finally follow the same road. For its famous Mart, the writing was on the wall by 1850. That year the local newspaper penned a tentative epitaph, remembering what had been and that 'in days of yore this mart was considered one of the largest trading fairs . . . and was the resort of traders from all parts of the kingdom, who supplied the inhabitants far and near with every description of goods, useful and ornamental, but of late years its trading character has sunk into comparative insignificance and it is now nothing more than a pleasure fair'. And as that it would survive, as would Nottingham's legendary Goose Fair, today a gigantic jamboree on an 18 acre site with around 55 rides (not including the 40 for children), over 200 games stalls and a further 400 or so for goods. Although still being patronised by good county families into the late nineteenth century, it too had lost its purpose about the mid-point of the century. Now not a single goose is left to strut its stuff on the Forest recreation ground on which the three-day October fair is held, a mile or so out from the Old Market Place that was its original venue.

When the city gave itself a facelift and a grand new Council House it was considered that its old fair was no longer appropriate in such a setting. The last one was held in the shade of the new building's girdered skeleton in 1927. There was protest at the time. Folk had got used to the fair in its setting in front of the Exchange and to the atmosphere of bacchanalian excess that was mysteriously hushed each year as the hands of the Exchange clock struck Saturday midnight. The silence was eerie as the lights flickered out one by one, letting the velvet dark cloak the city. Revellers took their leave through the adjoining streets. Soon in the dark, a flickering flame or two would silhouette the flitting figures of the exhausted fair people dismantling the rides, the swings and the amusement stalls, for the rule at Nottingham was as inviolable as that at Stourbridge. As the clock's morning chimes rang across the rooftops, early church-goers would find the market square desolate and deserted. The debris of three days' riotous revelry had been spirited away in the night by the city's cleansing department – fifty cartloads of it confetti. But the fair was

The silence was eerie as the fair lights flickered out, one by one . . .

no stranger to change or controversy: in 1876 it was curtailed to nine days, which the town council almost immediately reduced to five and in 1880 to the usual three.

At Tavistock the 'goosey' still has all the delights of the fair, only today you are more likely to buy a roast-goose supper than the bird itself. Cattle, sheep and ponies are still sold – to the knell of the auctioneer's hammer – as well as baskets, china and clothes, as the town gives itself over to the spirit of carnival in what is now a one-day affair, a great West Country get-together when the harvest is won. It was the laws on fowl pest that put an end to its serious dealing in geese. Time has mellowed its reputation for drunkenness. It has a traditional air, with the gallopers whirling in Bedford Square and the organ belting out the sound of the old-fashioned fair. Glastonbury's Tor Fair has retained its own ancient magnetism, though it is no longer staged on the south side of the magical Tor itself but in the Fair Field close by the old railway station. In Devon, unsung and almost unknown, the little village of Marldon is gallantly striving to keep alive what is probably the last of the nation's apple fairs, once a tradition in the region. Who knows for how long . . .

The horse fairs would be finally eclipsed by the internal combustion engine

Horse fairs, with their suspect copers and sometimes shady dealing, would endure better than most, well into the age of the internal combustion engine – and, in the case of the heavy breeds, as more localised affairs until the tractor's mechanical horse-power became a reliable alternative in the fields. Horncastle's August occasion was said once to be the most important horse fair in England. But it, too, was finally eclipsed by the railways and by the growth of the auction yards. It would shrink to cover in days what had once occupied it for weeks. Yet it survived as well as any of the great horse fairs, still attracting its cosmopolitan motley of buyers long after it was past its peak. In 1895 the *Horncastle News* was still reporting what had become a familiar story: 'A great number of dealers making their headquarters at the inns have had to sleep out. Beds have been obtained for the visitors all over town.' With the opening of the rail link in 1855 there had been concern. But the effect initially was quite different from what anyone had expected. The railway was a boon to buyers, giving quicker transportation for their persons as well as their animals – almost 1,000 for each fair at the close of the 1880s. It brought even more Irish dealers and breeders; in 1891 the *News* was marking the Irish ascendancy: 'The chief feature of the fair was the Irish hunters, the stables at the Red Lion Hotel, the Rodney Hotel, the New Inn and the Fighting Cocks containing some of the best class ever seen in Horncastle.' The Red Lion's 200-capacity stables were full. By 1895, however, and despite the local newspaper's upbeat stories, the future was being subtly signalled. Only 733 horses arrived by rail that year; by 1905 only 159 were brought into the station sidings and what had once been a three-week orgy of trading (and much else besides) was down to two days. With the end of the First World War it would become a local one-day event. Its struggle to survive, however, would continue through another world conflagration. It succumbed in 1948. Today Horncastle is a quiet town with a sense of history and a plethora of antique shops.

'Dartmoor Drift.' The old
name of the yearly round-
up of the moor's ponies for
fairs such as much-sung-
about Widecombe gave the
painter Arthur James Stark
(1831–1902) his title for
this strong and dramatic
1880s depiction of the
autumn ritual

The end came faster for Penkridge. By 1820 the much-vaunted horse fair had long slipped from its high position as Horncastle was outstripping its close rival Howden (both specialised to some extent in saddle and coach horses). In 1871, the *Goole & Marshland Gazette* was bemoaning the fact that the Yorkshire town's streets were no longer filled for days on end – 'the busy fair has disappeared in Howden town'. It got to the nub of the problem: 'the generally decreasing importance of all fairs, the facilities of railway communication enabling dealers and their agents to visit constantly all parts of the country and pick up anything likely to suit them'. Two years later, in 1873, after the five-day fair, the newspaper was being even more profound: 'No greater change has been wrought in any profession than the railway has in reference to this horse fair, and those, whose memories reach back to the time when George Stephenson's iron horse had not commenced to run on its own iron road through all parts of the country, must often view with astonishment, if not with wonder, the complete revolution it has affected.'

Brough Hill, after centuries during which it had been a great northern gathering point, was diminished when the great cattle droves ended. In 1865 the *Westmorland Gazette* was lamenting that the local farmers now moved their livestock by rail and that the fair that year was the smallest its regular attenders had ever seen. Brough was finished as a cattle fair by 1876, although it would have a few cattle pens until well into the present century, where local farmers would buy beasts to fatten for the area's butchers. But the horse-copers hung on, giving the Hill fresh life as a considerable fair for working farm animals, mainly Clydesdales, vanners (those interesting crossbreeds sometimes called Galloways), and dales and fell ponies. It was reduced to one day in the early twentieth century, but more than the southern horse fairs it was a thriving affair between the wars. It lacked their cachet, of course, and was becoming increasingly a fair for gypsy dealers. Effectively the historic fair ended with the Second World War and the wider introduction of the farm tractor, but it continues today. In the last days of September a handful of the travelling people congregate for what is now called the Romany Brough Hill Fair. The name explains its provenance. For those who remember its rascally character from the old days it has become a spectral feast, but it was always unrealistic to expect that both Brough and Appleby could continue to prosper so close in proximity.

Most of the old horse fairs in time would slip from the country scene; a few others would survive, but again as mere shadows of their former greatness. Lee Gap, held on St Bartholomew's Day (24 August), once lasted for three weeks and three days. Now the Yorkshire fair, at West Ardsley, near Wakefield, takes place, wittily and with a flawless logic, on the first and last of its days as First Lee and Latter Lee. Northampton's Rothwell would not be so fortunate; it is no more, though the fun of the fair continues. Dunningworth Fair, that Suffolk gathering that brought London dealers in search of the draught beasts to haul the capital's brewery drays, is a distant memory, like the old village that once hosted it. The fair died out at the end of the century. Things looked black for

Brough Hill would be diminished as the great droving days became a memory

Brigg as early as 1870; today the fair has dwindled down to a handful of horses and the desultory interest of a few dealers in the town's Stockmarket. Bampton, held for the disposal of Exmoor ponies in late October, was still a very sizeable affair as the century turned, with the ponies being driven in by mounted drovers and then corralled in stockades to await their turn in the sale ring, and as late as 1910 its tolls were still being collected for the lord of the manor. But it sold its last pony in 1985. Another, however, has managed to continue, selling a few ponies off the moor . . . that little fair that put Tom Pearce's grey mare at fatal risk. Widecombe, mainly one suspects on the strength of a song,

The golden fleece would lose its prestige to the dominance of Australia's flocks

> When the wind whistles cold on the moor of a night,
> Tom Pearce's old mare doth appear ghastly white

still draws a crowd of some 5,000 tourists on fair day to see a horseman ride a grey mare round the Dartmoor village and watch the now almost obligatory thatching demonstrations and horse-shoeing, and perhaps a parade of the hounds, along with the tug-of-war, and to feast alfresco from the barbecue. Widecombe, sadly, has become something of a cliché and one doubts whether Tom Cobley (or Cobbleigh) or any one of his comic cavalcade would now bother to bestir himself. Come to that, it is unlikely that he ever did: the only Tom Cobley in a nearby churchyard was laid there in 1794 at the age of ninety-six about sixty years before Widecombe's upstart fair began.

Only a few fairs now have even a vestige of the brisk aura of those grand old occasions that reeked with the fetid sweat of neckerchiefed men and the odour of horses' urine. At Barnet, where London's cabbies carefully selected their cobs, indulgent fathers now come to seek daughters' ponies. The deals may close with the grip of at least one horny hand but the payment is impeccably businesslike, by cheque. As the millennium approaches the gypsies still come – leisurely down from Appleby – but the 'higgling' is pallid by comparison with the old days. It is all over in a couple of hours. Come the evening a motley handful of ponies find themselves in fresh stalls. And clearly, at Appleby the fair's continuation lies in the hands of the travelling folk.

The golden fleece would lose its prestige after Australia became one vast sheep station, the merino breed's wool finally ousting the English product from its position of supremacy. It was both better in yield and finer in quality, though the same might not be said for the merino mutton. But after all the fleece's fluctuating fortunes – and its crucial role in England's history – this time the loss was permanent. The collapse of the trade in West Country cloth, which had gone panniered and by waggon to London's Blackwell Hall, came after 1815 in parallel with the fall of agriculture; it never recovered to challenge its competitor, the north of England.

Today Hudson's shepherd Caleb Bawcombe – his real name was James Lawes – would find his downland flock dramatically diminished. The chalkland sheep fairs would confirm the sad story, though a number would continue until the First World War and beyond, remote in their settings, far from the towns but eminently convenient as gathering points for the West Country flocks. Woodbury Hill, once so prominent, was in decline by 1770 and held its last sheep day in 1906. Weyhill, Cobbett's delight, came to an end just before the Second World War but like many is commemorated by a carnival, in July, a downcome from its days of fame. Hardy's Poundsbury, that September sheep fair first held on the banks of the River Frome, near Dorchester, only in 1848, gave the lie to his moving epitaph by a spirited resurrection in 1993, ten years after its closure. Ilsley's sheep market by the Second World War had dwindled to only a remnant few pens and the nadir of inactivity, and in its northern fastness Stagshawbank was staged for the last time in 1926, well past its prime, a lonely outpost that nobody wanted to come to any more.

A few would weather the years, such as Priddy on its Mendips hillside and also, notably considering its long enmity with Salisbury, Wilton, though its fairs in 1888 were but two in number, in May and September, and the sheep turnover by the early twentieth century was cut by half. Wilton Great Fair is still the biggest of the West Country's sheep fairs, bringing 20,000 animals into its stock pens for auction. Lesser rivals have fallen by the wayside: Cold Harbour faded in the 1860s; Bradford-on-Avon, a market town before 1086, with thirteen alehouses in 1628 each brewing its own malt, continued into the early years of this century; Bradford Leigh lapsed around the same time; Marlborough's 'great sheep fair' on the common was held until the 1960s; Bratton Down foundered with the First World War; Tan Hill, with all the attractions of the big fair in the eighteenth century, including horse-racing, would endure up to the Second; Warminster's once-notable October fair for sheep had become a pleasure fair by the 1960s.

So they faded from the country calendar, those landmarks that had punctuated the drudgery of the year for farmer and labourer alike. Through the years of change a strange thing would happen to the mop fair. That shaming occasion, held mainly after harvest, that brought the farmhands, the labourers and the servant girls to town in their Sunday best and clutching the tokens of their calling, to find new masters and mistresses amid scenes that mocked all human dignity, would slowly be transmuted. The high turnout for the statute fair would be maintained well into the 1860s. Stratford's mop, one of the most popular in the Midlands, was among the first to lose its original role; Warwick's started to fail as a true 'statty' soon after the labour-market peak of the mid-nineteenth century. By the mid-1880s Brigg hiring fair, too, was seeing a falling off that perhaps more truly reflected the national trend. (Of those attending the 'statty' of 1893, more than 2,200 people came by train.) Marlborough's mops by 1888 had lost all significance in the hurly-burly of their rides and amusement booths. Highworth's hiring fair in the market-place had already capitulated. Reporting the Michaelmas Fair of 1874, the *Swindon Advertiser* was of the opinion that 'the attractions of the pleasure fair though of a better class, were of the usual type . . . There were but few servants for hire.'

Through the years a strange thing would happen to the scandalous mop fairs

Wet and woolly flocks. They might have delighted Thomas Hardy had he been around but in Bridgwater's Sheepmarket in 1933 they still choke people's doors in a scene from the past. Time stood still, too, for the town's mop fair, which continued up to the Second World War

In 1888 'very little hiring appeared to be done'. But Newbury's mop, that trysting place for scattered families, was still the scene of hirings in the 1890s; Lincoln's 'statty' would be functioning as the century turned and Burford's was busy even in 1905.

Such fairs, as we have seen, had long caused concern; there was the growing disquiet about young girls parading themselves in the street, to say nothing of the ungodliness that invariably followed. The sensibilities of the quality and the clergy who had long come to hire their cooks and house help, grooms and gardeners – doubtless driving as hard a bargain as any of their rougher farming acquaintances – began to be stirred. The mop had become a mote in society's eye. But there were other forces influencing change: industry, particularly in the Midlands, was offering an alternative to those disenchanted with farm work and the servitude of domestic service. By the end of the century Yorkshire's farmers were having to go as far afield as Suffolk to hire the labour they needed at the wages they were prepared to pay. Very few of England's old mops would survive the First World War in their traditional role, though Bridgwater's unabashedly would call itself a hiring fair right up to the outbreak of the Second.

The mop indeed would move far from its roots, from that time when it had been as vital to agriculture as the sales of the heavy horses. By a bitter irony, in mid-England it would become, instead, an occasion that caused the same disquiet as the discreditable old mops themselves had done as the annual and even more frantic beano for those whose lives were dominated by the factory clock rather than the morning cock-crow and the immutable turn of the seasons. Excursions organised from Midlands towns swelled the fair crowds; Warwick's mop today draws thousands from Coventry and Birmingham; Gloucester flocks to Tewkesbury; Leicester to the 'statty' at Ashby-de-la-Zouch. Indeed, as early as the 1860s, it was often the behaviour of hooligans from the industrial towns rather than the high spirits of the farmboys that brought an urgency to the cries for the mop's suppression.

They live on today, these boisterous Michaelmas occasions, purely for pleasure – scenes of milling merriment but with that slightly dangerous explosive undercurrent that is never far from the surface of the fair. They still have the power to tangle the traffic and shatter a town's tranquillity; still they have a reputation for rowdiness if nothing worse. Nowadays, for the travelling showmen, they provide the cream of the year's takings – which is not to say that the showmen are not as anxious as anyone that they should be joyous and orderly affairs. Today's season of mops opens with Witney Feast in mid-September and ends with Warwick's runaway mop deep into October. At many of them an ox is still publicly roasted . . . in an attempt to recapture the atmosphere of the real thing, that time when the raw-boned farmboy, his future secure for another year, took his 'hiring penny' and wandered into the miasmic wonder of the fair – the coconut shies, the fat lady, the booths with barkers promising outrageous delights, at a price. But first he would hie him to the cheapjack's stall to buy his sweetheart a 'fairing', a token of the fair – some tawdry gift or sparkling bauble that would delight her country heart, or perhaps the ribbon she had begged him for, to tie up her bonny brown hair!

NEW SIGHTS, NEW THRILLS

The fair is not what it was; it is something else. The sheep, the horses, the clustered cattle pens have gone. It is no longer a venue for serious business where men with fat wallets wheel and deal. It has slipped from its central role, socially and economically. Once, too, it was the great gladiatorial circus of its time; it focused the wild spirits of the community; it brought that regular catharsis of the year that, as Dickens observed, cooled the blood for a six-month. It is no longer society's escape-valve, no longer in a multi-screened, televised world even the great entertainment event it once was; no longer central to life, urban or otherwise. It has lost most of its primitive excitement. Nobody gets lodged in the stocks (except with their consent); there is no piepowder court, no miracle plays (maybe they would be irrelevant now). Nothing today can recapture that magical atmosphere recalled by George Sturt in *A Small Boy in the Sixties* (the 1860s, that is) as he looked out fresh-eyed on Farnham's fair: 'in my earliest years the fair was in full blast o' mornings when I woke up for the day. Already could be heard unwonted noises from down in the street; and one had not to look long to see down below a hurry of strange sights – a herd of black Welsh bullocks coming over from Blackwater Fair, a dishevelled gang of gypsies, a flock of sheep thronging the street from side to side, sheepdogs rushing and barking to keep slow sheep on the move and in order, a little group of farmers (not, as on market days, in their best clothes), a show cart, a dirty gig or two, unkempt mumpers quarrelling and spoiling for a fight at public-house doors, hard-faced travelling women with sticky-looking brown hair; and at times, as if all this straggling, careless, swearing, jostling crowd were not enough, along the street would come yelling while the road was just cleared and no more by folk who gave no other heed . . . a horse-coper running a frightened horse for sale.' The sheep pens stretched all the way up one side of Farnham's Castle Street and round the corner out of sight. Farmers, drovers and idlers sat around. As the livestock left the 'arena' the sideshows moved in and the town gave itself over to pleasure. There were even performing birds: canaries hauling tiny buckets up tiny windlasses. And a man made a pudding in a chimney-pot hat borrowed from someone in the crowd. Thus did the traditional fair of Old England come to town.

In a way the fair has come full circle and returned to its roots as the Roman *feria*, a festive holiday. It can still bring chaos to a country town but no longer those raucous, raggedy folk from the lonely, outlying farms determined to break the monotony of their lives and make a day – and sometimes a night – of it. Time has changed all that; today the only wallet being lightened is Dad's – as he pays

Enduring emblem. Still a challenge for the faint of heart, today's Ferris Wheel is a towering monster that takes the brave to 100 feet above the crowd

for yet another ride on the latest space-age monster or subsidises another trip to the candyfloss stall. The fair's purpose now is pleasure, pure and sometimes not so simple. Those job-seeking, labouring men who came to stand soberly in their billycocks and later even in that emblem of probity, the bowler, would wander through it, as dazed as Priestley, lost in a gleaming technological wonderland, a complex maze of mobile multi-million-pound entertainment. Those Cockney ladies resplendent in their feathered hats with voluminous skirts under gay, protective aprons who came to Epping Forest trailing neckerchiefed men, would amble as they ate their jellied eels, bemused by a spectacle so different from the old travelling fair they had known.

In some ways, like so many other things, the fair has become a travesty, a pseudo-event, stage-managed, often commendably in aid of some deserving charity – but a charade none the less. Where an old fair has faltered the showmen themselves have often stepped in to save it – in their own best interests. Occasionally some of the hallowed protocol remains, a loose connection from the past that upholds the local tradition. Barnstaple's St Giles's Fair, in September, has been held without a break for close on 750 years, and begins still with the symbolic white glove – adorned with dahlias and displayed in front of the Guildhall – and the principal proclamation follows a civic ceremony at which spiced ale is served with toast and cheese. (The ale's ingredients are a secret, known only to the town's senior beadle who mixes the drinks.) Britain's largest, brashest fair of all, Nottingham's Goose Fair – some 700 years old and claimed even to be Europe's largest – for all its reputation as autumn's great merry-making occasion, never forgets to pay due attention to the past in its ancient and solemn ritual: at noon of the first day the Lord Mayor marks its opening by ringing two silver bells,

On a roll. An amazing sight and sure to thrill – and guaranteed to turn your stomach over; the High Roller at Hull Fair in 1997

following the town clerk's proclamation before the sheriff and a gathering of other civic VIPs. These are but two of many such ceremonies up and down summertime England that seek briefly to unite the centuries and revisit history.

There is something else that remains unchanged. Today's travelling fair, like those of the past, is designed to be erected and pulled down and fitted into transporters in the minimum time. That is important. Its composite pieces, like a jigsaw, must interlock without problems. Each year showmen and their families take their stalls and booths round the country to countless established venues between the traditional start of the season on St Valentine's Day and the autumn-tide mops, their operational year-end. On village greens and parish commons, or in small market squares and winding streets, they strive to recreate a period from the past, to rekindle a tradition – briefly.

Machine for the Millennium. The triumph of technology has changed the ambience and look of the fair with machines like the fearsome Top Gun

For the fair must always move on. It is an ephemeral thing; transient, like life itself. Maybe that is the secret of its enchantment. Addison, that urbane historian, knowing better than most its countless flaws and the blushes it has caused society, would look back down the years in 1953 in *English Fairs and Markets* and recall its former social significance: 'In every cottage the largest ham was taken down and cooked on fair day . . . And last came the music and dancing that went on till cock-crow or even milking-time in the great kitchens and barns. They are heart-warming scenes to remember.'

Truly they are. They are from another time, part of our rural past and a merrier England.

In a spin. A ride designed to give the fair-goer something of a turn and called, appropriately, Top Spin. Like the technological terror Top Gun, above, it is moving the fair on the summer common into a whole new realm of entertainment

INDEX